DATE DUE

OCT 2 1 1994	
FEB 2 9 1996	
MAR 14 /96	
OCT 1 6 1996	
MAR 3 0 2003	

The Anthropology of Breast-Feeding

Edited by

Vanessa Maher

This volume offers an 'ethnography' of breast-feeding by examining cultural norms and practices in a number of countries. A new light is thrown on gender and on social relationships in general. The volume calls into question current medical and demographic approaches to breast-feeding which, as these essays make clear, are ethnocentric and ill-informed as regards its nature. The significance of breast-feeding reaches far beyond its biological function and the essays show that in fact there is nothing 'natural' about breast-feeding itself. On the contrary, the authors argue, attitudes and practices are socially determined and breast-feeding has to be seen as an essential element in the cultural construction of sexuality.

Vanessa Maher is Associate Professor in Cultural Anthropology at the University of Turin.

Cross-Cultural Perspectives on Women
General Editors: Shirley Ardener and Helen Callaway,
for the Centre for Cross-Cultural Research on Women, Oxford

Dress and Gender: Making and Meaning
Edited by Ruth Barnes and Joanne B. Eicher

Persons and Powers of Women in Diverse Cultures
Edited by Shirley Ardener

—Forthcoming—

Servants and Gentlewomen to the Golden Land: The Emigration of Single Women to South Africa, 1820–1939
Cecillie Swaisland

Women and Space: Ground Rules and Social Maps (pb)
Edited by Shirley Ardener

Defining Females: The Nature of Women in Society (pb)
Edited by Shirley Ardener

Bilingual Women: Anthropological Approaches to Second Language Use
Edited by Pauline Wilkins, Ketaki Dyson and Shirley Ardener

Women and Missions: Past and Present Anthropological and Historical Perceptions
Edited by Fiona Bowie, Deborah Kirkwood and Shirley Ardener

Migrant Women: Crossing Boundaries and Changing Identities
Edited by Georgina C.V. Buijs

Gender: Symbols and Social Practices
Edited by Tony Bleie, Vigdis Broch-Due and Ingrid Rudie

Gender, Drink and Drugs
Edited by Maryon McDonald

Muslim Women's Choices: Religious Beliefs and Social Realities
Edited by Camillia Fawzi El-Solh and Judy Mabro

Women and Property, Women as Property
Edited by Renée Hirschon

Women in Ghana
Ellen Bortei-Doku

The Anthropology of Breast-Feeding

Natural Law or Social Construct

Edited by
Vanessa Maher

BERG

Oxford/Providence

Distributed exclusively in the US and Canada by
St Martin's Press, New York

First published in 1992 by
Berg Publishers Limited
Editorial offices:
165 Taber Avenue, Providence, RI 02906, USA
150 Cowley Road, Oxford, OX4 1JJ, UK

Library of Congress Cataloging-in-Publication Data
Applied for

British Library Cataloguing in Publication Data
A CIP catalogue record for this book is available from the British
Library.

ISBN 0 85496 721 4

Cover photograph by Sandra Assandri

Printed and bound in Great Britain by
Billing and Sons Ltd, Worcester

Contents

Notes on Contributors

Franca **Balsamo** is a sociologist at the Department of Social Sciences, University of Turin. She is the author of articles on childbirth and maternity and is particularly interested in the way they are represented in language. She has also taught trainee nurses and midwives at the Clinic of Gynaecology and Obstetrics, University of Turin.

Catherine **Panter-Brick** is a medical anthropologist engaged in long-term health studies in developing countries, in particular Nepal and India. She holds a position at Durham University. She has collaborated with the Indian Statistical Institute in a study of child-growth and behaviour in Calcutta.

Jane **Khatib-Chahidi** taught in England and abroad for many years before returning to full-time research. She specialised in Social Anthropology at Oxford University and was lecturer in this subject in Kerman University, Iran (before the revolution) and in the East Mediterranean University in Famagusta, Northern Cyprus. She also helped to establish an anthropological consultancy service, based in England.

Marie-Louise **Creyghton** was for many years a free-lance photo-journalist, then lecturer in Cultural Anthropology at the University of Amsterdam until 1985. She carried out research in Northern Tunisia on peasant ideas of well-being and misfortune, and in particular, made a study of children's illness (Ph.D thesis on 'Bad Milk'). She is currently interested in ideas on the relationship between health and place.

Gisella **De Mari** is a psychotherapist who has carried out research into maternity and the construction of sexuality. She is a member of the Leche League, Turin.

Kirsten **Hastrup** is Professor of Social Anthropology, University of Copenhagen, Denmark, and currently Chairperson of the European Association of Social Anthropologists. She has carried out research in Iceland, particularly with regard to systems of meaning and to the relationship between history and anthropology.

Vanessa **Maher** studied Social Anthropology at Cambridge and is presently Associate Professor of Cultural Anthropology at the University of Turin. She is author of publications on Moroccan women including *Women and Property in Morocco* (Cambridge University Press, 1974); and on various aspects of twentieth century Italian society. She has carried out research into maternal and infant mortality in developing countries and is currently engaged in a participative study of immigration from developing countries to Italy.

Rosalba **Serini** is a research sociologist attached to LARES, an institute which carries out sociological enquiries for local authorities and other clients. She has been involved in studies of child rearing and educational preferences in Turinese families, of childbirth in Turin and of the mother-child relationship in hospital. She teaches sociology to trainee midwives and nurses.

Preface

This book owes its existence to many people, most of them women, whose contribution I would like to acknowledge here. It is to discussions with Moroccan women in 1970–1 that I owe my first awareness that breast-feeding could pose a problem and that the choice of bottle-feeding was often a considered one, not born of ignorance.

Between 1986 and 1988, I had a rare opportunity of discussing the whole question at length with Franca Balsamo, Gisella De Mari and Rosalba Serini, during the research we carried out together into the infant-feeding choices of women in Turin. This was a period in which we participated in the first women's seminar to be held in the Faculty of Political Sciences and in the setting up of an Interdepartmental Centre of Women's Studies in Turin University. My three colleagues' experience of research with women has been the basis not only for enjoyable and fruitful 'team-work' but also for a respectful and important exchange with the mothers in Turin who agreed to talk to us about breast-feeding. We learnt much from the lucidity and courage with which our interlocutors analysed their experience; we would like to thank them here. We should also acknowledge our debt to the doctors of the infant ward and the maternity ward, respectively, of two Turin hospitals. The doctors' invitation to collaborate with them was an important stimulus to our work. They allowed me to interview women in their care and spent many hours in discussions with us over our findings, although our perception evidently differed from theirs.

During the academic year 1986–7, I was granted paid leave by the Faculty of Political Sciences of the University of Turin (to which I am grateful) to spend a year as Visiting Fellow at the Centre for Cross-Cultural Research on Women, Queen Elizabeth House, University of Oxford. I have to thank the Director and members of Queen Elizabeth House for their hospitality. I am particularly indebted to the members of the Centre for Cross-

Cultural Studies on Women and the Visiting Fellows, Stephen Ameyaw and A.B. Assensoh, for their friendship and the stimulus of many interesting discussions and suggestions. During the academic year 1986–7 I worked on maternal and infant mortality in connection with the problem of breast-feeding. Shirley Ardener encouraged me to organise a workshop on breast-feeding under the auspices of the Centre. During the year and particularly during the preparation of the workshop I received continuous support from Shirley herself, Pat Holden, Alison Smith, Iona Mayer, Helen Callaway, Jane Chahidi and other members of the Centre, whom I wish to thank. At a later stage Shirley Ardener, Helen Callaway and Iona Mayer gave me useful editorial advice. I would also like to thank Juliet Blair, Debbie Bryceson, Lucy Rushton, Hebe Welbourn and Mai Yamani for information and suggestions. I derived useful stimuli from seminars at the Centre for Cross-Cultural Research on Women and the Department of Biological Anthropology, University of Oxford, the History Workshop conference on 'Women, Technology and Reproduction' and the conference on 'Feminism and Anthropology' organised by Anna Aalten and Annalies Moors in 1988 at the University of Amsterdam, where I presented a first version of my chapter on maternal depletion. I was also set thinking by a paper by David Harley on breast-feeding in seventeenth-century Cheshire, which he gave at the Wellcome Foundation for the History of Medicine.

I am grateful to members of the Perinatal Epidemiology Unit, Radcliffe Infirmary, Oxford, to Jo Garcia and in particular to Sally Inch and Chloë Fisher, who agreed to give papers at the workshop, based on the research of the Unit and on their experience as professional midwives. The workshop was set up to examine infant feeding practices in their cultural context, rather than to promote one practice over another. I think our medical colleagues from the Perinatal Epidemiology Unit, who work hard to promote breast-feeding, were perplexed by this approach, but vice versa, their analyses of current breast-feeding practice in Britain, the obstacles to breast-feeding in hospital and the attitudes of midwives and doctors were invaluable to us.

I wish to thank Richard Burghart, Jane Chahidi, Catherine Panter-Brick, Nadja Reissland and Margot Waddell for giving papers at the workshop; and the other participants (anthropologists, demographers, historians and psychologists) for giving generously of their ideas and experience, making allowance for one another's disciplinary rigidities and providing an ideal atmosphere for a fruitful discussion. For the sake of coherence and argument, this book includes only anthropological contributions. It did not arise directly out of the workshop (only three of the authors were present at it), but the general approach developed there has informed all the papers to some extent. The papers were purpose written for this volume and represent, I believe, a new approach to breast-feeding as an aspect of culture.

I have to thank many people for insights and moral support, or for pointing out new research to me. Chief among them, in Italy, are Luisa Accati, Lanfranco Blanchetti Revelli who introduced me to Emily Martin's work, Rina Constantino and Paola Moltoni; in England, my sisters Fiona and Angela, and over many years, for their care and encouragement, Mary and Dick Palmer. I am also grateful to the Department of Political Studies, Turin, whose staff have always been a great help.

Finally I would like to thank my son Stefano, who taught me much of what I know about breast-feeding; and Mauro, to whose counter-cultural sense of paternity we both owe a great deal.

Vanessa Maher,
University of Turin

1

Breast-Feeding in Cross-cultural Perspective: Paradoxes and Proposals

Vanessa Maher

In the 1960s and early 1970s, maternity was not a prime feminist issue in the West. Women were more concerned with freeing themselves from childbearing and rearing than with realising the potential of these roles as a female resource. The 1980s have brought a widespread visibility to childbirth in medical and women's circles but breast-feeding does not share the limelight. The visibility of breast-feeding as an issue, or the custom of breast-feeding avoidance, needs critical interpretation in cultural terms, rather than in the positivist terms of the medical model (see Maher, final chapter; Raphael, 1979b). In the industrial West, interpretation in cultural terms is hard to come by.

This is true especially in hospitals, although it is these institutions which have been the focus of the discussion on childbirth. Hospitals may attempt to lay down rules, rather than encourage the mother herself to interpret the baby's behaviour and assess her own and the baby's needs within the framework of their relationship and particular social circumstances. Rules are likely to be inappropriate to the breast-feeding situation which, like the personalities of mother and child, is always in some aspect unique. Further, if we may judge from the immense variety of instructions for breast-feeding which appear in manuals of paediatric medicine, any set of rules is likely to be arbitrary. Research carried out in England shows that even the notion of demand feeding is apparently interpreted in widely differing ways in different hospitals. Various interpretations are found even among midwives working in the same hospital (Inch, 1987: 53–8). Since the mid-1980s, the

1

social and medical pressure on women to breast-feed has increased but new mothers receive conflicting information and advice. In any case, this volume should cast doubt on the idea that 'successful' breast-feeding is merely a matter of having the right information. More complex cultural conditioning and relationships are at stake.

It is significant that even Emily Martin, in her path-breaking study of the management of reproduction in the southern United States of America and in particular of the relationship between medical and popular images of women's bodies, barely mentions breast-feeding (Martin, 1987). This lack of emphasis may reflect the actual behaviour of the women Martin interviewed and the real replacement of breast-feeding by bottle-feeding with artificial powdered milk. The tendency to bottle-feed has gained momentum in most Western countries over the last hundred years but it was led by the United States. Recent trends, particularly among middle-class women, and fostered by such organisations as the Leche League, have helped to reverse the decline in breast-feeding. Groups such as the Leche League attempt to provide person-to-person support for women who wish to breast-feed (La Leche League International, 1988).

The practice of these groups has brought to light the neglect of breast-feeding in hospitals, the misleading advice which the (generally male) doctors and consultants have been giving to women, and the extent to which the medical establishment has become compromised by the enormous commercial interests involved in the production and sale of artificial baby foods. Women in the United States who now wish to breast-feed cannot call on the experience of the previous generation of mothers, since few of the latter actually breast-fed. On the other hand new mothers have to deal with considerable muddles in obstetric and paediatric thinking and practice. Some of the gravest of these muddles derive from the fact that the medical profession conceives of mothers and babies as belonging to separate fields of research, and thus, the partners to the breast-feeding relationship are dealt with by different specialists. These conditions may make the attempt to breast-feed a confused and frustrating one, as many accounts of Western infant feeding suggest (Martin, 1986; Balsamo, De Mari, Maher, Serini, this volume; Oakley, 1979b).

Writers on Africa, by contrast, never fail to discuss the long periods of breast-feeding and the weaning practices among African women. Indeed, breast-feeding looms large in medical recommendations and nutritional policies for developing countries in spite of its apparent decline in these areas. This prominence has drawn little comment from women, feminists or social anthropologists. The same medical establishment which has helped along the decline of breast-feeding in the West, in spite of a recent theoretical volte-face, remains, on the whole, remarkably innocent of what breast-feeding entails. It stands aloof from lobbies in the West which aim to help provide the conditions inside and outside the hospital for women to breast-feed as they wish. Yet it is this medical establishment which provides the most vocal apologists of breast-feeding by women in developing countries.

Many medical writers ignore the differences in local, social and cultural conditions in developing countries. Indeed, some even propose that breast-feeding practice in developing countries, regarded as a homogeneous whole, be taken as a model by Western women, regarded as another homogeneous category (see Maher, this volume). This disregard for the local, social and cultural conditions of breast-feeding has led to undue simplification of the issues involved. As far as infant feeding in the developing world is concerned, the essays in this volume, by restoring a social and cultural dimension to the discussion of breast-feeding, cast doubt on the accepted medical wisdom of many international organisations active in the field of healthcare.

Breast Versus Bottle: Is the Formula too Simple?

The 'baby-milk scandal' brought to light the fact that the feeding of artificial formula baby milk, in the form of powder to be added to water, to babies living in developing countries where their mothers had no access to clean water or refrigeration, had resulted in the death of great numbers of babies. Although this insight was important, in the wake of the campaign against bottle-feeding and the companies responsible for promoting formula in developing countries, the discussion of infant nutrition has become remarkably and misleadingly over-simplified. Commercial baby milk, it is suggested, is a vehicle for disease and death. Breast-milk is sterile and safe. Therefore mothers should be encouraged to breast-feed, particularly those whose 'ignorance' has made them an easy prey to the aggressive marketing of the baby milk companies.

The following advertisement by UNICEF (1989–90) appears intended to spread this message. Under a picture of a pretty, dark-skinned child, around four years old, runs the title: 'What would you like to be when you grow up? Alive!' Below this dramatic opening line, which suggests that the child's very survival depends on taking the advice given below, we read:

> Breast-milk is the most nutritious food for infants in any country, but in the developing world, its advantages over formula feeding can mean the difference between life and death. Breast-milk contains antibodies which protect babies against fatal diarrhoeal diseases. Bottle-feeding increases the risk of infection. UNICEF seeks various ways to protect and promote the practice of breast-feeding.

These general statements, which treat breast-feeding as a merely nutritional matter, and mothers as people needing to be informed of its importance, may actually not hold under particular social and cultural conditions. The picture of the child in the UNICEF poster is itself misleading. A child of four in a developing country does not owe its survival to breast-feeding only, but to the fact that it has lived through the dangerous weaning period and the period of peak mortality which immediately succeeds it (around one to two years). Its survival in the future will depend on many factors but certainly not only on having been breast-fed. More serious is the fact that important questions regarding the actual practice of breast-feeding are evaded in this advertisement, such as: under what conditions does a particular form of feeding endanger a baby's health?

In urban areas of the Philippines and of Tanzania, it has been shown that well babies are those whose parents have a higher than average income, which usually means piped water, proper sanitation, adequate medical care, good housing and mothers with higher than average education. Of these babies, some are breast-fed, some are bottle-fed and some 'mixed-fed'. The mode of feeding babies does not seem to be significant (see Maher, final chapter).

Another question in developing countries which the UNICEF advertisement appears to beg is the vexed one of: to what extent, under what conditions and for how long, do the antibodies present in breast-milk protect babies against diarrhoeal infections?

Many studies suggest that breast-feeding protects the baby only during the first three to six months. Others indicate that this protection is, in practice, sabotaged by frequent supplementation with teas, gruels or rice-water during this early period, and a

Philippine study reports that diarrhoeal disease accounted anyway for only 20 per cent of total illness among the sample during the study year – the sample under discussion included babies up to a year old in 1985 (see Maher, this volume). Perhaps the most important question side-stepped by the advertisement is: how long is it *safe* to rely exclusively on breast-feeding for the baby's nutrition?

Many studies indicate that babies breast-fed for longer than six months tend to be less healthy than those exclusively so fed for only three to six months (Maher, this volume). Yet the World Health Organisation recommends that mothers breast-feed for one to two years and a United Nations manual assumes that at nine months, as well as two solid meals a day, infants are still receiving 500 ml of breast-milk (Cameron and Hofvander, 1976). This is an overall maximum for most women in developing countries, and unlikely to be sustained up to nine months when the child is receiving solid food as well, and the mother has returned to a regime of undernutrition and heavy work (Maher, final chapter).

The WHO and UN recommendation (apart from the two solid meals, and the volume of the milk-feeds) are probably derived from women's actual practice in many developing countries, rather than from some Western discovery. It seems unrealistic to suppose that women have to be 'taught' the importance of breast-feeding when, as it is, most breast-feed their children for long periods. But the fact that lengthy breast-feeding is established practice in a given society does not necessarily make it 'natural' or even the best thing for mothers and babies. In most societies, there are strict controls, mediated by the political and symbolic system, on women's sexuality, reproductive capacities, and the form and content of their social relationships. We need to ask in what way, if any, these controls affect the practice of breast-feeding.

Given the limited nutritional or protective advantage for babies of exclusive breast-feeding past the six-month mark, some more questions need to be asked such as: Why is such practice the rule in many societies? What is the real contraceptive effect of lengthy breast-feeding? How safe is lengthy breast-feeding for the overworked, underfed, multiparous mothers of many developing societies? What is the relationship between overwork, undernutrition, high fertility, lengthy breast-feeding and the high morbidity and low life expectancy of women in many developing countries? What consequences can a mother's ill health and early death have for the rest of her family? Is it possible that less breast-feeding might improve her life chances and those of her family? If lengthy breast-feeding (past six months) provides only marginal advantage to the baby and to the mother, how is the method and period of breast-feeding determined, to what purpose and to whose advantage? In this chapter and the final one, we will pose these questions and suggest, at least, some possible answers.

While we recognise that breast-feeding may provide emotional and sensual gratification to both mother and child, it is not these benefits which are in the forefront of medical discussions, nor have the emotional and sensual gratification of women and children often been the point of cultural imperatives. The medical discussions focus on the prevention of malnutrition and disease. Many cultural imperatives mention the duty of a woman to her husband and children, and the duty of children to their parents, and particularly to their adult male relatives.

Breast-Feeding and Adult Male Privilege

Few societies appear to stress the duty of the father to care for his children and safeguard their welfare. Yet, as we will be demonstrating below, it is men in many societies who decide who shall be breast-fed by whom and for how long. Whether their decisions are likely to be to the advantage of children and their mothers in a regime of gender inequality, where the role of the father is more often associated with authority and privilege than with nurturing behaviour, is a moot point. How compatible, indeed, with responsible parenthood is the adult male privilege which characterises many societies?

Boys are not usually socialised to assume caretaking roles in relation to women and children, but rather to enjoy particular privileges at their expense. This emerges in the patterns of intra-family and intra-community food distribution, where in many societies, males, especially adult males, are assured a disproportionate share of food and the needs of women and children neglected (see Maher, final chapter). Men may also enjoy other privileges at the expense of women and children. In many European countries, in the sixteenth, seventeenth and eighteenth centuries, when it was believed that sexual intercourse 'spoiled the milk', middle-class husbands prevented their wives from breast-feeding rather than forego their sexual privilege. Gender inequality, and the general cultural priorities of which it is a symptom, is more significant for child and female morbidity and mortality in many countries, than is the mode of infant feeding.

Adult male privilege is reflected not only in the distribution of food but, in many societies nowadays, in the control of cash income. In sub-Saharan Africa, for example, women not only carry out 'domestic tasks', such as fetching water and fire wood, processing and preparing food, as well as caring for children, they also produce 75 per cent of the food, and contribute most of the labour to 'male' cash crops which encroach increasingly on the land needed for subsistence crops. But it is their husbands or male relatives who pocket the proceeds from crop sales, and often use them for their own ends and not for the needs of the family. Because of male migration and high divorce rates, up to 40 per cent of households have no adult male worker and little cash income. Migrants often have no cash to send home. It is in this combination of factors (male migration, the shrinkage of the sub-sistence sector in favour of cash crops, the disproportionate and increased burden of work which women have to assume, their lack of title to land, their lack of access to cash and credit and so incapacity to improve their land,) that we may identify some of the main causes of the drop in per capita food production in Africa over the past two decades.

During these decades, women have had few sources with which to feed their families. The fact that, in most societies, parenting is seen as an exclusively female task may contribute to the high level of both female and child mortality in many developing countries. Often men contribute little to the children's support, in terms of work, cash and material resources, and women and children must share 'short commons'. How are these women to squeeze cash out of their recalcitrant men, to make up the shortfall in the food supply?

The decline in breast-feeding and the increase in formula feeding may be associated with this dilemma. During field observation in Morocco in the 1970s, where women had little access to money, it seemed to me that they faced some of the problems described above. These observations (Maher, 1984) and my belief that women's behaviour is as rational as anyone else's, have led me to look for reasons other than 'ignorance' behind women's adoption of formula feeding. First of all, it is clear that formula feeding makes inroads on *male cash income* (since women get cash from men for milk powder) and not on female bodily resources. Women, in bottle-feeding, give up the impossible task of compensating with their own bodies for the shortcomings of a social and material environment which is hostile to women and children, and attempt to offload some of the burden of parenting and food production onto men. I have heard arguments between men and women in Morocco which made this explicit (Maher, 1984).

It is interesting that in Western industrial countries, too, many women explain their decision to bottle-feed in terms, among other things, of their wish to share the parental role with others, in particular with the father of the child. They describe this form of child rearing as one step towards a more equitable division of labour (see Balsamo, et al., this volume). They do not often expect the father to take on other aspects of the parenting role (cleaning and so forth) or to take over the housework to enable the mother to breast-feed. Bottle-feeding is often regarded as allowing a somewhat covert shift in the sexual division of labour, and as involving the father in parenting, by beginning with its most gratifying aspects.

It is sometimes argued that lengthy breast-feeding is the only solution to a situation in which there are no transitional or weaning foods for young children. This may be true in some societies, such as, for example, those of New Guinea, where most available foods have a high-bulk, low-nutrient content, or under emergency conditions of food shortage. It is hardly true of many contemporary societies in South or South East Asia, the Middle East or North Africa, where lengthy breast-feeding is nevertheless the rule. Here it appears that, although grown men are usually well nourished, scarcity is passed on to women and children. Breast-feeding compensates, somewhat ineffectually as we have seen, for a culturally created lack of food for children.[2]

Many societies which have the means to provide interim weaning foods for babies over six months may not do so, preferring to rely on lengthy breast-feeding for the nourishment of half-grown infants. It is possible that the pattern of lengthy breast-feeding may be explained more adequately in terms of the power structure, including gender inequality, within a given society than in terms of the biological benefits it confers on children.

The Cultural Meanings of Breast-Feeding

The assumption that breast-feeding is a merely nutritional, or at most psychological, matter lies behind both medical approaches and women's failure to take position with regard to these approaches. Breast-feeding, according to this assumption, is the same the world over, a matter of the 'successful' or 'unsuccessful' functioning of a physical or psychological relationship between two individuals.

The present collection, on the contrary, points out that breast-feeding involves much more than a relationship between individuals. The economic and social conditions of infant feeding have a fundamental effect on its chances of 'success'. Among these conditions are the extremely varied social and symbolic relationships which infant feeding creates and services in different cultures. Indeed, the notion of 'successful' breast-feeding varies cross-culturally, and includes timely weaning.

Infant feeding often entails not only the physical survival of the child but also complex forms of socialisation of mother and child. In fact, the forms of feeding considered culturally appropriate may put the child at risk. In Europe this has been true of wet-nursing, (which endangered both the child put out to nurse and the nurse's own child, though in different degrees,) bottle-feeding and other practices up to recent times. A striking example was the practice which prevailed in Iceland for over two centuries of feeding butter and cream to infants and not breast-feeding them at all (see Hastrup, this volume). Practices associated with some breast-feeding societies, for example, the denial of the cholostrum (the first breast-milk, rich in nutrients and antibodies) to the baby, may affect its chances of survival.

Here we underline the fact that breast-feeding, like female sexuality and childbirth, is the subject of considerable cultural elaboration in most societies. These essays point out that the 'nutritional uses' of breast-feeding are culturally determined, (even those recommended by WHO) and have only an indirect relationship with biological efficacy. They show that breast-feeding has other uses besides the nutritional. It is not only conditioned by cultural patterns but exerts a definite influence on them (see also Raphael, (ed.) 1979).

The mode of breast-feeding may influence fundamental cultural coordinates such as those which define the concept of the person, or of closeness of relationship and thus the 'structure of roles' within a society. It may serve to socialise the person to a given political and productive system, forging through this primary experience, for example, the socially accepted concept of time or more generally, the rules concerning the management of sexuality and emotion, on which the social order is founded (see Balsamo, below). It may provide the imagery for religious beliefs (Warner, 1978). Since the Counter-Reformation, the image of the Christ spurting blood and water from his side has frequently been juxtaposed iconographically with that of the breast-feeding Madonna, and the qualities associated with the priesthood are those of the nurturing mother (Bynum, 1987, Accati, 1990).

Breast-feeding may inform a universalist ethos: 'the milk of human kindness', in contrast to a restrictive one: 'blood is thicker than water'. At-Tabari, a tenth-century Arab chronicler and Koranic commentator, cited many warm comments of the Prophet Mohammed concerning the generosity of motherhood and the debt of children to their mother. Breast-feeding was rewarded in heaven:

> And when she delivers, not a mouthful of milk flows from her and not an instance of child's suck, but that she receives, for every mouthful and for every suck, the reward of one good deed. And if she is kept awake by her child at night, she receives the reward of one who frees seventy slaves for the sake of Allah (Schleifer, 1986: 53).

Wet-Nursing, Weaning and Social Structure

The culturally induced 'failure' of women to breast-feed, such as that which has characterised many Western industrial countries since the 1950s, or a taboo on breast-feeding like that which obtained in Iceland over a period of several hundred years (Hastrup, this volume), may make important cultural statements about the relation of man and woman to nature, about social priorities, the relations between the genders and between adults and children.

There is some indication that the curtailment of breast-feeding by mothers, whether this curtailment takes the form of early weaning, wet-nursing, hand-feeding, or latterly bottle-feeding, is common in those societies which emphasise marriage and having children as institutions for the confirmation of wealth and status, rather than as means to parenthood and the extension of kin ties. These are often sharply stratified societies. The control of breast-feeding is generally a male prerogative and serves to emphasise the husband-wife relationship, or that between holder and heir, not that between parents and child or mother and child. To some extent, and particularly in pre-industrial situations, we may identify these societies as those which Goody considered to be characterised by 'diverging devolution', that is, the inheritance of property and status by men and women from both their parents (Goody, 1976). Property is transmitted 'vertically' between parents and children (who are valued mainly as heirs) and so lateral kin fade in economic and political importance. Endogamy, monogamy, adoption, celibacy, late marriage and rarity of divorce characterise this pattern, which Goody finds exemplified mainly in Europe and some Asian societies.

In many societies in sub-Saharan Africa, on the other hand, marriage does not confer property on the new couple, nor indicate a unique achievement of economic and social status for them. It is, rather, characterised by transactions between their kin. Kin groups and status groups are often exogamous. Everyone gets married and there is no celibacy to speak of. Polygamy, divorce and remarriage are easier to arrange. Political authority derives from a person's position within the kinship system, and power from the number and influence of his kin and affines, including his children. Men inherit from men, women from women, and more often from lateral kin than from parents. Kin ties are often more important than the marriage relationship. In such cases it is rare to find men curtailing breast-feeding by their wives. On the contrary women may be encouraged by kin as well as husband to breast-feed as long as possible, commonly for two years or more.

The patterns described above may fit the behaviour of some strata within a society and not others, and in some historical periods and not others. However it seems fruitful to consider the possibility that changes in social structure may affect gender relations, child-adult relations, and so forms of infant feeding too. For example, it seems likely that the progressive closure and isolation of the Western nuclear family during the nineteenth century, and the patterns of conjugal and gender relations which developed within it, contributed to the decline of breast-feeding not only in Europe and the United States, but also in those countries which came under their economic and social influence.

The Sexualisation of Girls and Women within the Family

In an important chapter of her book on the psychoanalyst Karen Horney, Marcia Westcott (1986) describes Karen Horney's insights, rarely expressed in so many words, into what Westcott has defined as the 'sexualisation' of girls within the family. The closure and isolation of the Western nuclear family, combined with its power structure which stresses female dependence and male responsibility and privilege has particularly negative implications for women and girls. Foucault too (1978) has pointed out that, during the nineteenth century, the middle-class family became a 'close quarters . . . saturated with sexuality'. At the same time middle-class identity became associated with sexual repression. Anything which deviated from acceptable sexuality, that is, that of husband and wife, had to be obsessively controlled. It will be seen that this control came to be extended to the physical relationship between mother and child during breast-feeding (see Balsamo, et al., this volume).

'Thus, the emphasis on female subordination, the eroticisation of interpersonal power, and the gender differences in the simultaneous repression and incitement of sexuality contributed to a complex family dynamic in which daughters and sisters were treated in ways that were both sexually charged and repressed'. (Westcott, 1986: 101) It is this dynamic that underlies Horney's description of the family as an 'emotional hothouse' (1967) in which women of the feminine type were sexualised as girls.

Girls were expected, in their subordinate position to be submissive, seductive and nurturant towards the men of the household. The achievements, activities or aspirations of girls, anything which detracted from their sexualised femininity, were disparaged and ignored.

If the sexual abuse of girls within the European family is anything to go by, this situation appears to have worsened during the twentieth century, and affects not only the middle class. But fathers and brothers may merely indulge in the kinds of teasing, sexually-tinged concern with a girl's appearance, caresses and spying with which the girl has often to deal in the public sphere as well. The devaluation and sexualisation of women has become 'public' in the twentieth century, with sexual harassment of working women and the portrayal of women's bodies as playthings, building on their negative childhood experience. A situation which, according to Horney results in her 'feminine type's compulsive heterosexuality' and lack of sexual self-determination. Many women feel a disgust at their own bodily processes which only male interest can allay. These attitudes give rise to hostility and rivalry towards other women, so that mutual help and the transmission of knowledge is impeded (Horney, 1967; Westcott, 1986: 88–119).

Such attitudes spell disaster for breast-feeding. One English book on breast-feeding advises the breast-feeding mother never to forget that she is still her husband's 'mistress' (see below). Such advice, intended to prevent the husband from 'straying from the hearth', may be a contradiction in terms in that a stress on the husband's sexual privilege (rather than on his capacity to provide emotional and material support for the new mother) may put an end to breast-feeding. Certainly, some of the mothers we interviewed in Turin expressed the fear that if they were too concerned with the new baby their husbands would leave them.

Breast-Feeding and Male Sexual Privilege

Manuals on breast-feeding for Western readers do not always discuss its sexual implications, other than to suggest that women may be inhibited from breast-feeding by their awareness of the erotic value of the breasts for men. However, the authors of one relatively 'progressive' 1978 manual recognise that breast-feeding for many women can be a 'highly pleasurable experience', and that the hormones such as oxytocin are crucial in many sexual situations, such as orgasm and birth as well as for the 'let-down reflex' in breast-feeding. Further, both hormones and nervous pathways interconnect nipples, uterus and clitoris. On the other hand, the writers insist that a woman's pleasure in breast-feeding her baby should not interfere with male sexual privilege: 'If a woman gets pleasure from having her baby stimulate, play with and feed from her breasts, her husband may well not enjoy the baby's relationship with his wife. Until now, his wife's breasts have "belonged" to him and he may resent the little intruder.'

The doctor-authors provide, for good measure, the following hints on: 'How to combine a good sex life with a happy breast-feeding baby.':

1. Make sure your husband doesn't feel left out – physically or emotionally.
2. If feeding makes you feel sexy or even pleasantly relaxed, tell him so as to encourage him to make the most of it.
3. Wear a good nursing bra and remind him that you're doing it for his benefit so that he'll have your breasts looking good years from now.
4. Respect his wishes not to feed in public or in front of certain people if you know it upsets him.
5. Plan the odd trip out together once your let-down is well established. Express some breast-milk and leave it for the baby sitter to give. You can't expect your husband to look favourably on breast-feeding if he thinks he's going to be tied to the house for the next six months.
6. Keep up your previous "mistress" image as much as possible. (Stanway, 1978: 185–6).

It is difficult to imagine how a woman who tries so hard not to appear to breast-feed, particularly to her husband, is going to manage it at all. The total lack, in this passage, of any expectation of parental or caretaking behaviour on the part of the father is remarkable.

Contrariwise, some of our interviewees in the Turin research (those most articulate on the subject of their own sexuality) found that their psycho-physical relationship with the baby tended temporarily to diminish their interest in sexual relations with their husbands. It appears to be true that where the conjugal relationship, and not the parental one, is considered to be the corner-stone of the family, and the isolated nuclear family to be of central importance for the social identity of both women and men, breast-feeding may be inhibited (Goody, 1983: 153–6).

Christiane Klapisch points out that in fifteenth-century Florence, the merchant class acted on the belief that a new pregnancy would spoil the milk for the nursling who might die if he fed from a pregnant mother. That is, there was a post-partum taboo. Wet-nursing was seen as a solution which allowed the child's parents to resume having sexual intercourse soon after the birth of a child, as the spate of births at short intervals shows (Klapisch, 1980). In another vein, wealthy English mothers in the sixteenth century bewail the fact that they can give little attention to their babies and are obliged, in the first instance, to please and obey their husbands.

In 1662, the Puritan, William Gouge, said: 'Husbands for the most part are the cause that their wives nurse not their own children', and in 1753, the London apothecary James Nelson said: 'A man cannot be conversant with life and not see that many a sensible woman, many a tender mother, has her heart yearning to suckle her child, and is prevented by the misplaced authority of her husband'.

Mary Wollstonecraft was still convinced in 1772 that the father's desire for sexual relations was the reason for the survival of wet-nursing: 'There are many husbands so devoid of sense and parental affection that during the first effervescence of voluptuous fondness, they refuse to let their wives suckle their children' (Fildes, 1986: 104).

During the whole of this period poorer English women did breast-feed their children (as well as those of their richer sisters), often with explicitly contraceptive intentions and had longer birth intervals, fewer and healthier children. As Fildes points out, when the wishes of the rich for many children were matched by the wishes of their social inferiors for family limitation, then the ideal situation existed for the practice and perpetuation of wet-nursing (Fildes, 1986: 109). It would be interesting to examine the relative stress on conjugal and parental roles in these two milieux.

Where a woman's first consideration is her duty to her husband rather than that to her children and kin, she is often dependent on him economically and socially. The social and institutional emphasis on the conjugal relationship at the expense of wider networks of kin and others can be shown to be typical of most parts of Western Europe (Bott, 1957; Goody, 1976) in the twentieth century, and of certain social strata in earlier periods. To a certain extent, a woman becomes a mother under circumstances which her husband creates and conducts her maternal role according to his wishes, that is as subordinate to her conjugal role.

The effect of this on breast-feeding can de deduced from the example of Ghanaian women in Britain during the sixties. In Ghana these women were used to acting within the social framework provided by their female kin. In Britain, they found themselves, for the first time, far from both their own kin and other social networks and forced into a more nuclear and conjugal family situation than they would have lived in Ghana. Under these conditions of greater dependence of both spouses on the conjugal relationship and in the absence of those social controls which caused couples in Ghana to observe a lengthy post-partum taboo, women shortened the breast-feeding period. Apparently under pressure from their husbands to interrupt the post-partum taboo, and responding to an environment favourable to bottle-feeding (cheaper milk), women stopped breast-feeding after some months rather than after a couple of years (A.B. Assensoh, personal communication).

In West Africa, as in New Guinea, a post-partum taboo on the mother having sexual intercourse may last for two or three years. Frequently, the post-partum taboo is closely associated with the breast-feeding period. Such a taboo enables the mother to dedicate her undivided attention to the infant, relieves her of the fear of a new pregnancy which would endanger the young child, and makes it unnecessary for her to employ contraceptive measures (such as the pill which tends to inhibit lactation). A long period of breast-feeding reinforced by the post-partum taboo ensures a long interval between births to the advantage of both mother and child, where resources are scarce and a woman's work-burden heavy. In some, but by no means all of those societies where there is a post-partum taboo, men may have more than one wife or mistress. Under these conditions it is likely that a woman's role as mother, kinswoman and worker will be emphasised at the expense of her conjugal relationship. This is especially true if one considers that a woman may bear six or eight children, each of whom she nurses for a couple of years, during which time she must abstain from sexual intercourse. But the post-partum taboo also obtains in many monogamous societes. It may be considered necessary, in the interest of the child, that not only its mother, but also its father should abstain from any sexual relationship for a certain period of time (see Maher, final chapter). This is an unusual form of emphasis on the male parental role. Where parental rather than conjugal status is an important source of social identity, rivalry between father and children for the mother's attention may be less acute than in societies without a post-partum taboo, or at least, it may take other forms.

So it seems that there are many factors which influence the practice of breast-feeding. The facile hypothesis whereby it is women's work which interferes with breast-feeding is common in the West, especially in medical circles. But in Turin we found no association between women's employment and the absence of breast-feeding. Even in developing countries, there is little evidence to support this hypothesis. S. Taha remarks that the decline in breast-feeding in the Gezira (Sudan) is not due to women's salaried work, since no woman goes out to work (Taha, 1979: 199). On the other hand, Catherine Panter-Brick's article in this volume points out that in mountain areas of Nepal, breast-feeding mothers do not appear to work less than other women, and nurse their children during breaks in the work.

In areas of female farming such as sub-Saharan Africa where women do most of the agricultural work, they also breast-feed their children for one or two years. Yet, to say that agricultural work is 'compatible' with breast-feeding and child care is to ignore the fact that in order to carry out their work, breast-feeding mothers in widely differing cultural contexts, have tended to introduce early supplementation and sometimes use inexpert child care (by small children). In spite of breast-feeding, these societies are characterised by high infant mortality.

If a mother is unable to nurse her child in a relaxed way during the day, or if the child is too heavy to carry long distances and must be left at home in the care of a big sister or grandmother, he/she is often able to make up for lack of nourishment during the day by suckling at night. This is more easily arranged if there is a post-partum taboo and if mother and baby share sleeping quarters at night.

The stress by Western parents on conjugal intimacy and privacy, their fears for the safety of the baby and for their own daytime efficiency, mean that babies cannot sleep in their mother's bed and suckle at night. Western notions of hygiene and privacy in this sense are sometimes introduced together with Western pediatry into African or Asian contexts, with devastating effects on breast-feeding. In Western countries, then, babies are fed during the day, and the new mother sets herself the task of eliminating 'the night feed' as soon as possible. Since the industrial revolution and the separation of workplace from home, women are likely to be far from their children during the day. Occasionally the workplace provides day care for children and facilities in terms of both a time and a place for women to feed their babies three or four times during work hours, or on demand. Such facilities are rare in Western capitalist nations, or indeed in industrialised socialist (or ex-socialist) nations, where the proportion of breast-feeding mothers is no higher (Heitlinger, 1987).

Whose Milk is it Anyway?

It should be clear by now that in many societies the rules regarding breast-feeding are laid down by men and tend to support male-dominated institutions. For example, in those countries which observe Muslim civil law, the duty of the woman to feed her husband's children, the length of time she should feed them and the conditions under which she may feed children other than her own, thus establishing links of milk kinship, are all prescribed by a male-dominated legal system. Jane Chahidi's article in this volume points out that the suckling of one woman's child by another has been used in different societies to make peace between two tribes, to consolidate clan unity, to prevent marriages, to create clients, in sum, ritually to attain objectives which lie far beyond the nursing woman's own interest.

It has been pointed out that younger women's practice is often enforced by older women, not men, but this does not necessarily mean that the ideas behind such practices originated with women nor that they are to women's advantage. There are many examples of the contrary, of which infibulation and clitoridectomy (carried out in about half of all African societies) are the most striking. Nevertheless, a study of breast-feeding norms and practice reveals a tension in many societies between norms which suggest an association between men and breast-milk, and women's actual practice which may be in contradiction to those norms. In setting up and maintaining day by day a breast-feeding relationship with their children, women may come to value the kinds of physical and emotional experience it affords them. This experience may undermine the social relations which the norms are meant to safeguard. Indeed women themselves may use breast-feeding as a resource to manipulate social relations. The social norms concerning breast-feeding often include reference to male privilege, and to men's right to control the behaviour of women. The experience of her own sexuality which accompanies a woman's sensations during menstruation, pregnancy, childbirth and of course breast-feeding may contradict male representations of these processes, and in a more general way the male-dominated norms and symbolism which regulate them. These processes are often socially represented as manifestations of women's negativity, dangerous to men, and to be controlled by them, directly or indirectly. But at the same time, in many societies, we may find a 'muted' or 'counterpart model' (Ardener, 1975: vii–xiii) which stresses women's reproductive power and their intrinsic physical benevolence.

We might take as an example the common precept in Muslim societies which obliges a woman to breast-feed her husband's children for two years, a rule which underlines a woman's lack of bodily autonomy and her duty of devotion to husband and children. In fact the Koranic recommendation is less stringent than that of many contemporary Muslim societies.

> Mothers shall suckle their children for *haulain kamilain*, (two whole years), [that is] for those who wish to complete the suckling. The duty of feeding and clothing the nursing mother is upon the father of the child . . . If they desire to wean the child by mutual consent and [after] joint consultation, it is no sin for them; and if ye wish to give your children out to nurse, it is no sin for you, provided that ye pay what is due from you in fairness (Schleifer, 1986: 68).

Yet in these same societies, a woman's milk is a sign of the blessing and abundance (*baraka*) that she brings to her husband's household, fields, animals, and on which his prosperity depends. That is, breast-milk is a female resource, whose cultural and institutional importance is such that men and women contend for its control. Thus, on the one hand, it is suggested as in Saudi Arabia that 'the milk is from the man', or in northern Tunisia that the 'grandfather-saint' cures 'milk-illness' in children. On the other hand, in these same societies the bond established between siblings suckled by the same woman is said to oblige them to mutual support, that is it creates a matrilineal tie, and a female source of power, in an ostensibly patrilineal and patriarchal society (Altorki, 1980: 233; Creyghton, this volume).

Breast-Feeding and the Political Order

The question of breast-feeding is also bound up with the cultural organisation of space and relationships. State organisation has resulted in the normative separation of 'public', that is productive and collective space, from 'private', that is 'reproductive' and individual space. To these categories are also attached those of gender identity, such that the public space is 'male' and the private is 'female'. Further, the spatial categories imply categories of relationship whereby relations of emotional and physical intimacy are confined to the private sphere, and impersonal work, political or social relationships characterise the public sphere. Where political and private spheres are not so distinct, it is often true that the ideology which separates work from the home does not subsist either, nor are outside and inside work sex-linked. In areas of female farming, women work together or with kin. There is no private domestic sphere, where it is more proper to breast-feed than at work. In sexually segregated societies such as those of North Africa and the Middle East, women breast-feed in the company of other women, who are not always kin, though Mai Yamani reports that among the *'awa'il* of the Hejaz (Saudi Arabia) elderly women often talk about how an envious woman can, just by looking at another nursing, cause the latter's milk to stop or make her ill. To feed only in the presence of family is only one of many precautions which Hejazi women adopt to avoid the 'suppression' of their milk (Yamani, 1989). Bottle-feeding which made headway among the Saudi Arabian élite during the 1950s, 1960s and 1970s does not have to be hedged round with precautions. Recently there has been some return to breast-feeding for religious reasons.

I have elsewhere concurred with Michelle Rosaldo that the divisions in Western industrial society are not only normative but also evaluative, conferring greater power and cultural value on the public, male impersonal sphere. Most of real life crosses and recrosses the boundaries between spheres (Rosaldo, 1980). It is clear that women who cross these boundaries as workers are expected to leave behind all accretions of the 'private' sphere such as their relationship to their children. The sexual harassment to which women are often subjected is a reminder that their role in the work world is conditional on their subordination as a gender to the men who dominate the public sphere. The sex-linked character of the spheres emphasises that women should not only bear children but should take on all responsibility for the physical and emotional relationships that this involves. This work is considered secondary and unimportant, compared to the 'productive' work in the public sphere, and has tended to become increasingly subsumed in it.

That a woman should breast-feed at work or in public is a violation of cultural categories, of the deep-seated taboos which sustain a power structure. Jelliffe quotes the case of a woman, arrested on a charge of obscenity for breast-feeding in a public square in Washington (Jelliffe, 1978). The State authority which presides over the public sphere and its privilege with respect to the private sphere, that is over the preservation of cultural categories, was challenged by this violation of boundaries, and took steps to restore order. Whether the State is associated historically with a Protestant or a Catholic ethos does not appear significantly to affect people's reactions to the 'intrusion' of breast-feeding into the public sphere. The lack of a time and place to breast-feed at work is not the only reason preventing working women from breast-feeding.

Most Westerners, both men and women, feel discomfort, not to say disgust at the idea of a woman breast-feeding outside the home, or in public. In England television advertisements for baby care products always show even tiny babies being bottle-fed, never breast-fed. Elizabeth and John Newson, who carried out an important psycho-social study of child rearing among working-class families in Nottingham, England, during the 1960s and 1970s, remarked on the fact that women frequently felt ashamed to breast-feed, even at home. One mother explained that she had stopped breast-feeding because she felt too ashamed in front of her three-year-old son (Newson and Newson, 1968).

The Newsons maintain that in England this is a more working-class than middle-class pattern (Newson and Newson, 1974: 72). The reverse might be true in Italy (Balsamo et al., this volume). The assumption that what happens outside the home is more socially important than what happens inside it, results in people attaching shame to those activities which imply physical and emotional intimacy, or which refer to aspects of female sexuality, menstruation, childbirth or breast-feeding. In our Turin research, the very presence of breast-feeding mothers in a hospital appeared to be a source of embarassment and pollution, to be neutralised with disinfectant and the covering of the breasts, and never discussed among the mothers themselves. These are not circumstances likely to favour the let-down reflex (see below p. 30).

Patriarchy and the Mother-Child Relationship

Like other relationships, that between mother and child may receive various degrees of cultural emphasis and figure in insti-tutional terms to a greater or lesser extent. The discussion of the matrifocal family has underlined the fact that 'cultural emphasis' and social, not to say legal institutionalisation, do not necessarily mean the same thing (James, 1978). For example, there may be strong values attached to the maternal role even in patrilineal societies. The mode and circumstances of breast-feeding are considered in many societies to be fundamental in the definition of mother-child and in general of adult-child relationships. Usually tenderness and nurturant attitudes are considered to be the characteristics of the mother and not of the father, and it is she who must assure the child of a loving environment, especially through breast-feeding. It is not a question of the child's survival at this point, but of its emotional development.

At-Tabari says that, in Islam, although: 'there is no sin in weaning the child [before the term of two years], it should be kept in mind that if the child is separated from the bond that was between him and his mother, he is thereby denied both his mother's tenderness and the nourishment from her breast, nourishment which leads to the formation of the mature adult' (Schleifer, 1986: 71).

The degree to which the child, or even the mother is seen as an active partner in this relationship can vary according to social structure. For example, Nadia Reissland's work on child rearing in Mithila, Nepal, quotes her informants as saying that the child 'takes the breast' just as she 'takes birth'. Thus, although the 'quality' of the milk is affected by the mother's personality, her role in breast-feeding is represented as secondary to that of the child. This is perhaps coherent with a strong patrilineal emphasis. In fact, in Mithila the baby is nourished not only by her mother but also, and particularly, by her father's sister who is responsible for massaging her daily with oil, and who gradually establishes a close and important relationship with the child. The massage, which proceeds according to precise rules, is said to make the child 'fat'. That is, the father's side nourishes the child with massage to counterbalance the mother's role in breast-feeding. The mother is not allowed to intervene though she may demur at the more energetic exercises such as throwing the baby up in the air and catching her. According to Reissland, this treatment is intended to make the child courageous and self-confident, and according to her observations, Nepalese children have a much greater degree of physical co-ordination than their European equivalents (Burghart and Reissland, 1987a, 1987b).

Patriarchal Institutions and the Interruption of Breast-Feeding

Patriarchy means that the relationship between mother and child is defined or even controlled by the cultural emphasis or social institutionalisation accorded to relationships involving adult men in dominant positions. This may have implications for the way breast-feeding is regarded in symbolic terms and for women's practice. In some cases, and particularly among high status groups in stratified societies, the child is removed from the mother and the breast-feeding relationship is interrupted or prevented altogether in order to secure the patrilineal alignment of the child. In these cases, the breast-feeding relationship is believed to create powerful maternal loyalties which may upset institutional arrangements. The case material for these beliefs is to be found in other 'less patrilineal' strata of the society to which the group in question belongs. Sablonier points to the arrangements which James II of Aragon made for his children in fourteenth-century Spain, surrounding them with nurses and tutors, arranging early marriage (age six) for the girls, and separating the siblings from each other and their mother at an early age so that their main loyalty should be to himself, and that emotional ties should not hinder his political plans for them (Sablonier, 1984). This was not exceptional among the European aristocracy of the period.

Christiane Klapisch has described the custom in fifteenth-century Florence of sending children out for wet-nursing, a custom among the merchants and notaries whose family accounts, *Libri di Ricordanze*, she has studied (Klapisch, 1980, 1985). The child was removed from its mother at birth and placed with a wet-nurse, chosen and paid by the father, who also decided when the child should be weaned. When marriages were arranged in order to match the rank and wealth of husband and wife, there might have been a risk that the influence of the wife's family, *vis-à-vis* the husband's, might mitigate the personal authority of a man over his wife. The man's control over breast-feeding was one way of establishing the children as the 'property' of the paternal line, but it served also to weaken the woman's role as mother within the family and to emphasise her role as wife.

The success of this endeavour is moot, since mother-child relationships have many bases for development, other than breast-feeding. In fact, different societies exploit to different degrees the psycho-physical potential of the breast-feeding relationship. Aztec mothers were known to breast-feed without holding their infants at all. If this may be difficult for some readers to imagine, I recently received an eye witness account of a young mother in a rural area of Western Piedmont, who breast-fed her baby by bending over him while he lay on his back on the kitchen table. Her arms were outstretched on either side of him, her hands on the table supporting her weight without touching him. Thus, although breast-feeding is frequently taken by psychologists to offer maximum skin contact and to be an archetypical situation of 'holding', closeness and cuddling between mother and child, such as is held to promote 'bonding' (see Maher, final chapter), there appears to be considerable room for cultural variation in this area.

Dorothy McClaren points out that in England in the sixteenth and seventeenth centuries, well-to-do women sent their babies out to be nursed by poorer women who also breast-fed their own. The richer women bore many more children than the poorer ones. Moreover the mortality rate of children from well-to-do families was very high and so was that of their mothers. Poorer mothers bore fewer children who lived longer. McLaren hints that, with the example of their poorer sisters before them, richer mothers may have been aware that maternal breast-feeding would reduce their fertility and save some of their children, but they were under pressure from husbands and Church to send their children to be wet-nursed (McClaren, 1985). This pattern of infant feeding seems to jeopardise both children and their mothers and it is difficult to understand how it could obtain, unless in a situation where the survival of mothers and their children was not defined as a social problem. As we have suggested above, what appears to have been at stake in these families, was the conservation of status, property and male privilege. The conjugal role of well-to-do women, in England as in Florence, probably included the management of large and complex households as well as entertaining and being entertained. In sum, a wealthy man's wife was to exhibit in her person, her dress and her home, the social position of her husband and breast-feeding would have interfered with such a role.

In Iceland, between 1600 and 1900, women bore many children, fed them on dairy products rather than breast-fed them, and had a great many of them die. If we take into account the enormous swathes cut in the small Icelandic population by successive plagues, we might guess at a certain haste to replenish it by avoiding breast-feeding with its contraceptive effects and post-partum taboos on sexual intercourse. But if this avoidance had, over three centuries, the opposite of the desired effect, we must look for other 'more cultural' explanations (see Hastrup, this volume).

In the case of the English well-to-do, the 'demographic argument' seems difficult to sustain. It seems more fruitful to look at the avoidance of maternal breast-feeding as having the result of enhancing the conjugal relationship, the status and privileges of the husband within it and the exhibition of that status within the husband's social milieu. That is, the prevention of breast-feeding and indeed of intimacy between mothers and their children for the long periods when they were bearing more children or being replaced by nurses and wet-nurses, may have whittled away mothers' influence over the family destinies. The polarisation of roles in which the wife, whose social origin may have been as elevated as her husband's, nevertheless led a life of frequent confinement, possibly confirmed her social dependence on and subordination to her partner.

Thus breast-feeding or not breast-feeding may be seen not only as a means to promote or prevent the growth of mother-child relationships, but also as the condition for the creation of other kinds of social relationship, centred round neither the child nor the mother, but rather designed to teach both of them their place in the patriarchal system of kinship and property.

Weaning in Buganda

Nutritional considerations are not foremost in the obligation recognised by every Baganda man to wean his child abruptly at one year old and send it to live with its paternal grandmother. The transfer of the child was seen as the grandmother's right and a means of reinforcing the child's tie with his patrilateral relatives, thus placing the child correctly within the kinship system. According to Hebe Welbourn, a pediatrician who worked in Kampala in Uganda during the 1960s and 1970s, the weaning of the child at one year old appeared to threaten its life, and although morbidity increased also during the second six months, infant mortality peaked at one year. This was partly because of the lack of an adequate transitional food to bridge the gap between breast-milk and the adult diet.

During the 1950s and 1960s the psychologist John Bowlby in Britain was developing his theories on the traumatic effects of maternal deprivation. His research was mostly based on the observation of children separated from their mothers during the Second World War, or shortly afterwards. But following a study which applied his theories *tels quels* to the Ugandan weanling problem, many British paediatricians were led to believe that it was the trauma of separation which caused babies to die when they reached the year mark. Welbourn points out, however, that this interpretation of infant mortality in terms of individual psychology fails to take into account the variability in the fate of children after their removal from the mother. She attributes this variability to differences in the social circumstances of Bagandan weanlings. For example, she suggests that the weanling crisis was provoked not so much by the anguish of separation, for marriage was virilocal and therefore a child's grandmother usually lived in the same village as her son, and was often among the child's chief caretakers prior to his move. It was more likely that the problem arose when the grandmother's household was too poor to meet the child's special needs. Where the grandmother was still an active farmer or her household was prosperous there were few signs that the weanling suffered (Personal Communication).

Breast-Feeding and the Social Construction of the Person

If the 'management' of breast-feeding may mean preventing it or interrupting it at a certain point, we may presume that what are being interrupted and prevented are certain kinds of relationship in favour of others. But the 'management' of breast-feeding in a positive sense, not in that of preventing or interrupting it, but as a relationship between persons, may be considered necessary in order to define the 'person' in conformity with cultural requirements. Thus At-Tabari, advising his Arab readers in the tenth century, points out that breast-feeding is necessary to the formation of the 'mature adult'. In Italian society, boy babies may be breast-fed for a longer period than girl babies, and each feed may last longer, in conformity with the cultural expectation that men, in many spheres of their later lives, will be afforded more emotional, symbolic and physical nurturance than women (Gianini, Belotti, 1973).

In Northern Greece, breast-feeding is considered to be the

means by which both mother and child pass from a symbiotic relationship to their reciprocal definition as separate persons. The way in which this process comes about is governed by cultural norms, and the success of the enterprise is believed to influence the way mother and child relate to the rest of society. Lucy Rushton's research in Northern Greece has led her to the following conclusions:

> Breast-feeding is, from one point of view, a part of social give and take, a particular relationship between persons. But it is also a prolongation of the pains of birth for a mother and it represents the mother's and child's mutual difficulty in establishing the correct separation between them. The moment of weaning offers the opportunity to set a seal on that separation and create for the child an essential pattern for all other relationships (Rushton, 1988).

In our Turin research (see Balsamo et al., this volume), the difficulty which most women experienced in establishing breast-feeding and deciding when to wean may be attributed largely to the hospital 'productive system', and its persistent interferences in the relationship between mother and child. Far from facilitating a reciprocal boundary setting between persons, the hospital tended to 'depersonalise' mother and child by its objectifying treatment and by separating them at an early stage and ignoring their relationship. Later on the mother's subordination to the quantitative culture of scientific medicine led her to inculcate in the child a sense that time intervals and rules in general were more important than his desires and emotions or those of his mother. On the other hand, the mother tended to delegate decisions over breast-feeding and weaning to the doctors. In this way, irrespective of the mode of feeding attempted, neither she nor the child ever achieved a personal boundary *vis-à-vis* the other, since their relationship was constrained by a series of exogenous rules and both remained open to 'authoritative' or even authoritarian manipulation by outside 'experts'. Perhaps this is one way of ensuring dependence on the institutions of centralised states.

The Transmission of Personal Traits

Breast-feeding, culturally rather than emotionally managed, is believed, in some societies, to inculcate in the child a sense of his own and the other's personal boundaries, as culturally defined.

But, in many societies, it is also believed to form a person's character. Mai Yamani reports the saying from the Hejaz in Saudi Arabia. 'Character impressed by the mother's milk cannot be altered by anything except death' (Yamani, 1989; See also Chahidi, this volume). As long as it is the mother who nurses the child, this presents few problems and, indeed, the choice of a spouse may be influenced by the idea that a wife should also be a 'good mother' and that her qualities will be passed in her milk to her children. However, if she breast-feeds a boy too long or pampers him, he may absorb too many of her female qualities and become a 'milk-sop'.

Special care is usually exercised in the choice of a wet-nurse or of animal milk to feed to the child. This is done not only on the grounds that the milk of the nurse or of the animal may be nutritionally inadequate, but because of the fear that the child, in drinking it, may absorb undesirable mental and personal qualities. Sixteenth-century writers in Britain believed that infants fed on animal milk were 'fierce and not like men', and the practice of direct suckling from an animal, although more widespread in France, was never popular in Britain, where wet-nursing was the rule among the wealthy, at least until the late nineteenth century (Fildes, 1986: 271). Among the poor, hand-feeding with animal milk or pap was always preferred to direct suckling.

In a strongly patrilineal and virilocal society, a mother is usually blamed for her child's illness or character defects. Goat's milk is fed to Nepalese children in Mithila because its cathartic components are capable of cancelling the negative qualities of the mother, who is always regarded with diffidence in this patrilineal, virilocal society (Burghart and Reissland, 1987a). Among the Khmir of Northern Tunisia, described in this volume by Creyghton, some children's illnesses are attributed to 'bad milk'. A woman's milk is 'bad' when she herself is 'hot' and tired from work. In this state she should never breast-feed, or give in to the tenderness or exasperation she feels for her crying infant. If she does indulge in untimely feeding she is merely providing another example of the incapacity of women to exert self-control, even for the sake of their infants. It is to the male saint or *marabout* (a charismatic figure especially revered within the Sufi Muslim tradition) to whom women turn for a remedy for their child's milk illness, through the medium of a woman healer.

Creyghton points out that the mother and child are still considered to be a single unit long after the birth, but the intervention of the *marabout* (mediating between the divine and the earthly sphere) marks a breach in their symbiotic relationship and the beginning of the child's relationship with his patrilineal kin. In this way, male control of breast-milk is re-established, but, on the other hand, the woman is assured of the support of the patrilineal relatives of her husband (descendants of the saint, whom they call 'grandfather'), whose child she is nourishing with her substance.

Women's Practice, 'Reverie' and the Let-down Reflex

In spite of the fact that in many societies the norms governing breast-feeding do not appear to originate with the mother, it is she who is likely to decide on a daily basis how, when and for how long to feed her child, within the framework of their relationship. Several of the essays in this collection discuss the fact that, although they may receive advice from different quarters, women often take these daily decisions in contradiction to the cultural norm, in the light of several considerations. These may include, besides the welfare of the infant, that of their other children, their own physical and psychological health, the availability of food and the pressures of work.

Since biological reproduction is a matter of great social concern and rarely left normatively in the hands of women, any attempt by women to gain control over their own bodies and sexuality, and to develop personal relationships on such a basis, is often seen as an illegitimate appropriation of social resources. It would be strange if breast-feeding escaped these strictures. The degree of freedom with which women are able to manage breast-feeding appears to depend on the configuration of roles which they are called upon to play in any given society.

Kitzinger and others (Kitzinger, 1980) suggest that a mother, especially a first-time one, relives her childhood experience during the early breast-feeding period. She feels dependent and vulnerable; this regression is necessary for her to relate imaginatively to her infant and to make the transition to the status of mother. Anthropological studies of status change would seem to confirm such a hypothesis; in many societies the ritual which expresses and to a certain extent effects the changes in status (both mystical, and in the case of a new mother, social) of a mother allow for her to hand over all her social responsibilities to someone else and to remain with her child for a couple of weeks, while they are both looked after. However, if there is no one to sustain them during the puerperal period, for example with household help and care for mother and child, the mother's regression is hampered. Mother and child are unable to indulge in the 'reverie' which both need and which is perhaps a necessary condition of breast-feeding. The 'let-down reflex', a hormonally triggered psycho-physical reaction which enables a mother to release the rich hind milk, is particularly inhibited by the situation of emotional and physical stress to which an isolated or harassed mother is subject. Distractions of different kinds have also been observed to reduce the milk supply by half (Kitzinger, 1980: 214).

The pleasurable sensations which many women experience when breast-feeding and which vary from baby to baby are often associated with the let-down reflex. The hind milk released by the 'let-down' constitutes about two thirds of the milk available for a feed. A child who receives only fore milk will soon be ill for lack of nourishment.

In many cultures women are discouraged from breast-feeding when under stress, by the belief that the milk may harm the baby (see Creyghton, this volume). Maybe this helps towards the management of 'let-down'. Creyghton suggests that Tunisian women, when breast-feeding, may employ mental techniques such as those employed in ecstatic religious cults to achieve mental 'decontrol' and 'indifference' to the world. Certainly in many parts of the Maghreb, women participate directly in Sufi practices (Dwyer, 1978: 585–98; Maher, 1984: 103–28). Although Creyghton does not provide us with direct evidence for this in Northern Tunisia, it is significant that it is the *marabout* (probably the focal point of local ecstatic practices) who is asked to intervene when a child falls ill with 'milk illness'. That is, the negative relation of stress to 'let-down' is recognised in different ways, and managed by culturally legitimated ritual practices. Within Western medical culture this relationship is totally ignored.

Many observers have remarked on the beneficent effects of women helpers or close relatives at childbirth. Their emotional support appears to shorten labour and ease the birth in many ways. Others have pointed out, and not only in the context of non-European societies, that breast-feeding is easier to establish with the help of an expert woman helper or 'douala'. However, Jean A. Ball has remarked on the frustrations with which Western midwives have to deal, especially in the hospital setting, in trying to give personal postnatal care to a new mother (Ball, 1987).

It is sometimes assumed that a woman's mother can provide care and advice on breast-feeding. In our Turin research, the desire to breast-feed appeared, indeed, to be associated with a mother's internalised image of her own mother. However, in reality, many women had not seen a baby being breast-fed by their own mothers or anyone else. On the other hand, the new mothers were often working women who rejected the kind of gender identity implicit in their mothers' model. Not only did a woman tend to manage on her own, but she tried to avoid her mother's presence during the early puerperal period and indeed subsequently, relying in many cases on her husband for some limited help.

For some women, the husband is important, in particular as witness to and main counterpart of a woman's new status. In this model, a woman achieves maternal status by 'demothering' her own mother, and by assuming a more powerful role with respect to her husband, rather than by seeking a particular relationship with the child. Not breast-feeding, or breast-feeding for a short time only, on the one hand allows the husband to 'help' with the baby, on the other stresses the conjugal and sexual privilege of the husband, and, last but not least, enables the new mother to establish her independence of her own mother, in symbolic if not real terms. Paradoxically, not breast-feeding appears to some women to be a condition of emancipation.

Women, Breast-Feeding and Industrial Society

The social and cultural importance of breast-feeding is such that, even in Western industrial societies, it is rarely called into question. On the contrary, like many social imperatives associated with gender roles, it is considered 'natural' even though the majority of women do not breast-feed. The decline in breast-feeding over the last hundred years is interpreted nowadays, particularly in medical circles, as an instance of women's alienation from their biological nature, or from their 'natural' gender roles. However, there have been historical instances, exemplified by the American conversion to formula-feeding, or by the avoidance of breast-feeding for centuries in Iceland (see Hastrup, this volume), when not breast-feeding has been considered to be an improvement on nature.

We may also advance the hypothesis that the decline of breast-feeding in Western industrial societies is part of the process whereby, since the sixteenth century, women have lost control over their bodies as a symbolic and institutional resource, because of the medicalisation of reproduction, and its subordination to industrial ideology and forms of relationship.

The emotional and physical relationship of women and children has disappeared from view to be replaced by a symbolic order and a bureaucratic practice, in which women and children reappear as resources to be optimally manipulated for productive ends. The overwhelming majority of gynaecologists and paediatricians are men (particularly those in leading positions). It would be interesting to plot the proliferation of negative images of women's bodies in Europe since the sixteenth century (see Merchant, 1980) against the development, on the one hand, of a male-dominated gynaecological science, and, on the other, of male-dominated pornography, both of which have often perceived women as body-objects to be controlled. Breast-milk as a hidden, invisible resource has turned out to be particularly recalcitrant to male control. The continuous search for artificial alternatives is only one symptom of the misogyny intrinsic to much medical research.

By participating in the medicalisation of their bodies and in the view of breast-feeding as desirable almost exclusively for nutritional reasons women lose touch with their own desire (or reluctance) to breast-feed their babies. Women themselves contribute to the medical representation of the female body as a machine which has to be managed in order to fulfil its proper functions. This image favours the view of the body as composed of so many more or less related parts. Many women perceive their bodies not only as internally fragmented but as split off from themselves as persons and as incumbents of social roles (Martin, 1987: 71–91). Women in the industrial West are less aware that they create and acquire symbolic value by breast-feeding, than they are of the risk of being physically and psychologically manipulated by medical intervention and control of their bodies.

Breast-feeding is difficult under these conditions, and not breast-feeding may even be considered a symptom of unconscious resistance to medical invasion of the self. The article in this volume on breast-feeding in Turin reminds us that the mechanical imagery which pervades the medical representation of breast-feeding has resulted in the attempt to subject it to factory-like regulation. In many Western hospitals, mother and child are separated for most of the day, but the rigidity imposed on their meetings is also presented as a model for the mother to follow once she has arrived home. Intervals between feeds and the length of feeds are to be timed by the clock. The mother should weigh the child after each feed and make up artificial milk to compensate for any shortfall in the average amount of milk per feed considered by the doctors to be necessary. In this picture, the active figures are the clock, the scales and the doctor, who reduce the mother and baby to mechanisms in a productive process and considerably hamper the development of the relationship between the two, or of each with the father.

The hospitalisation of childbirth, that is, its integration into a public and productive sphere dominated by men, has led to a disregard for women's and children's physical and emotional needs and relationships in the interest of a sort of mechanisation of reproduction. But in a more general sense, human emotional and physical capacities are crushed by the productivist and industrial conception of reality which has come to pervade social life.

Notes

1. In her article on wet-nursing published in English in 1985 ('Blood parents and milk parents: wet-nursing in Florence, 1300–1530', in Klapisch-Zuber, C., *Women, Family and Ritual in Renaissance Italy*, Chicago, University of Chicago Press: 132–64) Klapisch provides further material on wet-nursing in Florence during the fourteenth and fifteenth centuries. She emphasises the fact that husbands decided on the way infants were fed, that girl children were more often sent out to be nursed than boys, that the children of wet-nurses were often 'abandoned' to religious institutions by their fathers who wished their wives to wet-nurse a rich man's child, or sell the milk; that wet-nursed children had a lower survival rate than 'home-nursed' ones but a higher rate than 'abandoned' ones.

Bibliographical References

Accati, L., 'La cronologia differita dei simboli', *Studi Medievali*, 1990

Altorki, S., 'Milk kinship in Arab Society: an Unexplored Problem in the Ethnography of Marriage', *Ethnology*, 14, 1980: 233–44

Ardener, S. (ed.), *Perceiving Women*, London, Dent, 1975

Ball, J., *Reactions to Motherhood: the role of post-natal care*, Cambridge, Cambridge University Press, 1987

Bott, E., *Family and Social Networks*, London, Tavistock, 1957

Bowlby, J., *Attachment and Loss*, New York, Basic Books, 1969

Burghart, R. and Reissland, N., 'The quality of a mother's milk and the health of her child: beliefs and practices of the women of Mithila (Nepal)', *Social Science and Medicine*, July, 1987a

——, 'The role of massage in South Asia: research note on child health and development', *Social Science and Medicine*, August, 1987b

Bynum, W.C., *Holy Feast and Holy Fast. The religious significance of food to medieval women*, Berkeley, University of California Press, 1987

Cameron, M. and Hofvander, Y., *Manual on Feeding Infants and Young Children*, Protein-calorie Advisory Group of the United Nations System, Second Edition, New York, 1976

Dwyer, D., 'Women, Sufism and Decision-making in Moroccan Islam', in Beck, L. and Keddie, N. (eds), *Women in the Muslim World*, Cambridge Mass, Harvard University Press, 1978: 585–98

Fildes, V., *Breasts, Bottles and Babies: a history of infant feeding*, Edinburgh, Edinburgh University Press, 1986

Foucault, M., *An Introduction. The History of Sexuality*, Vol. 1, New York, Vintage Books, 1978

Gianini Belotti, E., *Dalla Parte delle Bambine*, Milano, Feltrinelli, 1973

Goody, J., *Production and Reproduction: a comparative study of the domestic domain*, Cambridge, Cambridge University Press, 1976

——, *The Development of the Family and Marriage in Europe*, Cambridge, Cambridge University Press, 1983

Heitlinger, A., *Reproduction, Medicine and the Socialist State*, London, Macmillan, 1987

Horney, K., *Feminine Psychology*, New York, W. Norton, 1967

Inch, S., 'Difficulties with breast-feeding: midwives in disarray', Report on Meeting of Forum on Maternity and the Newborn, 2 Dec 1985, in *Journal of the Royal Society of Medicine*, Vol. 80, Jan 1987: 53–8

James, W., in Ardener, S. (ed.), *Defining Females*, London, Croom Helm, 1978

Kitzinger, S., *The Experience of Breast-feeding*, London, Pelican, 1980

Jelliffe, D.B. and Jelliffe, E.F., *Human Milk in the Modern World: psychological, nutritional and economic significance*, Oxford, Oxford University Press, 1978

Klapisch-Zuber, C., 'Genitori naturali e genitori di latte nella Firenze del quattrocento', *Quaderni Storici*, 44, agosto 1980: 543–63
——, *Women, Family and Ritual in Renaissance Italy*, Chicago, Chicago University Press, 1985
Levine, N.E., 'Women's work and infant feeding: a case from Nepal', *Ethnology*, July 1989: 231–51
Maher, V., 'Possession and dispossession: maternity and mortality in Morocco', in Medick, H. and Sabean, D. (eds), *Interest and Emotion: essays on the study of the family and kinship*, Cambridge, Cambridge University Press, 1984: 103–28
McLaren, D., 'Marital Fertility and Lactation, 1570–1720', in Prior, M. (ed.), *Women in English Society, 1500–1800*, London, Methuen, 1985: 23–53
Martin, E., *The Woman in the Body: a cultural analysis of reproduction*, Boston, Beacon Press, 1987
Medick, H. and Sabean, D., *Interest and Emotion: essays on the study of the family and kinship*, Cambridge, Cambridge University Press, 1984
Merchant, C., *The Death of Nature: Women, Ecology and the Scientific Revolution*, Berkeley, California University Press, 1980
Newson, J. and Newson, E., *Infant Care in an Urban Community*, London, Allen and Unwin, 1963
——, *Four Years Old in an Urban Community*, London, Allen and Unwin, 1968
——, 'Cultural aspects of child-rearing in the English-speaking world', in Richards, M. (ed.), *The Integration of the Child into a Social World*, Cambridge, Cambridge University Press, 1974: 53–82
Oakley, A., 'A Case of Maternity: Paradigms of Women as Maternity Cases', *Signs*, Vol. 4, no. 4, 1979a: 607–31
——, *Becoming a Mother*, Oxford, Martin Robertson, 1979b
Raphael, D. (ed.), *Breast-feeding and Food Policy in a Hungry World*, London, Academic Press, 1979
Richards, M. (ed.), *The Integration of the Child into a Social World*, Cambridge, Cambridge University Press, 1974
Rosaldo, M., 'The use and abuse of anthropology: reflections on feminism and cross-cultural understanding', *Signs*, Vol. 5, no. 3, 1980: 389–417
Rushton, L., 'Breast-feeding and the Evil Eye in Greece', typescript, 1988
Sablonier, R., 'The Aragonese royal family around 1300', in Medick, H. and Sabean, D., *Interest and Emotion: essays on the study of family and kinship*, Cambridge, Cambridge University Press, 1984: 210–39
Schleifer, A., *Motherhood in Islam*, Cambridge, The Islamic Academy, 1986
Stanway, P. and A., *Breast is Best*, London, Pan Books Ltd, 1978

Taha, S., 'Ecological factors underlying protein-calorie malnutrition in an irrigated area of the Sudan', *Ecology of Food and Nutrition*, 7, 1979: 193–201

Warner, M., *Alone of all her Sex: The Myth and the Cult of the Virgin Mary*, London, Quartet Books, 1978

Westcott, M., *The Feminist legacy of Karen Horney*, London, Yale University Press, 1986

Yamani, M., *Formality and Propriety in the Hejaz*, unpublished D.Phil thesis, Institute of Social Anthropology, University of Oxford, 1989

2

Breast-Feeding and *Baraka* in Northern Tunisia

Marie-Louise Creyghton

Today, as in the past, mother's milk is considered to be an extraordinary baby food. It is well packaged, free of dangerous germs and always at hand and ready for the baby to consume, qualities which have their advantages when kitchen equipment is very simple indeed. Furthermore, breast-feeding arouses agreeable physical sensations and has contraceptive virtues.

In the north-western mountains of Tunisia, the regions which the French colonists called the Khroumirie, where the Khroumir or Khmir people live, women have additional reasons for appreciating breast-feeding. Here it is a cultural axiom that the flowing of a mother's milk and her baby's evident thriving on it is a sign of *baraka*, a life sustaining force. When a mother transmits this force, it is not only the nursling who prospers, but also everybody and everything pertaining to the house. Hence people feel confidence in their general circumstances when a baby fares well. Also, it is by breast-feeding, not by pregnancy, that the strong emotional bond between mother and child is created, a bond which is extended automatically to the mother's siblings, the child's *akhwāli*.[1]

The Old Khmir Way of Life

When the French troops penetrated into the Khroumirian hills in the second half of the nineteenth century, they found a few small and far flung settlements. Most of them were situated near a stream where the soil was reasonably fertile. The inhabitants must have been a brave and rugged lot who fiercely resisted the European enemy. The bulk of them were nomads who had been forced

37

by stronger tribes to find new pastures. Others had fled from calamities such as plague, cholera and famine which descended on Tunisia like the Biblical plagues on Egypt, especially during the first half of the nineteenth century (Valensi, 1977: 266). Still others had been forced to flee for their lives when one of their close family members had become involved in a question of blood vengeance, as a result of which neither his brothers, nor his sons, nor any other male agnate liable to represent him, could have dealings with his enemy. The fugitives hid in the mountains where other dangers lurked. Safety there depended on the number of able-bodied men on whom a cohabiting group could count and, of course, on how quickly and how well they succeeded in dissuading other groups in the region from attacking them. For especially in times of scarcity a raid was not uncommon.

A raiding gang was called a *gum*. At the time I worked there,[2] raids were no longer necessary, nor possible. The term *gum* was used to indicate collective aggression, or even the mere possibility of it. People who felt menaced by a group called it a *gum*. The word was never used of one's own group. Members of domestic groups, living with other households within calling distance, used the term *douār*. A *douār* is more than a mere village. Those who dwell there reckon themselves to be of one family; they count themselves to be descendants of the same eponymic grandfather and through their real or ascribed kinship ties they owe each other loyalty in certain respects.

It has always been the aspiration of every man and every woman to create a *douār* in order to be well provided for in old age. In consequence, to give birth and keep children alive, to pull them through their first hazardous years, were highly valued social capacities. Yet when a woman gave birth to a row of sons, other women began to mumble about her *gum*. This suggests that the position of a successful mother was highly ambiguous. Many sons promised safety and a livelihood for the mother and her family. But if her house became a *douār* within the *douār*, the carefully established status quo was jeopardized. Others might feel threatened. Both the father and the mother of many sons were obliged to resort to diplomacy and stratagems of various kinds within their own network in order to convince others that their growing family offered no dangers.

Pioneering in the north-western mountains of Tunisia must have been very hard. It was still hard after Independence in 1956. But in a different way. Villages and hamlets were growing fast. During a hot summer, drinking water from wells and springs was far from sufficient so that here was a real source of conflict for women to cope with. For they were the ones who carried the water home in large earthenware jars. The grass for the huge roofs of their adobe huts had become scarce and expensive.[3] Firewood was becoming a problem. Gathering firewood was women's work. Although there were pack-animals in the region it was the tradition that women carry wood, burdens of some fifty kilograms, the weight of a woman's own body or more. Early in the morning they set out in groups of four to five, cord and hatchet over their shoulders. Towards noon, if you looked from the top of the hill into the distance, you could see a line of bundles of wood advancing slowly, carried by naked feet which carefully felt their way home. Sometimes the women rested, leaning against bundles as high as themselves. Their pale faces sweated profusely. When, entering the yard, one of them heard her baby cry, she did not hesitate a moment, but threw her burden down, hurried to the child and, though tired and dirty, put her nipple in his mouth. Peace, silence and relaxation descended on the house. Later, when the baby eventually showed symptoms of Milk Illness she was to say that the cause was 'her warm milk clotting in her breast' because of the great effort she had made.

This gesture of suckling a baby when the breast was not ready was interpreted either as a sign of the mother's tender feelings towards her child, her *hanāna*, or as the proof of a typical female inability to foresee the consequences of one's actions, or both. *Hanāna* stands for compassion, maternal instinct, the desire to cuddle and spread warmth. A hen, spreading her breast feathers and calling her young when she is about to sink down on a good spot is driven by *hanāna*. *Hanāna* or not, women told me that after carrying wood home (an enterprise which closely resembled a raid when the wood was taken from grounds claimed by the *Service des Forêts*), they were so exhausted that they just could not stand any noise. They preferred to take the risk of nursing a child rather than have to hear it cry.

From the foregoing data we may construe a preliminary image of the Khmir adult woman as:

    a. endowed with formidable strength

    b. overflowing with love for her young

    c. disposed neither to reflection nor to foresight

d. acting spontaneously

It is striking that physical strength is no feature of the traditional image of man. Nor does spontaneity figure in it, although it is mentioned in some stories about male saints. In the image of the Khmir man social training is stressed. He is cautious, capable of careful judgement of the situation, far-seeing and cunning if necessary. Above all he is able to protect his honour. Sometimes a young man bursts through the trammels of convention and sometimes an older man who should know better allows himself to be carried away by his emotions in public. But this reality hardly seems to influence the image of man which is less rich, intricate, and contradictory in its different components than that of woman. For that reason I prefer to think of *one* image of man and of *several* images of woman.

Public normative behaviour towards women ignores the image depicted just now. It is inspired by another image which stresses the relation between woman and her social guardian (husband, father, brother). For instance, any man should avert his head when meeting on his path a woman with whom he is not well acquainted. Not to look into her eyes is a sign of respect, respect for the female status in general, respect for himself as a trusted man who upholds the values of society and respect for her husband or father whose vulnerable side she represents. To give another example, the scene of a mother with child, trotting behind her husband who rides the donkey has no humiliating connotation for the Khmir. On the contrary, it tells them of protection and respect. 'Why!' they exclaim when hearing of European feelings about the situation: 'who do you think should lead the way? She? And who has to be most visible, she or he? For who is to be addressed, should someone want to do so? Tired? A woman is strong, if she cannot walk she stays at home'. Apart from these arguments it would be very inappropriate for a woman to be seen riding on a donkey, a donkey being a 'low' and lusty animal. Or rather, it would be very inappropriate for a father or a husband to be responsible for a woman riding on a donkey, it would mean 'trouble ahead!'.

Dress, too, evokes an image of woman. The common dress consists of a long flowered shirt and over it a simple piece of cotton (or lately nylon), arranged like a gown. A long belt of a striking colour supports the abdomen. It should be wound as tightly around the hips as the headkerchief is knotted around the head.

Very little variation is admitted. All gowns are either violet or purple. All headkerchiefs are dark with more or less the same design. The uniformity tells of the 'sameness' of women, of the prohibition to compete on the level of outward appearances, but also of jealousy which is much dreaded when it starts to grow in a woman's heart. It is acknowledged that man can be jealous too, but the consequences of his jealousy are not considered so disastrous for the family. The way in which the girdle is worn tells us that breast and womb are not separate, as many European modes of dressing suggest. It tells us too that the woman's body is 'closed' like a sack is closed by firmly tying a rope around it. Neither belt nor headkerchief are untied in public, with the exception of a certain ritual occasion when a wife lays her belt for a moment on the tomb of a saint, asking to become pregnant.

The Khmir, like many people who pass on an oral tradition, are fond of analogics and comparisons. Some of them sound astonishingly positive, such as 'the House is like the *marabout*' and 'the married woman is like the House'.[4] The message this saying carries is that just as the *marabout* spreads his *baraka*, the life giving and sustaining force, over the surrounding territory, the housewife spreads *baraka* over the house, its inhabitants, its flock, the cow and all its livestock, in short over all living things which enter the house or regularly come into close contact with it. It is especially this image that we encounter when getting acquainted with Khmir feelings about mother's milk. None of the images mentioned so far stands on its own. Before pursuing our theme, that of the nursing mother, we have to enter another very old and powerful chain of associations that dominates the way Khmir view married women.

Further Exploration of the Way Khmir Represent Women

Every peasant in North Africa knows the saying: 'the married woman is like the earth', *l mra kimma l ardh*. Khmir key informants agreed that this meant that both the earth and woman should be given their *haqq*, their rightful share, that which they could rightfully expect. As the earth may ask for water, or manure, or to be weeded in due time, or to be left in peace in certain moments, so a woman has her demands which should be met in order that the marriage may be fruitful. The earth knows the right time in which right actions should be performed in the right way; woman is no different. Both the earth and woman yearn for their *haqq*. This indigenous interpretation is interesting because it ignores the widespread notion that North African women are sexually insatiable and that their appetites drive them to infidelity. If the married woman is like the earth it means that perhaps some special treatment is needed, based on careful observation, or perhaps some experimentation should be tried. And that is just what a real husbandman who knows his plot is keen to do, informants said, adding that few men, alas, had the true love of the earth or the patience to experiment.

The notion of *haqq* is handled mainly by men; both agriculture and law are their domain. Since the chain of thoughts behind *haqq* is quite exceptional in not unconditionally defending the rights and prerogatives of males it deserves our full attention. When it is felt that a certain wife shows interest in men, people begin to suspect that her husband is weak. He may not be able to give her her *haqq*, in other words, he may not be virile, which by definition means that he is unable to act like a man should. No matter how he reacts to provocation at this stage, a frequent challenge in itself may be a clear signal that there are doubts as to whether he can really defend his goods and chattels and, with it, wife and honour. No wonder then that the same men, who speak intelligently about *haqq* when they think of trusted spouses, are tempted to defend with vigour the idea of women's insatiable lusts when they think with apprehension of their unmarried teenage daughters.

As Westerners we are inclined to think that the idea of *haqq* is reasonable and realistic while the idea of female lusts is a fantasy, inspired by male anxiety. All anthropologists know how difficult it is to gain more than superficial knowledge of intimate life in other cultures, so I shall not argue about reality or fantasy here. I simply want to point out that the idea of female lusts fits astonishingly well with the image of a person of great physical strength acting spontaneously and without much reflection, as she feels inclined. Insatiable sexual desires add the qualities of a She-devil to this image.[5] This new version is incompatible, in its lack of moderation, with the notion of *haqq* and it is self-evident that where a She-devil is concerned, it is irrelevant whether a man is virile or not.

This second image seems to be critical of woman and, moreover, incompatible with the former one which has its roots in *maraboutism*. But we must look beyond appearances. Essentially the idea of a She-devil offers a certain excuse for a woman's misbehaviour; it tells us that she cannot be responsible for herself and neither can men, who are her guardians, be called to account for her demeanour. The Khmir do not know where this strong sexual drive comes from (I am speaking of the way they represent women, not of reality) but they know it is very powerful, often beyond human control. They contemplate it with a certain awe, mingled with displeasure, because it affects their status on the social level where the opinion is cherished that women should and can be guided and ruled by men.

Reasonable as it appears, the notion of *haqq* has its unsuspected depths too. Regardless of whether a man is the owner of the plot he cultivates or not, the mere fact that he ploughs and sows it with his own hands creates an intimate relation with the earth, comparable to the relation with his wife. As the Algerian peasant public notaries did not wish to recognise that the direct physical contact with the earth, the fact that a man fertilised her, did not make him automatically her owner, even if she was in his possession (Charnay, 1965: 175), so Khmir husbands do not wish to accept that they are only to a certain extent possessors of their wives' bodies.

In former times a wife's brothers reminded him of this fact, if necessary. If their sister was not treated in a decent way the *akhwāli* could act as a group. If the worst came to the worst they took their sister and her small children back home, so it is said. Unfortunately, with the decline of the extended family and the current economic crisis, any additional mouth to feed might jeopardize a family's precarious food balance. So their actual influence is on the wane. In some respects a young wife is, more than used to be the case, given up to the occasional high-handedness or ill-will of a husband's mother, sisters or sisters-in-law. Clearly she no longer has male defenders and revengers, *aktāfi*, 'shoulders' as they used to be called. Yet she is still often seen as the *bint l baranīya*, the girl from outside the group, whose loyalties are with her own agnates, rather than with her husband's kin.

To be precise, a man does not possess the whole body of his wife. It is mainly the womb that his family has hired as a temporary shelter for his descendants. The womb is like the *tabūna*, the earthenware, locally constructed oven. The flat, round sponges of dough are stuck to its heated wall to bake. The oven contributes nothing to the bread itself, I was told. Its only function is to be a place where the fire can finish the work of the cook; likewise the *tabūna* is no more than a protective casing.

The Khmir deny explicitly that the mother's body may play a role in the creation of a child. She receives it as the *tabūna* receives the sponge and as the earth receives the seed. She is the environment where transformation occurs.

No married woman possesses her own womb. But no man is entitled to his wife's milk and, moreover, neither is his child. It is so self-evident that a child and his mother's milk cannot be conceived as separate entities that there is no stipulation in the unwritten local law, the *kanūn*, that a child has a right to his mother's milk.

This milk cannot be owned by a person or a group. It is a symbol which draws a circle around the group which includes the mother and child but also the mother's siblings. For they have shared the same milk which is passed on now to the nurseling, whose father stands outside the circle. The baby's mother's mother on the contrary may be included.[6] However, mother's milk is more than a symbol, more than another door leading to the world of the sacred where the *marabout* lives in his *baraka*. It is the very vehicle of that *baraka*.

Bad Milk

Ideas and other mental constructs concerning breast-feeding are hardly ever directly expressed by the Khmir. They hide them behind dark hints, evocative stories, behind ritual and symbolic behaviour. Moreover, there is never an ultimately 'true' interpretation. By shifting an accent, the commentator may build a bridge to other 'truths' which suit him better. Indigenous interpretation is often a form of *bricolage* in which, however, not just any possible construct is acceptable.

The best time to study ideas on nursing is when a baby falls ill. The Khmir think of a baby as a creature perfect by nature. No harm can come from inside. They would heartily agree with Bostock that the new-born baby should be viewed as an 'exterogestate' or external foetus (Jelliffe and Jelliffe, 1978: 4). In their eyes this stage does not last a mere nine months but as long as nursing continues, which is ideally two years. During that time only what comes from his mother can influence his health.[7] In practice this means that when a baby falls ill, the explanation that is given most frequently is that his mother's milk did not suit him. In that case we hear of *hlīb mšūma*. Bad Milk.

Bad Milk may occur at any stage of the lactation period, with the exception of the first forty days. We should not take this number literally. It is a symbolic number, standing for the fulfillment of motherhood and the perfect condition of the mother-child unity. After this period a painful process comes into operation in which the child very slowly becomes a separate being. 'My little liver' she calls him when he is young. Love is situated in the liver. When the baby grows and, as Westerners know, when the mother's milk becomes a less complete food, he moves to the outer fringe of her liver.

There are five variants of children's illness, caused by Bad Milk: *bunaghūt*, *ᶜafn*, *shedd*, *felg* and *helg*. They have no generic name. In the mountains we used to speak about 'children's illnesses which are healed by the *mra maᶜatielāha*, the female specialist'. For convenience's sake my assistant invented the term 'milk illness', *mardh al hlīb*, a term everybody understood immediately and which sounded more neutral than Bad Milk, an unpleasant term, as my interpreter pointed out. For by naming things you attract them. The differences among the five variants is not important here. Let us concentrate on *bunaghūt*, the illness which was mentioned most often. The symptoms by which it could be recognised were: stinking diarrhoea; dark rings under the eyes – in a later stage the pupils under the closed eyelids are turned upwards; general weakness and inability to move the head; weak neck; dark, swollen veins under the ears; bent fingers and toes which cannot be relaxed by light manipulation; refusing the breast.

A number of other symptoms like high fever, pimples, dirt in the eyes, vomiting and much crying were mentioned in other Milk Illnesses as well. A medical doctor, practising in a little town, just beyond the hills, and who was consulted from time to time by peasants from our region, supposed that Milk Illness might indicate toxicosis, but he was not sure, for mothers never visit the doctor when their baby is ill. At best they try the hospital when it is already late, even if they know that death, at this stage, is almost certain.[8]

A general opinion in the villages where I worked was that *bunaghūt* was caused by the baby's taking the breast just after the mother had come back from fetching wood in the mountains. People believe that the milk in the mother's breast becomes warm and churned up because of the overheated condition of the whole body. The milk in the breasts clots like milk in the *shaqwa*, the churning skin.

Here the analogy ceases. For unlike the milk in the _shaqwa_, the milk in the breasts returns to its normal state after half an hour. The milk may undergo physical transformation, not only if a mother works hard but also if she eats earth, (a common remedy for anaemia and much disapproved of by men), if she eats grain from the new harvest (first fruits) or drinks _lben_, buttermilk, from a cow who has recently calved. The change in the milk is never caused by supernatural agents.

The ingestion of dangerous food indicates, again, that women are incapable of foreseeing the possible consequences of their appetites. Or worse, it suggests a certain indifference to those consequences. However, though some people expressed doubts with respect to the current explanations of _bunaghūt_ it has not been recorded how many times a baby did _not_ get ill after having been nursed by a tired, hot and a sweaty mother. And I never heard women using work as an argument to deny personal guilt. As a matter of fact, women who had met with this illness did not seem to be weighed down by guilt at all. They accepted the folk belief, which links cause and consequencè, without a murmur. They did not dwell on it. Instead, when their baby fell ill, and when they wanted to offer an explanation, they described how they felt on hearing the baby cry and how the baby felt when craving for the breast. The listeners understood that here was true _hanāna_, which is a beautiful thing.

To my mind it is unwise, though from a Western standpoint quite understandable, to discard folk notions outright as mere fantasy, even if it is true that many women did not appear to behave as the model discussed here would lead us to expect. Some women who agreed with the folk definition of the situation did not remember having eaten dangerous/tabooed food or having eaten too much.

Milk Illness is cured by carrying out a ritual.[9] Though the ritual is performed on the baby, its main aim is not to heal the baby but to heal the situation in which the mother-child unit finds itself and which is relatively new. This new situation has been created by the crumbling social structure which, as we have seen, leaves a young wife less protected than she was at the beginning of the century (see note 1). On the one hand, she has to learn to live in the new social context of a nuclear family; on the other, she must adhere to the archaic religious framework within which rural people live and according to which she must learn to be what she in essence is: the

Centre of the House, the place from which supernatural blessing emanates.

This frame provides women with a strong and positive self-image. It states that the housewife is the transmitter of life, vitality and prosperity. In opposition to all negative remarks about women and overlooking her real or ascribed incapabilities, the healing ritual reminds the whole community of the great power of each woman to spread well-being around her. As this positive view is offered within the realm of *maraboutism* (which sees the *marabout* as a saintly channel of divine power), it is easy to see why women cling to this form of religion, although it is condemned as backward by the literate. It gives women status and respect.

The ritual affirms that the mother is indeed able to spread *baraka*. For after the treatment the baby accepts the breast again and the symptoms of Milk Illness disappear.[10] The ritual gives an implicit definition of the mother's true Self that is quite different from the one her critics give when they loosely mention her irresponsibility, her nonchalance, her indifference and even her joy in destruction, although they admit that this is never consciously aimed at her children. The definition of the mother's Self in the cult of the *marabout*, of which the healing ritual of Milk Illness is a part, is situated on a higher level than that of trivial reality. Not that this latter is denied. But it is not important.

In short, the healing ritual contains the following view: it may be true that babies fall ill due to the mother's irresponsible behaviour. But it is still more true, and demonstrably so, that they are healed by the touch of the female specialist who works with the 'hand of the *marabout*'. In the ritual the saint acts effectually in his capacity as 'grandfather', the highest authority in the lineage. As mother and child are one person, the mother too is affected by this treatment; she is cured of her Bad Milk. The healing enables the mother to prove that she is capable once again of transmitting the supernatural essence necessary to the well-being of her family, and this gives her the right to her place in the Centre of the House. The gesture of the grandfather overrules all social gestures of the woman's affines and puts her enemies to shame.

Western and Khmir Ideas on Lactational Failure

In modern scientific literature (I refer mainly to Jelliffe and Jelliffe, 1978), we find a number of concepts, among which I shall select two important themes, stress and quantity, which I shall compare with Khmir ideas.

Stress

'It has not been sufficiently appreciated in the past that environmental psychosocial stress can have an effect on lactation performance' (Jelliffe and Jelliffe, 1978: 62). We may wonder whether the Khmir show the same blindness as Westerners did to the results of stress in this field, or whether they ever mention it as a possible cause of nursing problems.

We have now some idea of the difficult economic situation in which the Khmir households lived around 1970. Young people tried to deal with it by imitating new types of household. But, in each case, the right to the new way of life had to be won. In the valleys where we used to work, most marriages were patrilocal and exogamous ('Never buy a chicken from the *douār!*'). It was the custom that the young couple was given a sleeping place in the parental one-room hut. For a short time the ideal of the harmonious extended family was realised in practice. Then the trouble started. The bride was considered as labour power, to be summoned by any member of the household, young girls excepted. In theory, the domestic chores were distributed equally among the women who lived in the same household. In reality, a hierarchy tended to develop rapidly, the new bride standing on the lowest rung. After the birth of her first child, and when lactation was fully established, this situation often escalated into a good row between the young mother and her mother-in-law or her husband's sisters. Tired of the constant bickering and the complaints of his womenfolk, the young father, if he was sufficiently self-confident, seized the opportunity to set up his own household. With the help of cousins and neighbours he built a new hut overnight and moved in. The rupture with the husband's family of origin was less dramatic than it seems. The new hut was erected on the father's premises and, after some days of sulking, the wife was usually allowed to draw water from her mother-in-law's well.

There is great variation in the degree of dependence of young married people on the co-operation of their families of origin. Once the couple had reached a state of relative independence, the locus of stress tended to shift towards the dyadic relation of husband and wife. It is not easy for a young, uneducated man, who owns neither land nor cattle, to provide for a family. Reproaches, quarrels between spouses and disillusion characterise this stage of the development cycle. So there may be plenty of stress for the young mother. Yet it is as if the Khmir expect her not to be harmed by it. As if they assume that she knows how to respond to it: empty her mind, settle down, spread her feathers over her chicks and allow milk and *baraka* to flow so that the harmonious atmosphere, thus created, will dissolve all stress. A peaceful picture which is highly deceptive. For the Khmir do not expect their women to be calm under all circumstances. They say so, yes. But the observer knows better once she has seen the delight of a husband whose wife has successfully fought with other women over a bale of grass, or heard him chuckle, sitting inside the hut as he listens to the astonishing invective with which she intimates to a trespassing shepherd to clear out as quick as lightning from her husband's fields.

There are things which a woman, so rash by nature, can do more efficiently than a man. Men frown at her taking initiatives but when her performances are intended to defend her family they laugh behind their hand. Older women are better fighters and young women seldom win in the end. So, the triumph goes to the former, the stress to the latter.

Intercultural study suggests plausibly that stress is an important cause of lactation failure (Jelliffe and Jelliffe, 1978: 62, 224, 300). Why then do the Khmir, who are fully aware of the stress in the life of a young wife, never mention it as a cause of Milk Illness? An obvious reason is that the mother-in-law can never be indicated as the source of all the trouble. It would undermine her authority. Nor can others be accused. In a little society where everybody is dependent on everybody else and where the art of living together calls for a great effort, stress in structural relationships is not an acceptable explanation for illness. Moreover, in the ideology of 'we are one big family', which is held up to outsiders, intra-family strife has no logical place.

Then there is a small number of women who learn in time not to withdraw into resentment, but to give vent to their anger and anxiety. A woman, who is pushed by strain into the role of the Formidable Housewife, a She-devil, who takes revenge for injustice done to her or to her house, derives not a little satisfaction from this. She knows how to turn stress into victory. As far as I know a She-devil does not suffer more from Bad Milk than meeker women do. Nor less, although she often prospers in other respects. In public opinion she has *baraka*, even when her behaviour does not conform with verbalised norms.

The great majority of young mothers, however, do not play this role. How then do they cope with the stress arising from the social and economic conditions, described above, and which many women must feel? A possibility which I can only tentatively put forward here is that Khmir women might use certain mental techniques in order to evade the harmful effects of stress. These techniques, consisting in a partly conscious, partly subconscious directing of awareness, may be derived from Sufi teaching, which we shall discuss briefly later on. Unfortunately, at the time of my fieldwork I had neither the knowledge, nor the preliminary training, necessary to pursue this line of inquiry.

Quantity

Lindblad et al. mention a too small production of milk as the most important variable in the lactation failure of poor women. As early as at four months the baby's growth stagnates because of '. . . the combined result of maternal disease, undernutrition, and the increasingly difficult living conditions in rapidly developing slum areas' (Jelliffe, 1978: 80).

Were the Khmir poor at the time of our research? According to Western standards, yes. They had no clothes other than those they were wearing, no furniture except an occasional sagging iron bed, and might be forced, in springtime, when the new harvest was not yet in, to sell the blanket that served to cover the whole family, sleeping in a row: that was poverty.

There was no pauperism, though, and no spiritual poverty. But the boundary between material poverty and 'making both ends meet' was sometimes very thin indeed. One really needed *baraka* to stay on the right side of it. 'It does not matter how much food there is', the Khmir used to say, 'food with *baraka* (meaning: prepared by women whose hands spread this quality) always feeds enough.' We may expect on the basis of this, that the Khmir should deny that a mother might ever not have enough milk. And that is what they do. Not quantity but quality is for the Khmir the most important aspect of lactation failure.

Nutritionists usually reduce it to insufficient quantity, resulting from a failure of the let-down reflex, a mechanism many people besides the Khmir may not be acquainted with. Khmir and Western scientists agree on at least one point: in principle the beginning of the lactation period shows no shortage of milk. Westerners meet the Khmir halfway by admitting that the quality of the milk of poorly nourished women is often not optimal, although in general it is 'surprisingly good' (Jelliffe and Jelliffe, 1978: 80).

In some other aspects the two parties disagree. Research tells us that the mother's milk is fully adequate as the sole source of a baby's food during four to six months, depending on the nutritional condition of the mother. After that supplementary food is desirable, and in the long run necessary, for reasons of both quantity and quality. The Khmir hold that a baby can prosper on the mother's milk alone for a much longer period. They do offer supplementary food, though. There are social reasons for doing so, rather than nutritional ones. It is true that they surmise that a mother's milk is of bad quality when they observe the languid behaviour of a young child. But they label this as an abnormal situation. Many Western nutritionists do not seem to recognise the sudden and temporary changes in mother's milk which the Khmir describe (Jelliffe and Jelliffe, 1978: 55). Maybe we should suspend judgement concerning these different views until comparative studies among various ethnic groups have been made.

There is an interesting cultural reason why the Khmir never think of quantity as a factor in Milk Illness. In the archaic world in which only the elderly, women and little children live nowadays, people are not in the habit of counting. Or so it is said. And to a certain extent, people comply with this social norm. Cattle were not counted, children were not counted but named in order of their age and land was not measured. But men knew its boundaries. All direct calculation of relative wealth was shunned. Measures and quantities were used in the market but not in the domestic sphere. Yet, as elsewhere in the world, every shepherd could tell, without counting his flock, when a lamb was missing. Counting is incompatible with *baraka* and *nīya*. In classical Arabic, *nīya* means 'good intention'. In Khmir society, however, it refers to an unconditional confidence in supernatural powers and a characteristic faith of the simple mind that formerly was common to everyone. Nowadays you find it more in women than in men, more in the illiterate than in the educated, more in children than in grown-ups. It resembles 'simple-mindedness' but it is of a completely different order. There existed people who 'were' *nīya*, that is, who were innocent as animals, *kif el haywān*. That did not mean that they were unable to bring about any harm. But harm was not intended. Nowadays many people have ambivalent feelings about *nīya*, especially if it seems to cause error. Then they call it sheer stupidity.

Modern people, especially women, are able to mobilise *nīya* for special occasions, for example when visiting a *marabout* to pray for his miraculous intervention. The visitor should turn to him with a child's faith. '*Normi nīya fi Abdelkader*' they say, 'I cast my *nīya* on Abdelkader.' They use that term to express the strong emotion which must accompany the prayer to make it effective. Women specialists who knew by experience that the *marabout* never failed them could afford a more composed attitude, verbalised by '*n ᶜaged nīya fi Abdelkader*' 'I tie my *nīya* to Abdelkader'.

Nīya is associated with the past when there was harmony and co-operation within the extended family. 'They worked with *nīya* and shared with *nīya*'. Indeed, the more new goods appear in the market, the more probable it is that there will be an uneven distribution of wealth, and that ill-feeling will arise because of this, especially between brothers and among women of the same household to whom the norm of sharing is applied most strongly. Now that exact counting is introduced, *nīya* disappears from the heart of man and with it the *ᶜašera*, the peaceful solidarity which kept the extended family together.

Baraka and a Mental Technique

A woman should not appear on the scene of present-day social life.[11, 12] She has no role there, no accepted social form makes her presence possible. She is represented by males, one male (a husband) or more of them (a father, brothers and even *auled ᶜamm*, patrilineal cousins). It is said that a woman has no honour, 'she lives in the honour of her husband', an expression which disguises the fact that she *is* his honour and that her behaviour affects him a great deal. Though she cannot figure socially, a woman possesses Power. Not the common social power which needs cunning and intelligence, but a religious power, contained in *baraka*, which is by definition a social and beneficial power. In order to wield it she must shed her negative thoughts and impulses and concentrate on her work.

Recently, in the West, much interest has been shown in research into altered states of consciousness, ranging from mystic experience, hypnagogic situations and dream consciousness, to those conditions induced by hypnosis and psychodelic drugs. In the wake of this research, studies have appeared on the role of imagination in the process of illness and healing (Tart, 1969; Achterberg, 1985). It is important that they were not done in the exotic frame of other cultures but in our own society and by scientists of different disciplines. Sooner or later the ideas developed here will influence the way we look at other traditions in other contexts, allowing us to take more seriously those indigenous claims which used to be registered as 'belief'. The first discovery we may make, then, may be that many cultures, whether primitive or highly developed, employ mental techniques for inducing particular states of consciousness.

In the eighteenth and nineteenth centuries the Khmir came into contact with Sufi holy men, itinerant members of religious brotherhoods, many of which originated in the Middle East. The holy men gathered adepts by travelling extensively and by building centres for their followers. Le Kef was such a centre. The lodge of the Qadiriyya, of the followers of Abdelqadir al Jilāni from Baghdad, was the centre where many Khmir received religious instruction. Anawati and Gardet call the Qadiriyya one of the most liberal brotherhoods, averse to religious or political fanaticism.

It was a two-day journey from the Khroumirie to le Kef. At a time when the only means of transport through a harassed country was by donkey or mule, the peasants could not visit the lodge as often as was necessary to learn the techniques taught in the centre. So in the mountains Sufi meeting places were built, *zāouia's*, where rituals were carried out, stories told or chanted, (*dhikr*) in a typically 'folk' version of the *hadīth*, the Islamic tradition. The *ḥadra*, the trance dance in honour of the *marabout*, was an occasion for religious instruction and experience, as well as for the healing of certain ailments. On all levels of the cult of the *marabout*, techniques for inducing altered states of consciousness and, perhaps more importantly, of subconsciousness, were learned.

The Khmir *fogra*, the trance dancers, claim that their 'sport' has a refreshing and invigorating effect. And better still, it helps them to leave their sorrows behind. *Dhikr* chanters have similar claims, though less outspoken. Is it not plausible to infer that the cult of the *marabout* offers certain mental techniques to free the mind and body from stress? And that it opens a door to abilities and powers, only a part of which are usually developed?

Many Khmir women must know the principles of these techniques at first or second hand, for although the brotherhoods have been abolished by the government, there are still many informal gatherings where Sufi rituals are performed. They might consciously or subconsciously apply these techniques to shed their sorrows and so evade the nasty consequences of stress.

When the mind is not too preoccupied on the social level it is easier to enter a slightly meditative mood that has a beneficial effect on the environment as well. Was this the aim of women's exclusion from public life? Needless to say that when no such natural or acquired disposition towards this mood and mental technique exists, forced seclusion can hardly be expected to produce the desired results.

There are a number of indications that might point to the occurrence of altered states of consciousness among women. They are said to fall very easily into trance, much more easily than men. There is a far greater number of women than men who claim to be possessed by *jnūn* (earth spirits, in this case). Women know that an abeyance of awareness plays an important role both in trance and possession and they warn the young never to allow their mind to fall vacant when sitting in dangerous places. Then we ought to consider the fact that Khmir believe women to be in almost continuous contact with *maraboutic* forces that must be handled carefully. Such forces may be contacted through strong emotion or in a more gentle way, according to the circumstances or the character of the person concerned. If this assumption concerning a mental technique, applied by Khmir nursing mothers, is valid, it suggests that there is a social/religious specialisation of Khmir housewives, which would explain the respect for women that Khmir men claim to feel and, indeed, often demonstrate.

Carrying on this line of thought we must look for evidence that *baraka* is more than an empty or theoretical explanation of well-being and prosperity. It may be more real than many Westerners have been willing to admit. In other words, we must accept the possibility that a married woman, aided by active or passive experiences in the cult of the *marabout*, learns to enter a state of mind which affects the members of her household, and especially her baby.

However, her 'technique' does not always produce the desired result, and the baby may fall ill with 'Milk Illness'. Whether the mother's mental training is inadequate or whether the physical situation is too difficult to change is hard to tell. The Khmir speak simply of a lack of *baraka*.

Ever since the nineteenth century it has been a Western axiom that women and fertility belong together. But there is no such direct link in Khmir thinking, as the analogy *tabūna*/womb shows. A woman's womb is a waiting room. It is true that it is a place of growth as well, but this growth is not stimulated by anything which is hers. This denial of woman's generative powers may seem remarkable, but we must not forget that the Khmir, unlike Westerners, never speak on a purely physiological level. Their idea of a mother's role in procreation reminds us in an oblique way of the trance dancers who call themselves *fogra*, 'poor men'. When they dance they have no power nor merit of their own, they have nothing; they are totally receptive, waiting to be filled with *baraka* by the *marabout*. All the miraculous feats they perform are His work, not theirs.

Their art is the model for the woman's task: to receive, to cherish, to transmit and to do all these things not by her own power, but with the blessed Power of the *marabout* to which every mother and housewife can open herself under certain conditions. To receive *baraka* a woman must possess *nīya*; to pass it on, especially to her baby who needs it most, *hanāna* helps, certainly if the mother is still young and inexperienced. Moreover, it is my guess that, aided by direct or indirect instruction from the Sufi schools, she must learn how to keep a quiet mind and to enter a meditative mood which we now would recognise as a particular state of consciousness, characterised by alpha brain rhythms (Kamiya, 1969).

When describing the strong emotions with which the Khmir approach the question of mother's milk, I related it to two images of women, both of which derive from religious tradition. A further image, that of the burdened, weak woman, does not seem to be operative in the context of Milk Illness. The image of the She-devil must be older than Islam. It is rather complex. I would have preferred not to mention it at all, here, but for its dark aspect which is in a certain sense the counterpart of *baraka* and which may jeopardise children and husband. In normal life the Khmir hardly ever refer to this image. At best it is used to poke fun at a person one dislikes or to express disapproval. Yet behind it lie doubts, reserve and fear.

The image may be compared with those associated with witchcraft in Black Africa. It is an ever present principle which may remain dormant during a whole lifetime. As is the case with *baraka* the power of the She-devil never becomes a woman's own power. When she has opened up to it, it blows through her being, it becomes part of her mental landscape without, however, merging with her Self. She is a conductor for certain elements which use her as a vehicle. In that respect again she may be compared to the trance dancers of the *marabout*.

So that is what a Khmir married woman seems to be: a field which may be taken over by both benevolent and destructive forces. The art of being a housewife and mother consists in being receptive to blessing, in transmitting it, and in keeping one's shadow at bay. The proof of the success of this endeavour is the flow of good mother's milk and the prosperity of all living beings in the House.

Notes

1. *Akhwāli*, pl. of *khāl*, mother's brother, stands for mother's siblings in general. In practice it refers mainly to her brothers because, under the rule of patrilocality, they stayed in their father's village, while their sister had moved. The *khāl* offers moral and material support to his sister's children. It is said that having shared his mother's milk with his sister, he has incorporated the same love and affection as his sister for the children to whom she transmits this milk. He and his sister's children are mutually attracted by bonds of milk, which counteract the stern rights and duties attached to blood-bonds in this patrilineal society. Which of the mother's brothers became *khāl* in practice depended on several factors such as personal choice, income, prestige and the relation between his own wife and his family of origin.
2. For some months each year from 1967 to 1971 and again in 1973 and 1974.
3. Well-meaning local authorities were at the time forcing the peasants to build houses with concrete walls and tiled roofs, causing unexpected heating problems.
4. The Khmir use the term *wāli* for a holy person or place. I shall use the anthropological terms *marabout* and *maraboutism*, introduced by the French. *Maraboutism* is the cult of local saints and places, so widely spread in North Africa. Its public forms are the pilgrimage, the

procession of the brotherhoods, a ritual dance (the *ḥadra*), and communal meals in honour of the saint. Apart from these public forms there exist private forms of this cult in which people – mainly women – venerate individually the saint by ritual visits to his tomb or to places where he left his *baraka*. The healing of Milk Illness is a recent form of the cult. It occurs in the private sphere.

5. The idea of women's insatiable sexual desires is a familiar one. Neumann writes of the Great Goddess that her 'orgiastic sexual character excels her fertility character'. (Neumann, 1963: 50) The image of the Great Mother is very alive in the Mediterranean, hence the need for 'masculine solidarity by which the Great Mother can be depotentiated'. (ibid: 61)

6. The question touched upon here is whether, in Arab culture, filiation is ever reckoned through a woman. Ever since W. Robertson Smith in his *Kinship and Marriage in Early Arabia* mentioned two subdivisions in the tribe, the *batn* and the *fakhd*, representing respectively members of the uterine and agnatic groups, its historical occurrence has been challenged. Chelhod rejects the possibility entirely (Chelhod, 1971: 58). It must suffice here to say that among the Khmir and adjoining groups, the matrilineal *principle* is certainly known. It is expressed in the notion of *silsla*, a genealogical line through mothers and daughters. It is very shallow, however and referred to for a limited number of purposes. That does not mean that on a certain level, the bonds of milk may not be as strong as the bonds of blood. The *akhwali* were supposed to act on behalf of their sister because of these bonds. Then we have the fact that in the Muslim world, children who have drunk the milk of the same woman cannot marry. (Altorki, 1980: 233–44)

7. Death, however, may also be explained by the aggression of mythical beings like *Umm Naush*, an invisible night bird that preys on newborn babies, and the *Tabaᶜa*, a female demon which is frequently thought of as woman's shadow side (Creyghton, 1987).

8. O. Boulakhbash working at the time in Jendouba.

9. The ritual is performed by the *mra maᶜatiellāha*, the 'woman to whom (the gift of healing) is given.' It is usually a woman who has several children. She received the gift either from the *marabout* who appeared to her in a dream, or from an older woman, who, by transmitting it, loses her own gift. The ritual consists in a light massage, making tiny incisions on the baby's fingers, toes, abdomen and face, and spitting a teaspoon of oil, mixed with a bitter herb, the ᶜ*arg Bunaghūt*, and her own spittle, in his mouth. (Creyghton, 1981: ch. IX)

10. This flat statement may scandalise some. Yet I choose to trust my own naive eyes and the statements of many mothers and specialists.

11. At the time of my field research, 1965–75. Although unexpected

changes may occur, it is unlikely that women's position, highly ambiguous as it is, will change much in the near future.

12. Anthropologists have referred to mental techniques for decennia, using other terms. In most cases it is difficult to understand what the actors actually do, probably because the techniques in question are pre-verbal or subconscious. It is risky for the social scientist to try to render them conscious because any information on the subject which reaches him must undergo a double translation, the first into words, the second into a level which he can understand.

Bibliographical References

Achterberg, J., _Imagery in Healing: Shamanism and Modern Medicine_, Boston and London, New Science Library, 1985

Altorki, S., 'Milk Kinship in Arab Society: an unexplored problem in the Ethnography of Marriage,' _Ethnology_, 1980

Charnay, J.P., _La Vie Musulmane en Algérie, d'apres la jurisprudence de la première moitié du XXe siecle_, Paris, Presses Universitaires de France, 1965

Chelhod, J., _Le Droit dans la Societé Bédouine_, Paris, Librairie Marcel Rivière, 1971

Creyghton, M.L., _Bad Milk: Perceptions and Healing of a Children's Illness in a North African Society_, Ph.D dissertation, Amsterdam, 1981

——, 'La Taba'a', _Cahiers et Traditions Populaires_, 6, 1987

Jelliffe, D.B. and Jelliffe, E.F.P., _Human Milk in the Modern World_, Oxford, Oxford University Press, 1978

Kamiya, J., 'Operant Control of the EEG Alpha-Rhythm and some of its Reported Effects on Consciousness', in Tart, C.T., _Altered States of Consciousness_, New York, John Wiley, 1969

Neumann, E., _The Great Mother: an Analysis of the Archetype_, Princeton, Princeton University Press, 1963

Robertson Smith, W., _Kinship and Marriage in Early Arabia_, Boston, Beacon Press, 1967, (First edition 1885)

Tart, C., (ed.), _Altered States of Consciousness_, London, John Wiley, 1969

Valensi, L., _Fellahs Tunisiens: L'économie rurale et la vie des campagnes aux 18e et 19e siècles_, Paris, Mouton, La Haye, 1977

3

Production and Pleasure: Research on Breast-Feeding in Turin

*Franca Balsamo, Gisella De Mari,
Vanessa Maher and Rosalba Serini*

Translated from the Italian by Mary Salvatorelli

In the late 1970s both the feminist movement and the medical profession – not often found in agreement – were still focusing attention on childbirth and ignoring the question of breast-feeding.[1] While delivery was seen as a social event to be piloted by institutional forms of socialisation such as antenatal classes, breast-feeding was long bound up with the concept of 'nature'. As a 'natural' phenomenon it belonged to the area still regarded as the mother's concern, a matter of maternal instinct, whereas the medical services had already taken over delivery and channelled it along institutional lines. On the other hand, while, in theory, breast-feeding was left to the mother and traditional female lore, in practice it was illogically bound up with feeding schedules and quantities laid down by the doctor. Actually, under cover of her natural role, the mother was being used as a machine for supplying milk and her efficiency tested by a simple time schedule to be followed like a medical prescription. The doctors themselves admit that the rules recommended for breast-feeding are merely translated from those applied for artificial feeding – the feeding times, length of feeds and intake of milk per feed (Bandelloni, Fabris, Mascherpa, Montrucchio, Sampieri, 1980).

At birth, medical practice left the field to the specialist in the newborn and the pediatrician, with all branches of study focused exclusively on the baby, as if the mother were only marginally concerned, seen purely as a means of feeding the child. There is still a break between the time of delivery and the time immediately

59

following. This break is not merely physical, it is a sign of a split at the symbolic level too, corresponding to social divisions between the maternity and pediatric clinics.

The Pediatricians' Alarm at Failure in Breast-Feeding

Little medical research has been done on breast-feeding and, at least in Italy, none carried out from the mother's point of view. On the whole the key words of these studies are 'breast-feeding', 'lactation', 'the newborn child', with no mention of the mother. Some research has been done at the Santa Croce Hospital in Turin on the effects of rooming-in and on how long breast-feeding is continued (Cattaneo, Ghiotti, Marra, 1981).

From the mid-1980s on, social awareness has changed radically, mainly thanks to steps taken by the feminist movement. Interest in breast-feeding has grown, partly as a result of an informal but thorough campaign in the mass media. Nowadays all pediatricians advise breast-feeding at least for the first three months of the child's life. Even the Health Service has set up a group of health workers who regularly visit mothers in their own homes after the birth and the local authorities have provided ample information through the press. Counselling and courses on childbirth, known as 'psychosomatic rehabilitation' courses have been started in several hospitals. The aim of these courses is to help women, partly through relaxation techniques, to adapt to their new experience and is based on the assumption that they undergo a change in 'bodily self-concept' in the post-delivery period. The term is a metaphor taken over from psychology (Elefante, 1985). The impression is sometimes given that the woman is being helped to respond to the new sexual expectations of her husband and the emotional needs of the child, to take on new burdens rather than being given practical help with breast-feeding. But at the same time the pediatric staff express the hope that:

> without placing undue pressure on the woman or influencing her choice excessively and without wishing to impose arguments and values we believe to be positive, an accurate body of information can be made available to underline with scientific data both the nutritional and psychological benefits of breast-feeding. This campaign might increase

the aptitude of mothers for breast-feeding, bringing the figures up to nearly 100 per cent (Bandelloni et al., 1980).

Notwithstanding the general move in child care towards breast-feeding, at least during the first few months, the challenge now being taken up by researchers in the clinical and pharmaceutical fields seems to be to find out how far mother's milk can be reproduced artificially. So we are getting a plethora of studies on 'adapted', 'modified' and 'formula' milk, if not presented as an alternative, at least advised at and after weaning time; rather like all the research on clonation in the field of biogenetics. It is paradoxical that while in theory mother's milk is held to be the best, research is moving towards the production of an ever more perfect surrogate, instead of enquiring, for example, into the circumstances that could support and help women who choose to breast-feed (Bottone, 1989).

Research carried out in 1982 on the choices made by a sample of seven hundred Turin families concerning the rearing of their children showed that even then only 39 per cent of the women interviewed were breast-feeding for at least a month, while 36 per cent of children were bottle-fed (with artificial or cow's milk) and 22 per cent had chosen mixed feeding. But the most interesting finding was that 90 per cent of the women who had not breast-fed said they had not been able to do so for reasons beyond their control.[2] More recent research seems to confirm this observation. A high percentage of women who say they wish to breast-feed prove, in practice, unable to do so. It was the very poor fit between the wish or intention and the carrying out of this wish that alarmed a group of pediatricians at the University of Turin with regard to the outlook for breast-feeding in our social and cultural context. Our research started quite by chance from this concern and later moved a long way from these initial questions, to follow its own course after divergences of opinion, in part of an epistemological nature, with our medical collaborators.[3] We now wanted to find out about the actual experience of breast-feeding, the things no one ever pays any attention to, or that are never expressed, because they are suppressed by the weight of social-medical and family injunctions that influence the mothers' behaviour, whether the mothers are isolated or whether they seem to be integrated into a network of effective social relationships.[4]

Our special interest in the research was to identify the socio-cultural circumstances that condition the mothers' feeding and other choices and to discover the various forms of adaptation or resistance expressed by the mothers in their day-to-day behaviour. We tried to avoid value judgements concerning the various choices, since we felt that every woman had different family, work and other circumstances to take into consideration when she opted for one or other type of feeding. But how far does she really make a choice?

Our Research

Our research is based on interviews with forty women. These interviews were partially open, partially in that they were centred on a series of topics previously discussed with reference to our own experience of research on women, as well as of breast-feeding. That is to say, an attempt was made to make the interviews comparable without depriving the woman being interviewed of her freedom of expression. We interviewed women belonging to various social categories, either by reason of their social and economic condition, or because of the place they had given birth in (small unit of a 'progressive' hospital, large town hospital, private nursing home). To make it easier to discuss such delicate subjects we chose most of the women to be interviewed from our neighbourhood networks, especially parents of children at local schools. The women who did not come from these networks were interviewed, where possible, several times. Because of the socio-economic differences between the three residential areas chosen, three quite clearly distinguishable categories of women, all between thirty and forty years of age, emerged. These women were interviewed in their own homes. A fourth, slightly younger group was interviewed in the State Hospital (University Obstetrics and University Pediatric Units) and subsequently at home.

The outstanding features of the groups were as follows:

1. The Vanchiglia District: this group included women from two different social classes; on the one hand working-class women, the wives of craftsmen with small workshops or immigrant workers, and on the other, women with a high level of education, (since it is an area of small enterprises, near the largest market in the town on one side and the university on the other). Most had given birth in a large city hospital, in one case eight years previously. *(Balsamo)*

2. Pino Torinese (the district on the hill): this group consisted mainly of upper middle class women. Most had given birth in private nursing homes. *(De Mari)*

(3) Moncalieri Hospital: this group was made up of middle class women and intellectuals. The special feature here was that delivery had taken place in one particular small, private hospital that provides very up-to-date antenatal classes and pays great attention to the period following the birth. *(Serini)*

4. A hospital maternity unit and the Children's Hospital: ten women from various socio-economic backgrounds were interviewed, first in the maternity unity of a large city hospital, just before and after delivery, and twice later, at one- or two-monthly intervals, either at home or on the phone. Six other women, whose babies had been taken to hospital but without serious disorders, were interviewed at the Children's Hospital's infant care unit. *(Maher and De Mari)*[5]

The Choice

Can we speak of the choice to breast-feed? The cultural imperative to breast-feed is so strong that it admits of no alternative. The women we interviewed who had bottle-fed their babies were convinced they had not nursed them and their sense of guilt generally put them on the defensive, causing them to list reasons and justifications for this 'deviance', widespread as it is. One reason, often attributed to obstetricians and eye specialists, is the risk that breast-feeding may worsen the sight. The mothers are faced with a double social message, the widespread injunction to breast-feed on the one hand, and the equally peremptory counter order from the doctor on the other. But the mother's responses may vary. Immigrant women go against the doctor's orders on the matter in order to breast-feed and face the risks to their health they are told they will be running.

No one now takes into account the advantage of breast-feeding that must have been decisive in times of more widespread economic hardship, the fact that it costs nothing in monetary terms.

Probably for the same reason, none of the women mention the contraceptive effects of breast-feeding, whereas some point out another advantage, that of being able to move around easily: 'It's so convenient. Wherever you are, you just take the kid and stick him to your breast'. The woman who does breast-feed does not advance any special reason for doing so and is not expected to, so she often wonders about it for the first time during the interview: 'I didn't think about it because it never occurred to me and no-one ever even had the brains to make me think about it'.

Breast-feeding is 'natural'. And there are no social differences in this deep conviction. So the concept of naturalness brings about a highly conditioned, only very partially free choice. Nature is presented as a source of authority, very nearly as a transcendental order. Few of the women we interviewed had seen their mothers or other female relatives breast-feeding when they were children. Nevertheless, there is sometimes an unconscious tradition that lies behind the concept of 'naturalness'. There is the shadow of another mother and the force of primary cultural imprinting. But the mothers of many of the women we interviewed, who to their daughters seem somehow to represent what is natural, were living under the Fascist regime and were influenced by the demographic propaganda of the time. So the fact that they breast-fed for long periods, for months or years, did not depend on their being close to nature, but rather on a conditioning that had something coercive about it. Breast-feeding was not always so 'natural', particularly at that time, when in the face of the development of the artificial milk industry and the spread of patterns of emancipation imported from the United States of America, doctors, who mediated between the state and the private individual, stigmatised mothers who did not breast-feed, as 'unnatural'. Nature can be invented by one carefully conditioned generation. This idea of 'naturalness' sometimes alludes to human life as one among many forms of animal life. The 'animal nature' of man as a species is seen as the basis of the 'naturalness' of breast-feeding, even though many scientists have pointed out that female monkeys, lemurs and other primates are often negligent about breast-feeding (Herman, 1979).

The new attempt to get closer to nature propounded in the antenatal classes is put forward paradoxically in the form of birth techniques which have to be learnt. But it is no less paradoxical to consider breast-feeding as 'natural'. Like delivery, it is one of the events in human life most heavily influenced by social custom, although there is no real, explicit instruction given in antenatal classes or elsewhere. In many of the interviews we find a kind of mutual reinforcement of the prescriptions to breast-feed, coming from nature and medicine respectively: 'All those theories about breast-feeding made me want to have a baby and breast-feed it'. (Luisa)

On the Breast-Feeding Scene

Three main figures direct and control the mother's behaviour. While the 'mother's mother' constitutes a primary symbolic point of reference and provides the first value imprinting, the hospital lays down the essential rules. In his turn the local children's doctor's function is mainly to keep a check on things and to act as mediator. Each of them intervenes with his or her specific culture and in the context of a specific kind of relationship with the mother-to-be. Then there are the background figures, who loom less in choice and decision-making even though they are important in giving practical help, as husbands are in some cases.

The husbands are often, though not always, extraordinarily helpful, even taking the mother's place in doing the housework. The impression is that as long as the mother is breast-feeding she is protected and defended and replaced in her ordinary household duties. But after the first few weeks, only a few mothers say their husbands help them, and then only when they can, when they are home from work. After the birth of the children many mothers have ended up by giving up their work and their activities outside the home. Our sample is not fully representative and we cannot claim that this is a general tendency. Nevertheless Carmen Belloni's survey on the use of time in Turin families shows that the married woman in this age group spends an average of six hours a day doing housework, while the husband does one (Belloni, 1988).

The Mother's Mother

She appears in various capacities, but generally breast-feeding provides the opportunity for a new understanding between mother and daughter. The daughters were almost all breast-fed by their mothers for more or less lengthy periods but in all cases longer than they themselves will continue breast-feeding. The mothers' fabulous feats of breast-feeding are told of proudly: 'Six children and all of them breast-fed for two years'. Theirs was 'real' breast-feeding. Sometimes the mother goes against the midwife or the children's doctor when they advise discontinuing breast-feeding: 'Whatever happens, you mustn't stop breast-feeding. A child without its mother's milk. . .' In particular, many of the mothers' mothers do not think the quantity of the milk or the weight of the baby matter: 'Look, he's growing well, obviously that's enough for him'. Another woman protested: 'I've got too little milk' and her mother and grandmother retorted: 'It's enough for the baby', though the pediatrician and midwife disagreed. Sometimes the mother's mother gives information about breast-feeding, emphasising its 'natural' character. Sometimes the mother insists on the merits of breast-feeding even when the daughter is against it and although her daughter is suffering from cracked nipples or is very run down. Other mothers help their daughters to stop under such conditions. But the mother is generally a great supporter of the value of motherhood, she represents the greatest control over her daughter's behaviour as a mother. This makes the daughter face up to the problem of becoming a mother, after always having seen herself as a daughter. In the behaviour of some women one gets a glimpse of a need to replace the mother, to do without her, so as to become the mother of their own children: 'I didn't do what she said, I did what I thought best'. 'They (the mother and mother-in-law) told me little enough and I told them to mind their own business'.

Lastly, there is the courageous mother who tries to transmit to her daughter her personal rejection of motherhood, pointing out the real costs of rearing a child. And there are daughters whose mothers go on leaning on them for support and not vice versa.

The Hospital and its Rules

The hospital is a constant feature in interviews with women, but the women we interviewed had had their children in the late 1970s and early 1980s, when normally 'they didn't say anything', in hospital, about feeding the baby. The milk was seen as contaminating, anomalous, the breast as a source of embarrassment: 'They only told me that I had to rub my nipples with disinfectant when the baby had its feed and keep them covered with a dressing all the time'. 'They told you "you feed him, you disinfect before and after, apply the solution" and that was that'. This is not the place to give advice on breast-feeding, but it may be noted that the La Leche League, which publishes the opinions of mothers who have breast-fed successfully, just advises 'rinse well with water' to clean the nipple and considers other substances harmful; they also advise leaving the nipples uncovered so that the air will harden them.

The ritual, purifying and disempowering effect of the disinfectant tends by its chemical symbolism to inhibit useful discussions on breast-feeding among young mothers in a ward, even when they become friends, chatter among themselves and help each other. It sometimes happens that competitive mechanisms are set in motion with regard to breast-feeding, with comparisons as to how vigorously and how much the baby sucks and so on. So the competitive tendency creeps in even here, in what in theory should be an essentially intimate sphere of life.

> We were breast-feeding and we talked a lot, because that was her second little boy and he was very voracious and on top of that she had more milk than she knew what to do with, so I was even more worried about it. When I used to see my baby girl falling asleep and her boy sucking like mad I suffered all the more.

The source of such mechanisms lies in a male-oriented ideology which binds the mother to the myth of maternal love which is expected to guide her behaviour and the choices she makes.

Supplementary Feeding and Engorgement

All our interviewees were misinformed, and this experience goes together with experiences of the mother's body being under-valued, as is her milk and her ability to establish relationships: 'They never asked you whether the baby had sucked properly or not. . . Then, when they came back, they weighed it and if it hadn't eaten much they gave it "a supplement" or else. . .' So the weighings before and after and the weight chart are often the only communication link between the newborn child, the clinical 'filter' and the mother. The mother is excluded from every other form of communication, support or recognition of competency, with the exception of a few formal items of information that she is asked for or receives concerning the state of health of her baby. And so the question of quantity, that will dog the baby throughout its early growth and which, as we shall see, will set some mothers struggling anxiously with the scales, is already at work in the hospital. Perhaps it is because of this external, visual concept of the mother's relationship with her child that obstetricians and oculists discourage breast-feeding by expressing fears for the mother's sight (see above, the importance of myopia given as a reason for not breast-feeding). The quantitative and visual version of the child's well-being leaves out the physical and emotional sensitivity between mother and child which provides a channel of reciprocal knowledge necessary to their relationship and their general development.

But this quantitative and visual perception derives not only from neopositivist medical culture but also from the lack of communication between the various units and centres of power in the hospital and the resulting separation of mother and child. The rigid, opaque dividing-lines of hospital organisation produce an incapacity to 'see' the physical-emotional relationship between mother and child. When right from the start the control of breast-feeding, entrusted to the impersonal eye of the medical staff, is separated from the woman breast-feeding and the child being breast-fed, the criteria for evaluating well-being shift from being qualitative, subjective signs to being objective indices measured by an instrument. The specialists in the newborn and their methods end up by taking the place of the mothers in feeding too, when according to expected standards the baby has not been sufficiently fed by the mother. And since the baby does not always grow at the same rate and his needs vary as time passes, the doctor often decides that the mother's milk is not enough for him. In hospital the result is that vicious supplementary feeding circle that even specialists in the newborn are familiar with. Often, when little or no help is given by the staff, the baby is not properly attached to the breast or, in the brief space of time for which he is left to the mother, he doesn't suck 'enough' (according to the standard growth trends). Then he may be given a supplementary feed shortly before being taken back to the mother for his next feed. Whereupon he falls asleep instead of sucking, reproducing the cycle that tends to maximise supplementary bottle-feeding and minimise breast-feeding. The descriptions the women we interviewed gave of the dead end towards which women are directed by hospital organisation are tales of real desperation.

They almost always brought my baby when she was asleep and so she didn't suck, she ate very little and slept almost all the time and I was desperate. She didn't take the breast and I didn't know what to do. One day I sent for that midwife who was with me in the delivery room. She came and tried to shake her out of her sleep. They used to give her the bottle and I just couldn't breast-feed her and I was desperate.

This was the beginning of an attempt at breast-feeding that gave way to bottle-feeding a few days after the mother and baby got home. In the meantime the mother's breast may become engorged by the milk she is unable to give her child. The staff do not give any real help beyond resorting to the breast pump which many women dislike, considering it as a further insult to their bodies, which are being treated as machines and imperfect machines at that, since they are unable to adapt to the industrial rhythms of the hospital. The mother empties her breast with the breast pump, while her baby is being fed with some sort of artificial milk, a questionable surrogate for the real thing.

Separation

The delivery had gone off well, and Luisa's baby had been taken to the nursery, but when her husband came to see her in the evening he couldn't find the baby. She had been put under the oxygen tent because she had been crying so desperately all the afternoon that she had gone blue in the face. The pediatrician was afraid she had some serious heart condition and suggested having an X-ray taken: 'You're all against X-rays, but when a doctor tells you a thing like that you can't make up your mind, you don't know what to do and you say – "give her an X-ray"'. In case of risk, the exiguity of the mother's knowledge in comparison with the doctor's compels her to give in. Only later does the mother realise she should have trusted her own intuition. There was nothing organically wrong with the baby. According to Luisa it wasn't her heart but the separation: 'very probably it was being separated from me that brought on this reaction'. She thinks that if the staff had shown more understanding, if they had brought the baby to her, she would have quietened down. Luisa says: 'she suffered from the effects of that for quite a time. After Sciaia left the hospital, if she got the feeling she was being left alone, she used to do just the same as she did there. . . She would hold her breath so long she went blue in the face'. Later, weaning was especially hard for Sciaia.

The social iatrogenesis of the hospital, the place of separation, is so pronounced and its effects last so long that it is hard to keep any subsequent check on it.[6] The separation of mother and child is taken so much for granted by the staff that they feel no obligation to give any but the most summary explanation if they don't bring the mother her child with the other babies on the trolley. As happened to Lina. The first time they didn't bring him they said he wasn't there because he was under the quartz lamp as he had got neonatal jaundice. Nothing else, and worry started to set in: 'I didn't know anything about it', says Lina, 'I thought that as long as he was under the lamp they wouldn't feed him.' The tension is much worse when the mother starts to have less milk because she isn't in contact with the child or when for the same reason there is a delay in the first flow of the milk. Since jaundice is quite frequent nowadays (apparently because of the medicines used to speed up contractions in labour), this situation not infrequently creates a state of collective anxiety in the maternity wards.

The hospital is organised in separate units and clinics which correspond to spheres of power with boundaries as clearly delineated and fixed as the geographical boundaries marking the limits of state power. These divisions leave an analogous network of symbolic dividing lines on the human body, assigning its various parts to the care of the respective domains and clinical competencies. That is to say, the hospital subordinates the newborn child and its relationship to its mother to the separations and divisions that grow out of latent or explicit conflicts and divisions of economic power, social prestige and political influence.

The abrupt, sometimes brutal separation of the woman and her baby occurs within this structure. It is rapid, aseptic, seemingly necessary, seemingly painless, merely because all the pain is transferred onto the physiological ordeal of the delivery room, where even the suffering caused by social organisation has to be expiated. The cutting of the umbilical cord which takes place here, corresponds to a social and symbolical cutting off that has no parallel in non-European, non-industrial societies. This separation is attributed to the requirements of hospital organisation, but the explanation is false, because there are hospitals in Italy too where rooming-in is practised and in other parts of the world there are hospitals where it is customary to leave the baby near its mother, even in her bed, and not for lack of space. Almost all the hospitals in Kenya do this, even the best-run ones, that come up to inter-national standards. Although the cradles are attached to the mothers' beds, the babies are normally allowed to sleep with the mothers, with no fear of their being suffocated. Indeed no cases of suffocation have ever been reported. Obviously demand feeding can be started easily and naturally in this way.

In Turin, the power structure of the hospital is not merely linked to the separation of mother and child, it is based on it. This is important because it is the mechanism through which other more general forms of social power based on the hidden deprivation of women are constructed, tried out and perfected in this laboratory. Here an impression of solitude and an experience of the other as absence is created both in the mother and in the child. The child's first cognitive and emotional processes grow out of solitude. The early separation of mother and child anticipates by many years the separation which only occurs during adolescence among other peoples (Herman, 1943). The consequences of early separation still have to be described, or perhaps they are already apparent but are not attributed aetiologically to these early experiences.

A Rite of Passage

Nowadays the separation of the child from the mother's world and his introduction into patriarchal society is accompanied by less formal ritual (less importance is given to rites such as baptism within Catholic-Christian culture) than there was in the early 1950s. At that time, baptisms often took place inside the hospital. Today the hospital has taken on a new function, that of carrying out the rite of passage, of separation and renewed aggregation, with its own sometimes oppressive, sometimes pleasant ceremonies. The post-delivery period is a sort of limbo between the separation of mother and child from their previous state of sym-biosis and the aggregation of the two separate individuals to the world of the father. The post-delivery period of this rite corre-sponds to the time when the woman is forced to lie in bed after delivery. There she is neither mother nor non-mother. She is waited on, her baby is brought to her, taken away from her and she has to stay there without moving, just waiting. The official reason given is that this ensures that the woman can get a thorough rest after delivery. This is not the only form of protection in our society that to the woman seems like a form of coercion, a being forced into passivity. The difficulty the woman has under these conditions in feeling responsible and active, capable of meeting the needs of her baby, may be a further obstacle to breast-feeding.

During this post-delivery period the doctors tend to prescribe treatment for the child without telling the parents about it beforehand. It seems as if, in the name of preventive medicine, they have to come between the mother and the child, making a specific contribution (material but decidedly symbolic) to the production of the child; as if to legitimise their presence and their role by the input of chemical and pharmaceutical 'semen'. The consequences are often unexpected and unpleasant.

Sandra decided to have her baby in a private nursing home because she was terrified of hospitals. From the first she was very active and took the nursing home in her stride. She walked around freely and took part in what was going on in the nursery. She remembers this as a pleasant experience, though here too the breast-feeding started off unsatisfactorily. The baby was born with a slight calcium deficiency; they gave her a gram of calcium, which is very little, only calcium causes diarrhoea. In this case it was the midwife who interpreted the symptom incorrectly, attributing it to the mother's milk and telling her to stop breast-feeding for the moment. When the pediatrician's advice was sought, he solved the matter by making Sandra give the baby her own milk, but with the bottle: 'He said to me "of course she's got diarrhoea, we gave her calcium, it's nothing to do with your milk. So you must just draw off your milk with the pump''. Then they brought me the pump, put the milk in a bottle, where they put that stuff, carob, that stops diarrhoea, and they gave it to her in the bottle'. The pediatrician can see no difference between breast-feeding and bottle-feeding. After all, you are depriving the baby of breast-feeding but not its mother's milk. In spite of all this, the baby continued to be breast-fed at home, with no further difficulty. Again in the case of Maria Rosa's baby, after giving her an X-ray, the doctors discovered what seemed to be an enlargement of the thymus and gave her cortisone treatment without asking for the parents' consent. When they didn't bring the baby to be breast-fed Maria Rosa was alarmed and it was only then that she was told about the cortisone treatment. Meanwhile the baby had had several X-rays, without any shield being placed over the ovaries or the rest of her body. When the pediatrician was consulted he found no enlargement of the thymus. Maria Rosa said there was a 'definite' connection between the cortisone treatment and the fact that the baby had great difficulty in suckling, later on as well. This is a typical case of complications originating in medical treatment, when preventive measures (or more strictly, diagnoses) have, paradoxically, just the opposite effect from that intended and produce pathological situations.

Home from Hospital: The Feeding Schedule

While disinfection is the first rule laid down by the hospital, the last, conferred as a kind of absolution, is the time schedule. The feeds, to be administered every three-and-a-half hours. If the mother keeps rigidly to this schedule at the beginning she may not produce enough milk, for lack of the stimulus that frequent suckling provides: 'When you leave the hospital they give you a sheet with the timetable you have to follow, more or less, to give you an idea. I think it's the hospital pediatrician who makes it out' (Lina). But neither Luisa, nor Lina nor Pina managed to keep to the timetables advised. Lina: 'Only I couldn't keep to it with Ivan because he used to cry every two hours'. Luisa: 'Then when I got home and started breast-feeding, although I wanted to do as they did in the hospital I just couldn't because Sciaia would have stuck to my breast all the time if she had had her way'. At first Pina kept to the time scheme (every four hours) 'but later on I didn't, later on, when the baby was hungry I fed her'.

Timetables can be respected in hospitals, thanks to the rigid organisation and because the staff are conditioned to be 'emotionally detached' from the patients, to adopt that neutral attitude that shields them from anxiety and over-identification. But it is very difficult to reproduce the rhythms laid down by the hospital in a flexible situation such as that of the family, where roles are superimposed on emotional relationships. It is difficult above all in the transitional period when the family even seems to suspend all its organisational structure to welcome the new baby. The mother has to set up her own much more fragile psychological 'barriers' in place of the physical barriers (the walls between the newborn and midwifery units) and the intermediary staff that the hospital uses to curb the baby's potentially 'insatiable greed' by objective necessity. For example, she has to put up with his crying and learn how to deal with him. Which is no easy task for a mother subject to many external controls, from whom a great deal is expected, although she is not always being given much help or practical advice. The flow of such help, formerly transmitted from one generation of mothers to another, has in many cases been interrupted by emigration. The mother is seldom very sure of her own decisions and lives in a state of stress, anxiety and depression, post-hospital rather than post-delivery. This is a form of social iatrogenesis rather than some hormonal alchemy, as some clinicians maintain in their biological line of research (Burton, 1974; Brunori et al., 1982).

However, apart from the mothers who were bottle-feeding, and who respected much stricter time schedules (Eleonora and Silvia, for example, kept to certain timetables) the mothers generally used their common sense about the time schedules advised and adapted them to the normal rhythms of their everyday lives and above all to their requirements with regard to rest and sleep. So in general, starting from the idea imposed by the hospital of following fixed times, almost all of the mothers ended up, more or less, by adopting demand feeding.

The Clockwork Baby

When the demand coincides with the time schedule, you get the baby 'regular as clockwork': 'My baby girls were regular as clockwork' (Angela). 'Some children are very regular' (Lina), while others are like Sandra's baby: 'after she'd been home for a few days she started messing up the timetable'. But later she too, except for that transgression, was always very regular: 'She got to be regular as clockwork'.

Paradoxically, in this simulation, the metaphorical mechanisation of the child's body is found side by side with the fact that he is spoken of as if he had an almost adult will. Some babies 'respect' the rules, others don't: 'He would suck a bit, drowse off and then, instead of keeping to those two or three hours, half an hour or so later he would be asking for more'. So breast-feeding becomes a social preparation for the ordering of time in our culture, hinged on commercial exchange and industrial production. In breast-feeding, together with the rules, the first forms of deviance from rules are defined. In this way, sometimes subtle and subterranean, sometimes imposed and coercive, an education in timetables and hence more generally in rules and their observance begins much earlier than in other cultures. Some mothers even seem to imagine the rules as part of the genetic heritage that babies come into the world with: 'Eliana fed in a very disorderly fashion for the first few days'. What is at stake is social conditioning to order. When the 'disorderliness' increases you get the opposite extreme: breast-feeding is experienced as never-ending and exhausting because it goes against 'the rules'.

At the Breast: Pleasure

It is significant that those who speak of breast-feeding with satis-faction do not keep to rigid timetables and prolong the length of feeding times beyond what the doctors prescribe: 'I let him have his fill! Lovely! When he was full he didn't want any more, I held him up until he burped and then I put him back in his cradle' (Pina). Giulia would let her baby feed 'for a long, long time because he wasn't lazy, he fed well, but he liked to fall asleep at the breast. He would suck for hours. Ten or twenty minutes, not likely. He would hang on until he closed his eyes. If I took him off he started to cry'. Luisa fed her baby girl at length because it was a pleasure for both of them.

> Generally she took twenty minutes, a good twenty minutes, really sucking, because then the twenty minutes became forty. What she really liked most was to lie against my body and she would relax like that. . .If I only held her while she was feeding, I realised afterwards that she enjoyed lying there. . .and I held her a bit longer. It was satisfying for both of us.

> 'It is a sensation stronger than hugging. . .it's just. . .it's something I felt in a very sensual way. More than hugging her, because of this contact I had. . . (Eleonora).

> Breast-feeding is not bad, said Giulia more cautiously: actually it's a wonderful sensation. . .it's really good to breast-feed, because the breast-fed baby gets more attached to his mother, at least that's my impression. . .The one that's breast-fed is physically nearer to the mother, it seems to me; the other wasn't (her second child, who was bottle-fed).

All these snippets from the interviews bear witness to a subtle kind of relationship that the pediatricians cannot and do not want to recog-nise. It is precisely this prolonged attachment that social control of breast-feeding aims at restricting and preventing, because it may be a risk for the only erotic feeling allowed to the mother in a patriarchal society, that connected with the adult male. While speaking to the researchers some pediatricians from the hospital deplored the tendency of the relationship between mother and child to become 'erotic' during breast-feeding, suggesting that the mothers should keep the length of feeds down to a few minutes, so as 'not to tire themselves or risk feeling they would like to give up breast-feeding.' Many failures in breast-feeding can be attributed to advice of this kind.

Many authors have pointed out that in Catholic countries, after the Counter-Reformation, women's sexual life has been ever more stigmatised by the Church. Through the figure of the Virgin Mary, seen on the one hand through the Immaculate Conception and on the other as Our Lady of Sorrows, the Church sanctions the repression of pleasure in women and its substitution by the myth of the mother's chaste, long-suffering love for her child (Accati, 1987). In the attitude towards breast-feeding of the women we interviewed and of the doctors, one gets a glimpse of the persistence at the cultural level of the myth of suffering mother-love. The mother must devote herself to her child with sacrifice and self-denial. The woman's own subjective life and sexuality should not appear either in this relationship or ideally in her relationship with the adult male (the Madonna is a Virgin, the mother is chaste).

In the doctors' misogynist attitude to the woman, the negation of the woman's pleasure in her child can be glimpsed. The new feature is that in the antenatal classes (in which delivery is compared to an orgasm), in the father's presence in the delivery room and in the post-delivery advice given to the woman, the relationship of the couple is underlined. Women are encouraged at both the cultural and medical levels, to move towards sexual relations with the adult male, the only relation regarded as legitimate, very soon after delivery. One of the women interviewed, who had spent years in feminist discussion groups, and was hence better equipped to express herself on the subject of sex than others (who hinted however at similar situations) noted that her relations with her husband changed after delivery. She spoke of her 'diminished sexual urge. He makes sexual approaches, but if it were left to me I wouldn't. . .I try to avoid it'. They talked a lot about it because they are very fond of each other. She hesitates between asserting her right to do as she feels and satisfying his wishes at least occasionally.

Tiredness apart, this mother's erotic sensitivity seems to be directed towards the child and to be satisfied in her relationship with him.

Luisa Accati thinks that medical misogyny is actually aimed at the priests who, through their power over women and repression of female sexual drives, have made the role of the husband/father within the family humiliating (Accati, 1987). The lay man/doctor has his revenge, denying the woman her psycho-physical relationship with her son and leading her in the direction of the conjugal relationship. The myth of motherly love on the sacrificial pattern is the only one compatible with this approach.

Early Attachment and Detachment

Demand feeding can be achieved either by increasing the length of feeds or by giving short, frequent feeds, as Lina did: 'There I was every two hours, having to let him feed . . .' In the end Lina slept with him and ate with him 'attached to her breast all the time'. With some variations and intermediate patterns, two ways in which breast-feeding and the relationship with the child are experienced and practised can be traced back to the cultures of origin: the tendency to attachment and the tendency to detachment. The two factors that have most influence on the mother's behaviour seem to be immigration, with its imported practices and traditions, more or less integrated into the new background and perhaps with some experience of loneliness to be compensated for; and the socio-economic conditions of the women interviewed. When the tendency is to attachment, the mother prolongs togetherness with the child as long as possible and delays the moment of separation. This in general is the attitude of the mother who has immigrated from the south of Italy and is not economically well-off. The early detachment model is typical of the middle class mother from Turin, who wants independence for herself and her child.

Mothers who prolong feeding times do not seem to perceive their child as part of themselves because of this; indeed they tend to see him as 'other'. A will of his own, wishes and preferences are attributed to him and attention has to be paid to them, they have to be interpreted and respected. If the child is kept at length on and often attached to the breast it is because, 'he wants it', though probably the infant's wish is recognised to the extent that it coincides with that of the mother.

When the tendency is to detachment, the mother thinks less of meeting the child's wishes (which may become 'whims') than of impressing the right behaviour on him, for his own good, which he is as yet unable to recognise. The mother keeps for herself a level of cognition and regulation which is different from that of the child. In the 'attachment' pattern the mother places herself on the same level as the child; either she meets his wishes (prolonging attachment) or she lives in a state of conflict (each of them has to conquer his/her own ground). Hence, while one behavioural pattern aims to satisfy the child's desires, the other seems to favour the opportunity to educate and socialise him or her. In the context of these two attitudes there are two ways of dealing with feeding times, the child's crying, bodily nearness (holding or not) and weaning.

Here is an example of the idea of physical contact that informs the behaviour tending to detachment, in which features due to the influence of clinical patterns emerge, the mother's role being restricted to her function in feeding the baby:

> I never held her. . .I never never held her in my arms. Absolutely not! It ruins one's back. . .they need their own place to sleep in too, their cradles. That's their place. She needed me to feed her, that's all. . .I held her up until she burped and then put her down again, face down in her cradle (Sandra).

Here the territories of mother and child are kept quite separate (as in the nursing home) right from birth and the newborn baby is considered to have her own 'autonomy'; whereas in the behaviour tending to attachment there is still a fusion and merging of spaces. Even when she is 'detached' the mother interprets her child's needs, but partly according to her own needs and partly according to the 'expert's' schemes of child growth and rearing. Here too there is a different time concept involved. The mothers who satisfy the child's immediate wishes seem to live the experience in the present, while those who prefer 'detachment' have a plan, a strategy of behaviour directed towards the future. The few women we interviewed who said right from the start that they intended to bottle-feed, were sometimes planning to share looking after the baby with their husbands. A Piedmontese woman worker, employed in a firm that granted eight months away from work after delivery and had a nursery in the factory (Olivetti) had decided not to breast-feed because the baby had got to get used straight away to a 'regular' timetable, like that the mother would have to keep to when she went back to the factory.

Crying

While for one group the child's crying is his way of 'communicating' his wishes, the other group, thanks to the interpretations of the pediatrician, feels that it may convey other meanings and provide the opportunity for teaching the child a lesson. As we have already seen, those mothers who increase the length or frequency of feeding times do so because the baby is crying. Attachment seems to be a response to this crying. But this is not simply a reaction common to all mothers. Actually it is bound up with different images, of cultural origin, of what a baby is, what its needs are and what the role of the mother is. So Luisa, Giulia and Lina put their babies to the breast again when they cry. To them it is always the same signal, which they always interpret in the same way, giving themselves and their bodies at the child's request. The child's crying replaces the timetable and the clock: 'If I realised she was crying because she was hungry, I gave her the breast and that was that'. Pina too thinks that if children are well and happy they don't cry: 'But my children, perhaps because they were always satisfied even when they were babies, my children never cried very much'.

Angela's attitude was different. She decided to be stricter with her twins, after her first child, who was 'always crying'. She never held the twins, even to feed them: 'I was alone during the day and I gave them their bottles in their cradles . . . When these children were little I never heard them, I never heard them cry'. Some mothers think that with demand feeding: 'the nights are tragic'. 'Then I started to try letting him cry. Then I let him cry. Little by little he got used to it'. So at a certain stage, Giulia managed to distinguish her own needs from those of the baby and give them precedence.

Then I Spoke to the Doctor

Others never manage to establish an autonomy like this. In such an anomic situation – in which the specialist in the newborn lays down rules but the baby breaks them by the brute force of his crying – the mother ends up by turning to the pediatrician for a solution to the problem and above all for her own relief and a chance to survive:

> When the baby started to upset the timetable, obviously I realised that at this stage I had no life of my own any more. Everything was chaotic. So I spoke to the doctor. He said "Don't worry. Let her cry", and I let her cry. But I didn't worry about it. Sometimes she cried for a long time but thanks to the doctor I knew that was the right thing to do and I wasn't a bit worried. And the time came when she got used to it (Sandra).

The role played by the pediatrician at the clinic or when called into the home is often that of defending the mother from the excessive encroachment of the child's needs and excessive social expectations. In particular, the pediatrician often takes over and justifies the mother's wish to stop breast-feeding and wean the baby. Often he advises the mother not to breast-feed if he thinks she has health troubles. In other cases he suggests switching to the bottle at once as a solution to small ailments in the child or to breast-feeding problems which he is not competent to solve. In a more flexible version than the hospital's, but still ineluctable, the pediatrician presents the mother with his quantitative criteria, according to which the child's health is to be measured in ounces of milk consumed and ounces of weight gained, both ensured by weighing the baby after feeds, or at least once a week.

Some mothers look on the pediatrician with suspicion and consult him only in case of illness, thus emphasising their independence: 'I managed on my own, always on my own. I've seen very little of the doctors, I got along on my own, even when they had a temperature. I gave my children very little medicine' (Pina). Giulia too, with the authoritative figure of her mother to back her up, avoided doctors' lore: 'I only called in the doctors when the children had temperatures and weren't well. Apart from that, I always decided for myself'.

The mothers' relationship with the pediatrician, the extent to which they rely or do not rely on him, is greatly affected by the socio-cultural background they come from. The middle- or upper-class women, often housewives, well-educated but with no social network to turn to, attribute great value to the doctor's knowledge. They not only place great trust in him but somehow give themselves entirely into his hands. The working-class women, above all immigrants, often rely on tradition and their mother's example. And when the mother's mother is there with help and advice, as in the case of Giulia, the doctor loses his authority almost completely and takes on an almost exclusively bureaucratic role.

The Culture of Quantity

The mothers' relationship with the pediatrician varies, but none of them quite escape his quantitative criteria. The specialist in the newborn and the pediatrician employ almost exclusively quantitative means for checking the child's state of health and growth, since they are considered 'objective' and hence exclude any subjective competence of the mother, precisely when this would be most necessary. As we have seen, supplementary feeding in the hospital, which already puts breast-feeding at risk, is a consequence of the practice of double weighing (contrast Creyghton, this volume).

'Otherwise, how do you know', asked an obstetrician we interviewed, 'whether the baby is well or not?'. The obstetrician can think of no other indicators, such as crying, the quality of response in the relationship with the mother and other figures, the tone of the muscles, the smile and so on. Doctors who have no share in the mother-child relationship, except indirectly and for short periods of time, (and in any case have a relationship that differs from the long-lasting one between the baby's and the mother's body) need a support, a means, not entrusted to the live, non-measurable subjectivity of women. An analogous sort of barrier is created between the gynaecologist and the pregnant woman.

Trusting to instruments and the faculty of sight is a trait which runs through the whole history of Western clinical practice and its control of the body. Of course, the scales are only a rudimentary instrument, but their value is mostly symbolic, as a means of social control rather than of measurement. The reasons for the use of quantitative parameters lie mainly in the role played by medical control in the reproduction process. It might be said that they illustrate a prototype of 'male', Cartesian thought in which the subject and object of knowledge face each other; since the Scientific Revolution it is more likely that the relation of subject to object will be mediated by an instrument (Bordo, 1986; Merchant, 1980). Hence the hegemony of quantitative scientific language serves to keep women, during this extremely important phase of reproduction, in a state of cultural, material and symbolic dependence on man, the doctor and producer. Men's social control over reproduction also involves restraining and hampering one aspect of breast-feeding as deep as it is forbidden, that is, pleasure. So the quantitative code would seem to act as a restraint, neutralising female sexual expression where, by tending to take on forms not institutionally permitted, it might favour ties that undermine social organisation based on privilege for adult males.

The quantitative criteria which associate time schedules and quantity with breast-feeding correspond perfectly to the model of industrial and economic planning which deals with every problem of production in terms of an efficient combination of scarce resources, time among them. So breast-feeding, like delivery, also becomes a question of planning (Martin, 1987) that is of rational calculation of the combination of resources: 'quantity of milk by length of breast-feeding time equals weight of the child'. The research begun by the hospital pediatricians from Turin was called: 'The optimum in breast-feeding'. The aim of the model is efficiency, certainly not pleasure. For women, using this terminology inevitably involves being alienated from their bodies, which they experience from the outside as objects, as one resource among others, available not to them but to the delivery 'system' and the breast-feeding 'system'. Within these systems the fundamental roles in decision-making seem to be that of the doctor on the one hand and the baby on the other. The mother is often left powerless, split between the two conflicting demands.

Nevertheless, the ways in which this culture is experienced, internalised or rejected by the mothers vary. They include different forms of resistance, which can partly be detected in the language mothers use. In particular, the mother who talks about quantity links it with 'tiredness', which is not always a trivial symptom.

Such a Lot of Milk, Good and Bad

Maternal assimilation of the medical concept of quantity leads to the conclusion that an abundant supply of milk makes a good mother; Sandra was proud of her 'oodles of milk'.

> I had a whole lot of milk, they all told me I had enough for two. In the morning I would wake up streaming with milk and I had to keep

washing, I had so much. And it was good; because often, when you have so much, it's poor quality.

Mother's milk is 'a fine thing', You can 'trust' it, unlike 'artificial' milk (Pina). When it's good it may be 'milk that comes from the shoulder'. I ate well and my milk was good, from the shoulder. . .you feel as if there's something there.

Pina explained that the milk is better when you do the housework. So 'milk from the shoulder', besides the fact that 'you feel that it comes from above, from the shoulder' from the upper, noble part of the body, is perhaps also the product of effort, of the strong woman, the working mother.[7]

But mother's milk can be 'dangerous' too, and this is a term often used by the pediatrician. It may be 'too fat'. And it was to this milk too rich in fats that Lina, accepting the diagnosis of her pediatrician, who had had her milk 'tested', attributed the fact that her baby cried every two hours. Or else, the opposite danger, the milk can 'turn to water': 'The baby drank my milk and brought it up; it was nothing but water' (Lina). And milk takes on all the negative power of the mother, or rather of her helplessness. It is not uncommon for milk and blood to be associated, but here the milk, white and generally good, is seen as positive, while the blood (from cracked nipples, and sometimes mixed with the milk) is negative. The blood was thought to be the reason why Maria Rosa's baby was unwell: 'She threw up and wasn't well'. The second time Lina was breast-feeding it was the same. Besides the fact that she was run down, it was the milk, this time 'like water' that made her stop. It meant admitting that her body was 'harmful': 'the baby drank my milk and brought it up'. In any case, indirectly, together with the milk, it is always the mother who is blamed, to the extent that it allows her to escape from the blind alley of breast-feeding, but only by accepting a negative image of her body and her psycho-physical make-up. The pediatrician and the 'scientific test' of her milk (seen as a sort of magic rite, like consulting the oracle) allow her to disobey the social dictate on breast-feeding but only at the cost of having her body branded medically as inadequate.

When breast-feeding is interrupted, behind the ostensible reason that the milk is 'too fat' or 'too watery', the psycho-social conditions of breast-feeding must be sought for. Outstanding among these are the difficulties the mothers face in coping with the baby's crying, in establishing the early relationship with him, finding a compromise between identification and difference, between feelings of love and conflicts of interest. Mother and baby must find the boundaries and links between them, as two people who are not fully recognised as persons in many private and public contexts. These difficulties cannot be expressed openly by the mother, because that would involve an unadmissible form of deviance in our society and our culture – going against the principle of absolute and unqualified 'motherly love', which props up so much of our social structure.

It is easier to justify oneself by hiding behind the excuse of milk: 'There was something wrong with the milk, that's what it was' (Lina). The shortcomings of the mother are projected onto the milk. This involves alienation of the self, the body and its products, which are experienced as outside the self. The milk 'comes' or 'doesn't come'. The mother feels it is something that does not belong to her. A split occurs between the speaking self and the breast-feeding self, reified as 'recalcitrant' milk. The symbolic alienation of mother's milk is a collective, social fact and does not concern the individual woman alone. Very often the woman does not include her bodily self (physical, sexual and maternal) in the make-up of her own identity. This split between the psychological and physical self is the result of imperatives that leave no room for choice.

Breast-Feeding: Social Practice and Symbol

Breast-feeding marks a second phase of 'separation' of mother and child, the first being delivery. Paradoxically this 'passage' is accompanied by a flow of milk which creates a new and eminently social relationship of the child with his/her environment. This flow, the first nourishment and at the same time a 'natural symbol', now plentiful, now threatening to dry up, can be interrupted or strengthened. How and by whom it is controlled are important matters because they tell us about the conditions under which the child and hence future society pass from symbiosis with the mother (or with the mother's culture) into patriarchal society. It is in breast-feeding, day by day, that, together with the most important social values (including 'social time'), family roles and relationships are reproduced within their licit bounds and the social limits placed on sexual life are reaffirmed.

During their children's early infancy, and in particular during the breast-feeding period, women undertake a difficult journey, full of material significance and symbolic meaning, not only for themselves but for the social order in general. This journey starts at the hospital, where they are given instructions about time schedules and quantities, rules which in the whirl of family life they are unable to apply. They end up with demand feeding, which soon becomes chaotic and dangerous for themselves. Then they go back to the source of law and order, the doctor, the social authority who helps them to defend themselves against the child's encroachment and the exacting example of their mothers, either by insisting on keeping to the timetables and encouraging resistence to the child's crying, or by suggesting that breast-feeding should be stopped. At the same time, the medical authority moves in to take over the woman's responsibility and decision-making capacity, often humiliating the woman's body in the process, through the milk symbol.

It seems important to emphasise that what is played out through the woman's body (the 'breast', the 'shoulders') and her psyche, in this first period of human life, in this socially invisible day-to-day procedure (sleepless nights, tiredness, exhaustion, desperation), is the re-organisation and reproduction of social time. Time schedules are imposed on the primary experience which is outside time. Social time is a cultural category, never established once and for all but continually negotiated and socially reproduced. At childbirth it is especially subject to pressure, in this dramatic and unrecognised struggle in which not only the physical and mental health of the mother and child is at stake, but their reciprocal freedom as well. Milk comes as the contractions of labour come, and then the child and before them all, menstruation, breaking into the patterns of social time. They have rhythms of their own, linked to the relationship of the woman to her physical and social background. They constitute a disturbance to the organisation of labour. And thus 'natural', individual time and the 'social' time of production come into conflict through the body of the woman. This conflict is even more dramatic today because production times have been accelerated with respect to 'natural' time, but also because women are becoming more and more integrated into the world of production and its forms of knowledge and are ever more dominated by it.

To come back to the question posed at the beginning of this essay. It grew out of the concern felt in medical circles about the crisis that breast-feeding appears to be going through at the moment, though pediatricians, feminists and ecologists all seem in favour of women breast-feeding. How is it that the question of maternal 'insolvency', of women's desertion from breast-feeding, interpreted as 'failure', is brought up periodically in the course of history? The figure of the 'bad mother', of the 'unnatural mother', seems to re-emerge every time deep social changes are taking place, particularly with regard to women and their role in society. In the eighteenth century Rousseau took middle-class mothers to task for putting their children out to nurse, and urged them to nurse their children themselves, so that breast-feeding became a kind of fashion much discussed in the salons of the aristocracy (Sullerot, 1968). In the years between the two World Wars, the 'ignorant' mother became a dominant theme in imperialist-minded policy throughout most of Europe. Great Britain was first in the field in setting up schools to prepare girls for motherhood (Davin, 1978). In Italy, under the Fascist regime, the weeklies were full of articles by doctors condemning 'unnatural' mothers who had stopped breast-feeding their children – victims, on the one hand of the propaganda of the new powdered-milk industry and on the other of ideas about the emancipation of women. Like some pediatricians we interviewed in 1986, those writers were in favour of obligatory breast-feeding.

And so we are facing a new wave of concern about women who do not breast-feed (or do not have children). What have these periods in common, to cause such concern that mothers may not fulfil their primary duty? On the one hand, they are all times when emphasis has been laid on productivity and a more stringent socialisation of the men and women who have to provide the labour for production. But other factors should be taken into consideration too. Today, the majority of the women in Turin with children are working. Many of the life histories we have collected are not merely stories of motherhood but, above all, of work. Women often consider themselves more as workers than as mothers if we understand this word in the old and still latent religious and symbolic sense of the mother who sacrifices herself for her child. Perhaps these periods also have in common some increase in the power exerted by women in public life. Or even simply the fear that it may be exerted.

Notes

1. Obstetricians and pediatricians themselves have recognised this in research carried out on the attitudes and behaviour of mothers with respect to breast-feeding (Bandelloni et al., 1980: 1). Again in 1984 a gynaecologist pointed out that the puerperium, unlike pregnancy, 'is characterised and marked by a lack of assistance' and that 'the woman is left to herself to face all the new problems and difficulties of the postnatal period' (Elefante, 1985). At the 1987 Congress of Obstetric Psychoprophylaxis in Nice, only one paper dealt with breast-feeding (Battagliarin et al., 1987).

2. A research project carried out by the Centro Ricerche Educazione for the Assessorato all'Istruzione of the Municipal Council of Turin in 1982.

3. These divergences concerned many epistemological questions and matters of principle. In particular, the medical approach considers the mother and child as biological individuals, neglecting both the emotional and social reality of their relationship and the network of relationships and the cultural context that influence their interaction. The doctors in question attributed the difficulties of the women who wanted to breast-feed, but couldn't, to three factors: the psychological problems of the mother (seen as an individual); the lack of adequate medical guidance; the ignorance of the mothers and doctors concerning the right technique to adopt in breast-feeding. They held that this technique should be sought among the more 'natural' mothers of the Third World and that it consisted in feeds of a few minutes in length. We disagreed with all these views and deplored the scarce attention paid to the opinions of the mothers. Other misogynous attitudes were expressed by the doctors as the discussions proceeded.

4. The reference to an 'effective network' concerns that part of a network of social relationships that involves a person most directly in his/her daily activities (Epstein, 1961). See also the concept of the 'closed', as opposed to the 'open' part of a network, as formulated by Bott (Bott, 1957).

5. In this essay we have only been able to touch on a few of the themes raised by the research. We have chosen to quote a small number of the women interviewed, so as to be able to give their opinions without fragmenting them excessively and so that the reader will be able to see the same women in different situations. Those quoted have almost all been taken from the first (Vanchiglia) group, which, together with the last (hospital) one, brought out particularly well the contrast between 'attachment' and 'detachment' during the early weeks of breast-feeding, between different attitudes to the mother, medical culture and so on. Franca Balsamo actually wrote most of the essay.

6. Long-term effects have also been hypothesised by some pediatricians and specialists in the newborn. 'We do not yet know what short-term and above all what long-term effects the transfer of childbirth from the home to the hospital may have on human society'. Or again, 'It is rather interesting to note how the mother-child relationship can be influenced by hospital routine, even in the long-term' (Fabris et al., 1985).

7. 'Milk from the shoulder' is a notion that comes from the women of Apulia and Calabria who have immigrated to Turin. One is greatly tempted to compare this expression with the idea of the Khmir of Tunisia, described in this volume by Creyghton, that a woman is protected in her husband's house in so far as she is supported by her 'shoulders', her uterine relatives who were fed by the same mother.

Bibliographical References

Accati, L., 'Il padre naturale. Tra simboli dominanti e categorie scientifiche,' *Memoria*, n. 21, 1987: 79–106.

Bandelloni, A., Fabris, C., Mascherpa, F., Montrucchio, F., Sampieri, G.A., 'Motivazioni e comportamenti delle madri nei riguardi dell'allattamento al seno', *Minerva Pediatrica*, Torino, Edizioni Minerva Medica, 1980

Battagliarin, G., Iacobone, N., 'La mamma italiana nei primi quaranta giorni dopo il parto: risultati di un'indagine statistica', *Congresso Mediterraneo di Psicoprofilassi Ostetrica*, Nice, 1987

Belloni, C., 'Tempo e spazio come indicatori della specificità di genere', in Balsamo, F. e Sarti, M.A., (eds), *Tematiche Femminili*, Torino, Il Segnalibro, 1988

Bordo, S., 'The Cartesian masculinisation of thought', *Signs*, spring, 1986, Vol. II, no. 3: 447–60.

Bott, E., *Family and Social Networks*, London, Tavistock, 1957

Bottone, E., 'Il significato del latte di proseguimento nell'alimentazione del bambino', in Bona, G., Chiappo, G., Zannino, L., (eds), *Prevention and Cure*, Torino, Edizioni CMS, 1989

Bowlby, J., *Attachment and Loss*, New York, Basic Books, 1969

Brunori -De Luca, I., Vaccaro, A., et al., 'Il "maternity blues": studio epidemiologico preliminare', in Meluzzi, A. e Menaldo, G., (eds), *Il Sesso e il Nascere: comportamento sessualità riproduzione*, Torino, Ecosistema Edizioni, 1985

——, et al., 'Ipoprolattinemia e stati depressivi', *Contraccezione, fertilità, sessualità*, 6, 1982: 513–8

Burton, J.L., 'Prolactin and depression', *Lancet*, 26, 1, 1974

Bynum, W.C., *Jesus as Mother: Studies in the Spirituality of the High Middle Ages*, Berkeley, University of California Press, 1982

Cattaneo, G., Ghiotti, M., Marra, P., 'Incremento dell'allattamento al seno in funzione di una assistenza alla coppia madre-bambino più individualizzata', in *Il ruolo della medicina fetale e perinatale nel centro ospedaliero e sul territorio, per una equilibrata eugenetica*, Torino, Regione Piemonte, Assessorato alla Sanità, 1981

Cavazzuti, G.B., Frigieri, 'La promozione dell'allattamento el seno', *La Pediatria Medica e Chirurgica*, 3, II, 1980

Davin, A., 'Maternità e imperialismo', in *Nuova Donna Woman Femme*, 6/7, 1978

Deleuze, G. et Guattari, F., *L'Anti-Oedipe*, Paris, Editions de Minuit, 1972

Elefante, G., 'Riabilitazione psicosomatica in puerperio,' in Meluzzi, A. e Menaldo, G., (eds) *Il Sesso e il Nascere*, Torino, Regional Piemonte 1985

Epstein, A.L., 'The network and urban social organisation', *Rhodes-Livingstone Journal*, xxlx: 29–62 1961

Fabris, C., Prandi, G.M., Tamburin, L., 'Interazioni precoci madre-bambino: fondamenti biologici e problematische assistenziali', in Meluzzi, A. e Menaldo, G., *Il Sesso e il Nascere*, Torino, 1985

Goffman, E., *Asylums. Essays on the social situation of mental patients and other inmates*, New York, Doubleday and Co., 1961

Handley, S., 'Mood changes in puerperium and plasma trytophan and cortisol concentrations,' *British Medical Journal*, 2, 1977: 18–22

Herman, I., *L'istinto filiale*, Milan, Bompiani, 1979 (first edition, Budapest, 1943)

Kitzinger, S., *The Experience of Breast-feeding*, London, Pan Books, 1980

La Leche League, *Quando Allattate il Vostro Bambino al Seno*, (Italian edition), Illinois, 1966

Martin, E., *The Woman in the Body: a cultural analysis of reproduction*, Boston, Beacon Press, 1987

Mastropasqua, S., Esposito, D., Mazzarello, V., Budetta, L., Pugliese, A., Paludetto, R., Rubino, A., 'Effetti di un parziale "rooming-in" sull'incidenza dell'allattamento al seno', *Congresso Italiana di Niprologia*, Bologna, 1979

Merchant, C., *The Death of Nature: Women, Ecology and the Scientific Revolution*, Berkeley, California University Press 1980

Moretti, M., 'Funzioni del pediatra e prospettive di intervento nella realtà dell'alimentazione del lattante', *Minerva Pediatrica*, 5, 1978

Nordio, S., Faraguma, D., Levi, N., Piazzo, G., Di Giacomo, 'Allattamento al seno. Unicità del latte materno', *Rivista Italiana di Pediatrica*, 5, 1979

Paludetto, R., 'Allattamento al seno', *Atti del IV Corso di Aggiornamento di Neonatologia*, Roma, 1980

Sullerot, E., *Histoire et Sociologie du Travail Féminin*, Paris, Editions Gauthier, 1968 (Italian translation, Milano, Bompiani, 1977)

Volpato, S., Chierici, R., 'La superiorità biologica del latte della donna,' *La Pediatria Medica e Chirurgica*, 3, II, 1980

4

A Question of Reason: Breast-Feeding Patterns in Seventeenth- and Eighteenth-Century Iceland

Kirsten Hastrup

The reproductive role of women is recognised every-where, and in most cultures motherhood is a positively marked aspect of female biology. During her child-bearing phase, the woman is generally classified as unambiguously female, and her fertility is not only an asset but part of her definition as a normal adult woman (Hastrup, 1978: 59–60). The biological functions of the female body are always marked, although the relative 'mark-ing' of the various stages of a woman's life may vary from one culture to the next (S. Ardener, 1978: 40–3). One result of this biological marking has been the well-known association between women and nature, as contrasted to men and culture (Bourdieu, 1973; Ortner, 1974).

Fifteen years of cross-cultural research on women has taught us that this association is of limited explanatory value. It has been suggested that we replace the sexual distinction made in terms of nature and culture by the distinction between domestic and public spheres of society (Rosaldo, 1974). However, this is only to replace one mismatch with another, and there is no way of reduc-ing the sexual difference to any other universal distinction than that of – gender (MacCormack and Strathern, 1980).

As already noted by Hertz at the beginning of this century the facts of nature are always transformed by culture (Hertz, 1973). When studying motherhood in various societies, we are, therefore, studying cultural representations as much as biology, as Callaway has pointed out (1978). Although the categories of male and female are primarily differentiated by their sexual complementarity in procreation, they are essentially asymmetrical (Callaway, 1978: 164). The 'pre-eminence of the right hand' (Hertz, 1973) extends to the pre-eminence of the male in most cultures. In the folk-models, as Callaway (1978) noted, this asymmetry is often attributed to the requirements of 'the most essentially female function at all: giving birth'.

Giving birth implies, first, a long and internal phase of foetal growth and, next, a long and external phase of lactation. Both of these phases – separated by the event of birth itself – are visible and apparently natural. By this I refer to the fact that the foetus grows and the breast-milk flows apparently by no act of will on the part of the woman. Naturalness in this sense, however, does not imply that there are no choices to be made by the women or no decisions to be taken by mothers. Contraceptives, abortions, and weaning are part of a larger field of decision making, wherein women maintain that biology is *not* destiny. Or, at least, that endless procreation is not necessarily part of their own definition of what it is to be female.

In this paper I am going to discuss breast-feeding as an aspect of this. Instead of seeing it as natural behaviour, I suggest that we consider it a cultural action – that is a deliberate and meaningful act (E. Ardener, 1973). When the option of lactation is *not* taken by mothers, this immediately calls for an explanation, but the point is that this applies to any breast-feeding practice.

The basic assumption of the present paper is that we cannot study the practice or absence of breast-feeding in any particular society without considering the larger cultural context. Evidently, within any one society, individual mothers may choose to breast- or bottle-feed according to a variety of whims and/or actual capabilities. Case studies among village women in the Third World document how breast-feeding and weaning patterns are not governed by blind adherence to tradition, but are products of rational considerations on the part of mothers (Millard and Graham, 1985). This is of no great surprise to anthropologists.

When the focus shifts from individual to collective patterns of lactation we face a slightly different situation, however. Even 'rationality' has a different set of connotations at this level. And if an entire society abandons breast-feeding we must try to understand it on the same scale, as it were. That is, we have to look to social and cultural factors, which cannot be reduced to a sum of individual choices for an explanation. The example we are concerned with here is seventeenth- and eighteenth-century Iceland. We now know that Icelandic mothers did not breast-feed their children for a couple of centuries, and we believe that this had severe demographic consequences (Sigurðardóttir, 1982). So far, we have been offered very little in terms of interpretation, however. One reason for this lack of interest is the fact that it is only recently that the tenacity of this feature of Icelandic society has been brought to light. Another reason is the inherent difficulty in comprehending any 'unnatural' behaviour, and especially of a kind which was so obviously disadvantageous to society. It is intellectually intriguing and emotionally provocative to most of us that mothers should choose to overlook the needs of their infants and silently watch them die from malnutrition, when the remedy was so close at hand. There is all the more reason to widen the scope of analysis from the narrow domestic space of the mother-infant dyad and individual action to the wider social space – which is an entity of thought, speech and action (E. Ardener, 1988).

As a result of the research on women of recent years, we are now in a position to take up the dialogue with the medical specialists and psychologists who have so far dominated the professional discussion of the importance of breast-feeding. And we are able to discuss its value, not only from a nutritional and emotional perspective but also culturally. We are in a position to study its *valeur* in the Saussurean sense, that is, its meaning as derived from its particular position within a larger system of meanings (Saussure, 1916).

My aim here is, first, to present the Icelandic case, and next to analyse it with a view to the difficult question of why breast-feeding was not practised by some ten generations of women in Iceland. Ultimately this will allow me to discuss 'reason' in human society as a general anthropological problem.

Iceland 1600–1900: Demographic Crisis

The first complete census of Iceland was made in 1703. By then the Icelanders numbered some 50,300 people; the age ratio and the household composition clearly show a population in decline (Hajnal, 1965: 137), and there is ample evidence from a variety of sources that Iceland had a severe demographic problem for some three centuries.[1] This is not the place to make a detailed demographic analysis of Iceland through the centuries. I simply note that for some centuries at least, social reproduction was at risk. Biological reproduction was an element in this, but not the ultimate cause. As I have discussed elsewhere, the patterns of causation in Icelandic history are very complex and not reducible to any single factor.[2]

If social demographic studies show that the population of Iceland was declining in the seventeenth and eighteenth centuries, they also demonstrate that this was correlated with a very low marriage ratio. The census of 1703 shows that only 27.8 per cent of the women between fifteen and forty-nine years of age were married, and they married late (Statistics of Iceland, 1960: 48–50). Although delayed marriage was no exception in pre-industrial Europe (Macfarlane, 1986), the Icelandic marriage ratio was 'staggeringly low even for a European population' (Hajnal, 1965: 137). Marriage was a legal precondition for procreation and for setting up an independent household. Thus it is of no surprise that the household structure of Iceland includes a high proportion of unmarried servants and farmhands, whom poverty prevented from changing their situation.

The ethnography of fertility, however, shows that within marriage there was a high birth ratio, which theoretically might have outweighed the demographic consequences of the low marriage ratio. Prior to the census, we have various reports about the fertility of Icelandic women. Thus, in late sixteenth century the Icelandic bishop, Oddur Einarsson wrote that many mothers gave birth to twenty to thirty children 'and I am not talking about the fathers here, who in their second and third marriages get many more' (1971: 85). Two centuries later an English observer noted that 'it is no rare thing to meet with a mother who has had twelve or fifteen children' (von Troil, 1780: 120–1). And the Enlightenment reformer Eggert Ólafsson echoes this when he says of married couples that they often have ten, twelve or fifteen children (1772: 451). Successive marriages were probably quite common for both men and women, as can be inferred also from the disparity in age between the spouses (Tomasson, 1980: 77–8). This was due to untimely death, according to both folk and other models. There is no indication that the purpose of marriage was to reach a comfortable widowhood as has been suggested for England (Macfarlane, 1986: 149); on the contrary, households needed the presidency of a married couple. The high mortality rate made successive marriages a logical corollary.

The parish registers from the early eighteenth century confirm that it was not uncommon for a woman to give birth to eight to ten children, that is almost one for every year in her (relatively late) married life (Guttormsson, 1983b: 153–4). The 1703 census ascertains this. The fertility rate was high, yet the number of children in the household was relatively small, and the population was stagnant or in decline. Explanations were called for by contemporary observers also.

In 1580 the Norwegian Peder Claussøn Friis wrote about the demographic problems of the Icelanders, and attributed them to their aggressive nature. If only they would stop murdering one another in defence of their honour, Iceland would abound in people (Friis, 1881: 196). In 1731 another commentator explained the continuous demographic crisis in terms of the poverty and bad health of the Icelanders (Jochumssen, 1977). Implicit in this statement was a high infant mortality rate, which also explains the family size. It was not until the late nineteenth century that the infant death rate started to decline (Tomasson, 1980: 67). During the eighteenth century, when the quantitative sources became comprehensive, the death rate for infants was about 300 per thousand (Guttormsson, 1983b: 149; 1983a: 147), possibly even more, given the nature of registration and of later evidence of the death rate approaching 400 (Guttormsson, 1983b: 149; 1983a: 147, Tomasson 1980: 67). Further, a high ratio of still births seems to have prevailed (Steffensen, 1975: 231).

Adding to high infant mortality was a generally very high mortality rate, affecting young children in particular. Mothers experienced loss of their infants and other children at a stark rate. Sigurður Breiðfjörð (1788–1846) gave a picture of this in a poem called *Móðurin við gröfina*, 'the mother at the grave' (*Íslenzkt Ljóðasafn* II: 275). The grief of the mother is implicitly recognised, but a sensation of relief is also noted: now, the child is in the grave, no pain or sickness can ever touch it again.[3] Eggert Ólafsson, a mid-eighteenth-century observer, was less forbearing about the Icelandic mothers. He accused them of almost deliberately killing their young, in their going against nature (1832). They hardly knew how to give birth any more, and they would rather that their infants died instantly. We know that maternal 'love' is no natural instinct (Badinter, 1982), and that even 'child-hood' may be a cultural invention (Ariès, 1973). Nevertheless, the imputation that mothers kill their offspring warrants closer inspection.

When Eggert Ólafsson travelled Iceland for some seven years in the mid-eighteenth century, a young physician was with him. Their mission was to describe the state of economy and health in this remote corner of the Danish kingdom (*Lovsamling for Island* III:70–2). Among their results was an explanation of the disastrous infant mortality rate: it was attributed to the fact that Icelandic mothers did not breast-feed their children (Ólafsson, 1772: 450–3).[4]

Of the twelve to fifteen children born to a married couple only two or three would grow up (Ólafsson, 1772: 450–3). To this statement, our observer adds that most of them die immediately after birth or during their first year, because they are given cow's milk and suffer from severe problems of digestion. Those who can afford it even give the infants cream, raw like the milk (Ólafsson, 1772). In addition to this they are given chewed fish or meat diluted with milk, cream, or butter. While it was clear to Eggert Ólafsson and Bjarni Pálsson that this diet virtually killed the infants, the Icelanders saw no such connection and attributed the deaths to external powers beyond their control (Ólafsson: 1972: 452).

The explanation of infant death offered by the eighteenth-century observers appears convincing, but it is only partial and must be seen in the light of the generally poor standards of hygiene and health in contemporary Iceland (Hastrup, 1990a: 228–41). Most houses only had one room for living, sleeping, working and cooking. The cooking was done on an open fireplace with dried manure as the main fuel; there was no smoke-hole in the roof. Diseases were common not only among people but also among the cattle; recurrent 'plagues' took their heavy toll on both popula-tions. Resistence to foreign diseases was scant; measles and small-pox epidemics hit the small Icelandic population hard during these centuries. All this contributed to the high infant mortality, which was further aggravated by early weaning.

These brief observations on the general pattern of health pro-vide some background to the high infant mortality rate. But they cannot explain the apparently 'irrational' behaviour of abandoning breast-feeding at a time when doing so threatened the life of the infants.

The Breast-Feeding Pattern

The amount of evidence on the absence of breast-feeding points to a social practice which cannot readily be explained by any functional virtues. Contemporary reporters are unanimous in their statements about the early weaning in Iceland, and are struck by the lax treatment of infants. A 1746 observer tells us that that children were breast-fed for only eight days, or perhaps fourteen if they were weak (Andersson, 1746: 117). In an attempt to defend the Icelanders this picture is actually confirmed for 'most' of the mothers (Horrebow, 1752: 283–4). It is noted that infants were left on the earth floor and fed on milk, bread, and fish, while the adults were otherwise occupied (Horrebow, 1752; von Troil, 1780: 120; Eggers, 1786: 176–7). The Icelandic household usually numbered several adult women, including servants, and many tasks were carried out indoors. There is thus no practical explanation as to why children should be left to themselves. The observation that infants are left on the floor must of course be read in the light of the general standard of housing of Icelandic peasants in the period, which was rather low in comparison with contemporary European standards, consisting of a simple turf and stone construction with earthen floors and often earthen sleeping platforms.

In a nineteenth-century medical book by Jón Pétursson, mothers are strongly advised to breast-feed – on the assumption that they do not generally do so (1834: 15). It is beyond dispute, then, that from sometime in the sixteenth and well into the nineteenth century it was the custom not to nurse infants (Jónasson, 1961: 263, 311, 332; Steffensen, 1975: 216–34; Sigurðardóttir, 1982; Guttormsson, 1983b: 155). One of the reasons given by contemporary Icelanders was that it was unhealthy (Guttormsson 1983b: 155).

Parallel cases are known from elsewhere, but none, it seems, that endured for such a long period of time.[5] The question therefore remains: why did Icelandic mothers not breast-feed their children for two or three centuries? One of the consequences was a narrow spacing between births and one might wonder whether the combined effect of a low marriage rate, a high marriage age and a high mortality rate could have motivated the Icelandic couples to have a child a year. But even if this was possibly a subconscious motive, the poverty of most Icelandic households would, it seems to me, certainly rule it out at the conscious level, owing to the general lack of means of subsistence. Children were often sent away from their own families to be brought up elsewhere, thus evening out both the work force and the numbers of mouths to be fed. While we cannot entirely rule out the wish to conceive again quickly after birth, it cannot of itself explain the early weaning. Culturally speaking, children were not unwelcome (Þorláksson, 1986), but they did pose parents with serious practical problems as far as feeding was concerned.

It could possibly also be argued that undernourished Icelandic women actually had very little milk for their infants. The (biological) interrelationship between undernourishment and lactation is important, yet in the Icelandic case I still believe that we are facing a problem of a different order. We note for instance, how an eighteenth-century observer said that only among the poorest would the infants survive, because the mother could not afford to give them cow's milk (Ólafsson, 1772: 451).

A change in the religious imagery may also have played some role in the abandonment of breast-feeding. Until the Reformation, the Virgin Mary had a supremely important position in popular religious practice, and during the purification rite after childbirth, the women would pray to Mary in their local church, even some time after the Reformation. In European art, Mary was often depicted in the act of suckling the infant Jesus (Warner, 1978: ch. 13). Her milk was both a sign of 'nature' and of her magical powers (Warner, 1978: 194). In Iceland, too, breast-milk was an important ingredient in magical ailments, prescribed in the medical books from before the Reformation (Kålund, 1907: 365, 394; Larsen 1931: 91). Thus, the destruction of the image of Mary may have some correlation with the abandonment of breast-feeding, but, again, it cannot of itself 'explain' the behaviour.

I think we may come closer to at least a partial explanation if we concentrate on the alternative diet: cow's milk, cream, and butter. In 1752 Horrebow says: 'the mothers never give their children whey but feed them on good cow's milk, into which cream is even poured by some people, so that it becomes fatter and in their opinion better' (Horrebow, 1752: 283–4). This is the clue; in comparison with breast-milk, cow's milk was better, and cream the best. Says Eggers in 1786: 'Many people believe that they do their children a favour by giving them cream instead of milk; they want them to eat fat' (1786: 77). In this country of farming and of ancient peasant values, the measure of wealth was farm produce. Cream and butter were tokens of success, and in all likelihood they became images of the most potent food item in a country struck by increasing poverty. In popular poetry, butter was not only a token of wealth but also a sign of 'Icelandicness'.[6] Foreign food habits were to be avoided, and butter gave strength to both body and soul. When very young children were given solid food like fish, it was mixed with butter, if it was available (Eggers, 1786: 77). In doing the best for their children, and in (socially) reproducing the ancient honour-and-butter values, biological reproduction was placed in jeopardy.

There are probably a good number of factors contributing to the same trend, including foreign influence (Sigurðardóttir, 1982: 29; Guttormsson, 1983b: 156). However, I believe that no explanation can avoid the consideration of a particular Icelandic culture or 'mentality', which was to express itself in a demographically inappropriate behaviour. The praise expressed by the poet Bjarni Gissurarsson (1621–1712) for the products of the land testifies to the high valuation of farming. When he tells how *mjölkurbrunnurin margar kýr/mettar börnin smáu* ('The well of milk from many cows/satisfies the young children') (IL II: 80) his testimonial reaches further – into the somewhat sinister reality of infant mortality and the 'unnatural' ways of Icelandic mothers.

The Meaning of Milk: Women's Values

The preceding remarks already position the matter of breast-feeding within a larger cultural context. In this context, cow's milk was attributed with a particularly high value, to the point where we may actually talk of an honour-and-butter complex.

A value system is one thing; a practice which takes it to such an extreme that infants' lives are endangered is quite another. From a global perspective, it is not the only practice involving women that seems to imply a shockingly destructive relation to life. We know that widows would follow their husbands onto the funeral pyre in some areas of India, and although this practice was probably never widespread it focuses our attention on a culture of emotionality – as well as rationality. We also know how in some places women are circumcised; and how, to our astonishment, they themselves uphold this custom. In facing up to such evidence, where women more or less voluntarily engage in practices that appear to be hostile to the female sex, our ideas of 'the oppression of women' become more complex.

Anyway, the choice made by Icelandic women not to breast-feed their infants cannot be explained by reference to their position in a particular power structure alone. Unlike the Moroccan case discussed by Maher, where a husband has the legal right to demand that his wife breast-feed the children (Maher, 1984: 107), the Icelandic women and their bodies were never the property of their husbands. Also, in spite of patronyms and of a general favouring of sons in terms of inheritance, kinship in Iceland was always bilateral. But like the Moroccan mothers who chose an alternative diet for their infants the Icelandic mothers never realised that they, too, killed off their infants, even though the structural conditions for the choice were quite different (Maher, 1984: 112). We must resort to a more general evaluation of the gender categories before we can get any further towards a comprehension of the breast-feeding practice.

Elsewhere, I have made a sketch of the categories of male and female in Icelandic culture (Hastrup, 1985), and it suffices to give a brief summary here. In the Middle Ages Icelandic women were noted for running their own lives to a considerable extent. They held the 'keys', it was said, meaning that they were in charge of the stores and of consumption in general. *Innan stokks*, indoors, they were in authority. After the Middle Ages, the Icelanders became greatly impoverished and stores were meagre, if not actually exhausted. Probably even iron for locks on the granaries had become too expensive, and keys were therefore superfluous. Yet the women retained their influence on the farm, or inside the social world – to phrase it more generally. In this sense they were on a par with the men who, however, had an additional 'wild' space to themselves.

Inside the 'social', which was very literally within the fence separating a domesticated space from the untamed wilderness, women were closely associated with the cows. Not only through their task of tending and milking them, but also conceptually in that cows were distinctly classified as 'female' (Hastrup, 1985). Cows were a measure of wealth, not only in the direct sense of being a form of individual success, but also in the sense of being a general standard of value in Icelandic society. The value of land and other major prizes were given in *kúgildi*, being the value of a three-to-ten-year-old fertile cow.

Women were in charge of the domestic space; it was their only domain of pride and honour. Whereas the men, in order to be 'male', occasionally had to leap out into the wild and defend their honour (and household economy) there, 'femaleness' was unambiguously associated with the domesticated environment. Women's skills and economic abilities were measured in terms of their success in transforming the raw natural products of farming into 'cooked' or at least edible items for consumption (Gísladóttir, 1985). During the sixteenth, seventeenth and eighteenth centuries, Iceland as a whole experienced increasing impoverishment. One consequence was that fewer women were married, since marriage presupposed a minimum property of three cows' worth. Marriage was, again, a precondition for setting up an independent household, and as a result of these combined factors households were composed of a married couple, their offspring, and often a parent, unmarried siblings and servants of both sexes.

We begin to perceive how the women, who find their domain of authority shrinking during the centuries of impoverishment, want to exploit their space of pride to the extreme. Cow's milk, butter, and sour whey had always been important items for daily consumption; even if (dried) fish provided the staple of the diet, no meal was complete without farm produce (Hastrup, 1991). Gradually, farm produce seems to have become a symbol of women's values, at the expense of the women's own natural capacities. Women undervalued their own milk and gave their infants cow's milk instead. To expand their domesticated space, they 'denaturalised' the feeding of the infants, as it were.

The point is that no single answer provides the solution to the puzzle of why Icelandic mothers did not breast-feed their children. It requires a thorough analysis of cultural values to get a glimpse of a possible reason for this unhappy neglect.

Reason and Rationality

Although breast-feeding habits cannot be understood with reference to biology and nutrition alone, we should not forget the biological component. Reading Shorter's *A History of Women's Bodies* (Shorter, 1984), for instance, makes us acutely aware of the risks to which women have been subjected through their reproductive role. It literally hurts to read the accounts of complicated births and so forth. We also know, medically, that breast-feeding not only improves the life chances of weak infants but also helps women get back to 'normal', as it were, after birth. No doubt, breast-feeding is a biological component in having children. The role of mothers varies greatly, however, between cultures as well as within them, and over the course of time. A recent American study relates the changing views of motherhood to a changing class structure and to a changing material basis (Margolis, 1984). Personally, I am very sceptical about such a crude materialist viewpoint. Neither biology nor economy are destiny, of themselves.

This is not to deny that material factors may play a crucial role in the choices made by women in matters of reproduction, as convincingly shown by Maher (1984). Certainly, the Icelandic case confirms that the semantics of breast-feeding are firmly locked into a changing material reality. However, to reduce women and their actions to a response to the needs of capitalism, as Margolis does, is not only to do an injustice to women as persons it is also to overlook the fundamental simultaneity between the material and the ideal world. Neither of these can ever be reduced to the 'effect' of the other, because in the real world the empirical and the definitional aspects of any phenomenon merge and dissolve the ossified opposition between materialism and idealism (E. Ardener, 1982: Hastrup, 1987).

Thus, we cannot explain the breast-feeding 'taboo' in Iceland by reference to either material factors or ideas alone. Nor can we explain it by reference to a particular power structure, or for that matter to a social function. What we can do is to establish a correlation between the breast-feeding pattern and a particular cultural system of values, and we are now to explore that further. We have to seek an explanation beyond the level of the obvious and discuss the nature of human reason in order to understand why it can be so 'unreasonable' as the Icelandic case implies. As anthropologists we cannot grant sovereignty to the physical world, because 'there is no material logic apart from practical interest, and the practical interest of men in production [and for women in reproduction, I would add] is symbolically constituted' (Sahlins, 1976: 207).

Icelandic women were responsible for social as well as biological reproduction, given the dominant position of the household in the Icelandic conceptual universe (Hastrup, 1990). The women were not muted within the social space (S. Ardener, 1975), and their contribution to social reproduction was in loud and clear speech – about domestication.

As it happened, the Icelandic social space as a whole became increasingly 'muted' by the external structure of (Danish) rule, and in order to manifest Icelandic autonomy the stress on old farming virtues became increasingly important. As a 'remote island' (E. Ardener, 1987) Iceland was increasingly vulnerable and as a reaction to this the Icelanders stressed their singularities to an ever more destructive degree (Hastrup, 1990b). Ever since the first settlements during the Viking Age, Icelandicness had been defined by the domestication of nature. Farming remained the essence of Icelandicness, and in the course of history the stress upon this particular characteristic had more or less fatal consequences.

Among other things it meant that the ancient practice of trans-humance, where shepherdesses and dairy maids had tended the milking cattle in pastures away from the farm over the summer, was abandoned. As I have written in more detail elsewhere (Hastrup, 1990c) this implied that the women were called home from the ambiguous space between the social and the wild, to become once again unambiguously associated with the domesticated space of the farmstead. There were other consequences, but suffice it to state that the distinct trend towards an increasing cultural emphasis on the household and on farming was part of the symbolic order which constituted practical reason in seventeenth- and eighteenth-century Iceland.

Thus we are back at a major anthropological issue, that is, the role of Reason in human culture. It is part of the Kantian heritage that we tend to think of pure reason as opposed to unreason and associate it with science as opposed to religion or magic. Needless to say, in the West the former pole of these dualisms is the more highly valued. As demonstrated by Joanna Overing among others, the series of dualisms of which these oppositions are part, may be substantially shattered by a few reversals whose validity is easily demonstrated (Overing, 1985: 15–16). The point is that there is no absolute scale of value which can be applied universally to oppositional constructs of this kind.

The hierarchical oppositions inherent in Western thinking (about 'others' in particular – whether savages or women) would immediately lead us to classify the infant feeding habits of Icelandic mothers as belonging to unreason. Their irrational behaviour killed the infants, and we might interpret it as a hidden population check, were it not for the fact that the Icelanders were conscious of a demographic problem and that they explicitly wanted their children to get the best of all possible food. Even if it were a kind of subconscious population check, this could be deemed neither functional nor rational under conditions of population decline, and we would be back at unreason.

Fortunately, other theories of knowledge have provided us with an excellent antidote to the power of Western hierarchical oppositions (Overing, 1985: 17). These theories have helped us realise that there is no 'pure' knowledge or reason separated from moral knowledge or ethics. To advocate breast-feeding is therefore also to advocate a particular morality, however much it is apparently based in scientific investigations into nutrition, immunity and what have you. Conversely, we cannot claim particular weaning patterns to be absolutely irrational or immoral. We have no unified standards of value which would allow us to draw such a conclusion.

It seems to me that with the absence of breast-feeding in Iceland, we are in the realm of the non-rational rather than the irrational. 'There are cases where canons of rationality, validity, truth, and efficiency are simply beside the point – irrelevant' (Shweder, 1984: 38). That is what anthropology's 'romantic rebellion' against the enlightenment is all about (Schweder, 1984). To be a romantic in this sense is to be anti-normative and to be suspicious of the concept of progress (Schweder, 1984: 47). From this perspective it is no coincidence that it was the Enlightenment that finally re-educated Icelandic mothers to breast-feed their infants when in the late eighteenth century it was transposed to Iceland also in the shape of a trained physician.

Just as we may see tribal society as an implicit refutation of the state, with all that implies in terms of hierarchy and centralisation (Clastres, 1977), so we may see the Icelandic infant-feeding practice as a rebellion against modernism, with all that implied in terms of centralisation and a unified standard of value. It was possibly to that threat of assimilation that the Icelanders reacted, by a continuous stress upon their own singularity, as tied up with their farming values. The implications of feeding infants on cow's milk take us to the ultimate conclusion, that breast-feeding is always a question of reason.

Notes

1. Thus Tomasson speaks of a 'millennium of misery' when discussing Icelandic demography in general (Tomasson, 1977), and states that 'the population of Iceland saw no sustained growth from after the Black Death [1402–4] until the end of the 1820s' (1980: 68).
2. A more detailed exposition is found in Hastrup (1990a).
3. To give the gist of the poem I shall quote the first verse:

> Kære barn mitt, korríró,
> kúrðu vært og sof nú lengi.
> Vekja þig af vænni ró,
> verkjatök né meinsemd engi.
>
> My dear child, *korriro*,
> crouch you calmly and sleep long.
> No pain or sickness
> can now wake you from blissful peace.

4. This also in part explains the narrow spacing between births (Lithell, 1981).
5. See for instance Knodel and van de Walle (1967), and Lithell (1981).
6. In Hastrup (1990a) I discuss the 'honour-and-butter-complex' more thoroughly.

Bibliographical References

Andersson, J., *Nachtrichten von Island* Hamburg, G.C. Grund, 1746

Ardener, E., 'Behaviour: A social anthropological criticism', *Journal of the anthropological society of Oxford*, vol. IV, no. 3, 1973

——, Social Anthropology, Language and Reality', in D. Parkin, ed., *Semantic Anthropology*, London, Academic Press 1982, ASA Monographs no. 22

——, 'Remote areas: Some Theoretical Considerations', A. Jackson, (ed.) *Anthropology at Home*, London, Tavistock, 1987, ASA Monographs no. 22

——, 'Ritual and the social space' (forthcoming)

Ardener, S. (ed.) *Perceiving Women*, London, Malaby Press, 1975

——, 'Introduction: The Nature of Women in Society', in S. Ardener (ed.), *Defining Females: The Nature of Women In Society*, London, Croom-Helm, 1978

Ariès, P., *L'enfant et la vie familiale sous l'Ancien Régime*, Paris, Seuil, 1973

Badinter, E., *The Myth of Motherhood: an Historical View of the Maternal Instinct*, London, Souvenir Press, 1982.

Bourdieu, P., 'The Berber House', in M. Douglas (ed.), *Rules and Meaning: The Anthropology of Everyday Knowledge*, Harmondsworth, Penguin, 1973

Callaway, H., 'The most essentially female function of all: Giving birth', in S. Ardener (ed.), *Defining Females: The Nature of Women in Society*, London, Croom-Helm, 1978

Clastres, P., *Society Against the State*, Oxford, Blackwell, 1977

Einarsson, O., *Islandslýsing. Qualiscunque descripto Islandiae*, (transl. by Sveinn Pálsson and with introductions by Jakob Benediktsson and Sigurður þórarinsson), Reykjavik, Menningarsjóður, 1971, (first edition, 1589)

Eggers, C.V.D., *Philosophische Schilderung der gegenwärtigen Verfassung von Island*, Altona, J.D.V. Eckhardt, 1786

Friis, P.C., *Samlede skrifter*, Gustav Storm, (ed.), Kristiania, Den norske historiske forening, 1881

Gísladóttir, H., 'Kvinner og Matstell på Island i Middelalderen', in *Kvinnearbeid i Norden fra vikingtiden til reformasjonen*, Bergen, Universitetet i Bergen, 1985

Guttormsson, L., *Bernska, ungdómur og uppeldí á Einveldisöld*, Reykjavik Ritsafn Sagnfræðistofnunar, 10, 1983a

——, Barnaeldi, Ungbarnadauði og Viðkoma á Íslandi 1750–1860, in *Athöfn og Orð: Afmælisrit helgað Matthias Jónassyni*, Reykjavik, Mál og Menning, 1983b

Hajnal, J., 'European Marriage Patterns in Perspective', in D.V. Glass and D.E.C. Eversly, (eds), *Population in History: Essays in Historical Demography*, London, Edward Arnold Publishers Ltd., 1965

Hastrup, K., 'The Semantics of Biology: Virginity', in S. Ardener (ed.), *Defining Females: The Nature of Women in Society*, London, Croom Helm, 1978

——, 'Male and female in Icelandic Culture: A preliminary sketch', *Folk*, vol. 27, 1985

——, 'The reality of anthropology', *Ethnos*, vol. 52: 3–4, 1987

——, *Nature and Policy in Iceland 1400–1800: An Anthropological Analysis of History and Mentality*, Oxford, Clarendon 1990a

——, 'Studying a remote island: Inside and outside Icelandic culture', in Hastrup, K., *Island of Anthropology: Studies in past and present Iceland*, Odense, Odense University Press, 1990b

——, 'The Meaning of Migration', In Hastrup, K., *Island of Anthropology: Studies in Past and Present Iceland*, Odense, Odense University Press, 1990c

——, 'Eating the Past: Notes on an Icelandic Food-Ritual', *Folk*, vol. 33, 1991

Hertz, R., 'The Pre-eminence of the Right Hand: A Study in Religious Polarity' (1909), in Needham, R., (ed.), *Right and Left: Essays on Dual Symbolic Classification*, Chicago and London, Chicago University Press, 1973

Horrebow, N., *Tilforladelige Efterretninger om Island*, Copenhagen 1752

——, *Íslenzkt ljóðasafn*, vol I–IV. Kristján Karlsson, (ed.) Reykjavik, Almenna bókfélagið, 1975–8

Jochumssen, M., *Anmærkninger ofver Island og dessen indbyggere. Innberetning etter reisen på Island i årene 1729–1731*, Oddvar Vastveit, (ed.), Oslo, Universitetsbiblioteket i Oslo, Skrifter, no. 5, 1977

Jónasson, J., *Íslenzkir þjóðhættir*, 3rd edn., Reykjavik, Ísafold, 1961

Knodel, J. and van de Walle, E., 'Breast Feeding, Fertility and Mortality', *Demography* vol. 14 (4) pp. 391–409, 1967

Kålund, Kr., (ed.), *Den islandske lægebog: Cod. Arnam. 434 a, 12 mo.*, (ed. and with an introduction by K.K.), Copenhagen, Det Kgl, Danske Videnskabernes Selskabs Skrifter, 6. række. Hist. Fil. afd. VI, 4, 1907

Larsen, H., *An Old Icelandic Medical Miscellany*, (ed., with an introduction and translation by H.L.), Oslo, Det Norske Videnskabsakademi, 1931

——, *Lovsamling for Island*. vol I, ff. Copenhagen 1853 ff.

Lithell, V.B., 'Breast-Feeding Habits and their Relations to Infant Mortality and Marital Fertility', *Journal of Family History* 6, 2 (1981): 182–94

MacCormack, C., and Strathern, M., (eds), *Nature, Culture and Gender*, Cambridge, Cambridge University Press, 1980

Macfarlane, A., *Marriage and Love in England 1300–1840*, Oxford, Blackwell, 1986

Maher, V., 'Possession and dispossession: maternity and mortality in Morocco', in H. Medick and D. Sabean (eds), *Interest and Emotion*, Cambridge, Cambridge University Press, 1984

Millard, A.V. and Graham, M.A., 'Principles that guide weaning in rural Mexico', *Ecology of Food and Nutrition*, Vol 16, pp. 171–88, 1985

Margolis, M.L., *Mothers and such: Views of American Women and Why they Changed*, Berkeley, Los Angeles, London, University of California Press, 1984

Ólafsson, E., *Reise igiennem Island*, Sorøe, Videnskabernes Selskab, 1772

——, 'Búnaðarbálkur', in *Kvæði Eggerts Ólafssonar*, Copenhagen 1832

Ortner, S., 'Is Female to Male as Nature Is to Culture', in M.Z. Rosaldo and L. Lamphere (eds), *Women, Culture and Society*, Stanford, Stanford University Press, 1974

Overing, J., 'Introduction', in J. Overing (ed.), *Reason and Morality*,

London, Tavistock, (ASA Monographs 24), 1985

Pétursson, J., *Lækningabók fýrrir almuga*, Copenhagen, 1834

Rosaldo, M.Z., 'Women, Culture and Society: A Theoretical Overview', in M.Z. Rosaldo and L. Lamphere (eds), *Women, Culture and Society*, Stanford, Stanford University Press, 1974

Sahlins, M.D., *Culture and Practical Reason*, Chicago, The University of Chicago Press, 1976

Saussure, F. de, *Course in General Linguistics*, Translated W. Baskin, New York, Philosophical Library, 1959

Shorter, E., *A History of Women's Bodies*, Harmondsworth, Pelican, 1984

Shweder, R.A., *Culture Theory: Essays on Mind, Self and Emotion*, Cambridge, Cambridge University Press, 1984

Sigurðardóttir, S., 'Höfðu konur börn á brjósti 1700–1900?', *Sagnir*, vol. 3, 1982

Statistics of Iceland *Manntalið 1703*

——, *Population Census 1703* Reykjavik, 1960

Steffensen, J., *Menning og meinsemdir: Ritgerðasafn um mótunarsögu íslenzkrar þjóðar og baráttu hennar við hungur og sóttir*, Reykjavik, Sögufelagið, 1975

Tomasson, R.F., 'A Millenium of Misery: The Demography of the Icelanders', *Population Studies* no. 3, 1977

——, *Iceland: The First New Society*, Reykjavik, Iceland Review in co-operation with University of Minnesota Press, 1980

von Troil, U., *Letters on Iceland*, London, J. Robson, 1780

Warner, M., *Alone of all her Sex. The Myth and the Cult of the Virgin Mary*, London, Quartet Books, 1978

þorláksson, H., 'Óvelkominn börn?', *Sagnir*, 1986

5

Milk Kinship in Shi'ite Islamic Iran

Jane Khatib-Chahidi

Islamic Law defines three types of kinship: relationship by blood, marriage and milk. The last is referred to as *al-rida'a* in Arabic, *shiri* or *reza'i* in Persian, and suffixed to the appropriate kinship term. All three involve an impediment to marriage between certain persons so related. The prohibition in the case of milk kinship extends, broadly speaking, to all who would be within the prohibited degrees of consanguinity if the act of suckling had been an act of procreation on the part of the woman who suckles another's child (the milk mother) and her husband (the milk father and 'owner' of the milk) (Wilson, 1921: 57). The milk relationship, however, is a restricted form of legally recognized kinship: milk kin cannot inherit from each other; milk parents have no legal duty to maintain their milk children; nor do they have any form of guardianship over them. Also, in cases where a milk child steals from the milk parents, the act is considered as theft and incurs the usual punishment (Hamilton, 1791, II: 99).

The milk relationship comes into existence through a woman suckling another's child at the breast. No amount of rearing a child, for whatever period, can create the relationship. As such it differs basically from institutions of fosterage which created kinship ties cited by several nineteenth- and early twentieth-century writers, despite the fact that it is often referred to as 'fosterage' and classified as being an example of the same institution (ERE, VI, 104–9). Although for all practical purposes the milk mother herself fulfils the same role as the wet-nurse in former times in Europe, it differs basically from that institution, too, since the latter did not involve the child and nurse in any legally recognised relationship, even though a deep emotional attachment might well develop between them.

The institution of milk kinship remains largely unexplored in anthropological literature in spite of the fact that anthropologists have shown a great interest in all forms of kinship and quasi-kinship since the emergence of their subject as a separate discipline in the late nineteenth century. In the current Encyclopaedia Britannica, for example, mention is made of blood brotherhood amongst the Azande in Africa, ghost marriage amongst the Nuer of Sudan, the *compadrazgo* relationship of godfather/godchild in Europe and Latin America and the quasi-father/son relationship between certain Japanese craftsmen and their assistants. No mention is made of milk kinship for which in Islam there exists a whole body of detailed laws and regulations. Altorki (1980: 233–244) appears to be the first anthropologist to have written in any detail on the subject in English and this in regard to Saudi Arabian society.[1]

Nor is the institution confined to Islam: as might be expected with a custom which deals with such a basic necessity as giving sustenance to an infant who would otherwise die in the absence of dried milk, it is found in many societies scattered across the world (Frazer, 1913, VII: 371; XI: 138).

Milk Kinship: A Transcultural Perspective

It is reported that when the Masai of East Africa wanted to make a lasting peace with an enemy tribe, the respective tribes would bring a cow with a calf and a woman with a baby. The two cows would be exchanged and the enemy's child suckled at the breast of the Masai woman; the Masai baby would be suckled by the woman from the enemy tribe (Hollis, 1905: 321–2).

Akbar, the Mogul Emperor of Delhi and descendant of Gengis Khan, would only inflict the lightest of punishments upon a milk brother who persistently offended him because 'Between me and Aziz is a river of milk which I cannot cross' (Malleson, 1890: 177). Although Akbar was Muslim, the institution of milk kinship certainly predates the Moguls' conversion to Islam: the terms used to designate the milk mother, her husband and their son are Turkish words used amongst the Turco-Tatar tribes from which the Mogul emperors were drawn. If the Osman Turks allowed milk brothers free access to the *harim*, usually permitted only to close kinsmen, it was probably due more to a previous custom than to their recent adoption of Islam (ERE, 1913, VI: 105). Although the Hindus of India do not recognise the milk tie in law, Lyall (1882:

221) mentions that the royal Rajputs usually chose their children's wet-nurse from a well-known pastoral tribe. The family of the nurse held a recognised hereditary status of 'kinship by milk' within the royal clan and the child's milk brothers wielded great power at court.

Biddulph (1880) gives several examples of the importance of milk kinship in the Hindu Kush amongst tribes which, although Muslim, had only been recently converted.[2] He comments that the milk relationship – which he refers to as foster kinship – was maintained amongst all the ruling families and its ties seemed more binding than those of blood kinship. All children were placed at birth with a foster mother and brought up by her family. Frequently the father did not see his child until he/she was six or seven. The whole family of the nurse placed themselves at the disposal of their foster child with whom, for the rest of their lives, their fortunes were inalterably bound up. If the foster child was exiled, they would go into exile with him; if he rose to influence, the foster father and brothers would be given positions and duties of importance. In the Ashimadek clans of Chitral in the Hindu Kush every infant was suckled in turn by every nursing mother of the clan. There was consequently a constant interchange of infants going on among the mothers 'for the purpose of strengthening tribal unity'. In instances where conclusive proof of adultery was lacking, and therefore punishment/vengeance could not be inflicted, Biddulph reported that the case would be brought before the ruler for settlement. A guarantee would be taken for the future by the accused placing his lips on the breast of the woman involved in the suspected act. She was thenceforth regarded as his foster mother and no other relations but those of mother and son could exist between them. The tie was deemed so sacred that it had never been known to be broken (Biddulph 1880: 77–83).

A similar example exists of how suspected adultery was dealt with in nineteenth-century Russia amongst the Svans (Charachidze, 1968, cited by Dragadze, 1987: 169). Dragadze herself found no record of such a custom in Ratcha, South Georgia, where she did her research, but she states that *rdzis nat'esaoba* (the milk relationship) is an institution which although nearly extinct, still forms an integral part of the conceptual framework of Georgian kinship in its wider sense. Nowadays when a mother in a maternity hospital breast-feeds the child of another woman because of an emergency, the two families will come together to declare milk brotherhood. The parents of the children will exchange visits, favours and gifts; when the milk siblings grow up, they will be expected to be on close terms with each other throughout their adult life. The relationship brings with it an impediment for marriage: the children of milk siblings cannot marry. Although in theory, as with blood kin, this should apply up to seven generations, there is little evidence that this is so (Dragadze, 1987: 166–9).

In nineteenth-century Ratcha, and elsewhere in Georgia, a custom called *skhvisshviloba* (another child) was still in existence. This appears to have been practised in order to gain trading partners who could be relied upon in potentially hostile areas. The Christian Georgians would send a new-born child to their Muslim trading partner in North Caucasia if the latter's wife was known to be breast-feeding. The Muslims would do the same but with another trading partner. It seems that the custom served the purpose of demonstrating that there was complete confidence between the parties concerned. The child would remain in the family until he/she was ten or eleven but would be returned then as proof that the foster parents had not acquired a cheap source of labour. The 'investment' was made mainly for the future genera-tion: the milk siblings would speak the same language, know the same traditions; they would help each other with trade, transport and hospitality. The relationship continued for seven generations and, as with the prohibition on intermarriage, the descendants of the milk siblings could not enter into another *skhvisshviloba* rela-tionship; nor could they intermarry even if their respective reli-gions and social status had permitted it (Rekhiashvili, 1974, cited by Dragadze, 1987: 166–9).

The Christian Slavs of southern and eastern Europe also recog-nised milk kinship as an impediment to marriage and used it, along with other 'fictitious' kinship ties such as *gossipred* (spiritual parentage), to prevent intermarriage (Maine, 1891: 257). Although the custom may have been adopted by the Southern Slavs from their Muslim neighbours (ERE, 1913: VI: 104), it would seem more likely, given the material from Georgia, that the institution predates Islam and was current amongst many more societies as Maine (1893: 241) suggests.[3]

Kinship in Islam

Before elaborating upon milk kinship with particular reference to Shi'ite Islam in Iran, it is necessary to consider the role kinship in general plays in Islamic societies and how it affects practising Muslims in their daily lives. In other words, milk kinship must be seen in the context of other forms of kinship if the Islamic rulings on the institution are to be fully understood.

It is often said that Islam is not just a religion but a way of life. The *Shari'a*, the law of Islam, is based partly on the Koran and partly on *hadiths* which are the pronouncements or acts of the Prophet reported by reliable authorities. In each of the four orthodox schools of Islamic jurisprudence recognised by the Sunnis (Maleki, Hanbali, Hanafi and Shafi'i) and the book of rules which each *mujtahed* (religious leader) in Shi'ite Iran compiles for the use of his followers, it is laid down, often in minute detail, how the devout Muslim must conduct him or herself in daily life. The differences between the various schools of law stem from the fact that *hadiths* accepted by one may differ from those accepted by another or the same *hadith* may have given rise to differing interpretations.[4]

A great number of rules are devoted to the prohibited degrees of kinship for marriage because kinship ties dictate the kind of behaviour and social interaction permitted between the sexes. Basically Islamic rulings state that potential marriage partners, referred to as *na-mahram* (whether related or not) may not mix: strict veiling is required on the part of the woman and suitably reserved behaviour on the part of both man and woman. Contravention of these rules can affect the validity of the devout Muslim's daily prayers. Those who cannot marry because of a kinship tie – by blood, marriage or milk – referred to as *mahram* relatives, on the other hand, are the men and women who can mix freely: veiling is not required and there is an easy familiarity in the relationship. Thus the laws which restrict the range of potential marriage partners, almost paradoxically, extend the range of social relationships with the opposite sex experienced by practising Muslims in their daily lives. In a sense it is this paradox which is being exploited by practising Muslims when they contract 'marriages of convenience' to enable people of the opposite sex to be together without infringing Islamic rulings (Khatib-Chahidi, 1981: 125–7); and in the case of milk kinship, deliberately creating a milk relationship for the same purpose (Altorki, 1980: 240; Khatib-Chahidi, 1981: 125), or to prevent a marriage which they deem undesirable (Altorki, 1980: 240–1).

Most commentators look upon the institution of milk kinship as pre-Islamic (Wilson, 1921: 57) and as having its origins in customs prevalent in Arabia at the time of the Prophet. Muhammad himself was put out to nurse with a woman of the Beni Sad who reared him amongst her own tribe until he was five (ERE, 1913: 104). Prominent Meccans up until comparatively recent times used to have Bedouin nurses for their children (SEI, 1953: 463). The Koran itself devotes little attention to the institution, confining itself to the impediment to marriage incurred between a man and his milk mother and milk sister (Sura IV.23). It is in the Traditions – based on *hadiths* – that the elaboration of the custom is to be found. Although there is a broad agreement on the principles involved, there exist many differences of opinion in specific details, particularly between the four Sunni schools; amongst Shi'a religious leaders, past and present, however, there appears little disagreement. The differences in opinion centre on the amount of breast-feeding that has to take place for the relationship to be legally recognised; whether the milk has to be taken direct from the breast; the period of the child's life in which the suckling should occur; the extent of the prohibition to marriage between milk kin. As regards this last point an added complication arises in Shi'ite Islamic Law because the milk relatives of the milk mother and her husband ('owner' of the milk), if they were nursed by someone other than their own mothers, are also included in this range of prohibited potential marriage partners.

Milk Kinship in Shi'ite Iran

The Shi'ite Islamic rulings which appear in this section are based upon the Persian text of Ayatollah Khomeini's book '*Resale touzih al-masael*' (n.d.: 392–9) 2464–2474 and 2487–2497 which, as mentioned above, differ very little from those of other Iranian religious leaders in the present day, such as Khoyi, Khonsari and Shahrestani, or from those of religious leaders living in previous centuries.[5]

The Marriage Prohibition Incurred by Milk Kinship

The child is forbidden in marriage to the following persons:

1. The milk mother
2. The husband of the milk mother, the milk father, who is owner of the milk
3. The milk mother's father and mother and their ascendants, including her milk father and mother
4. The children born to the milk mother before and after the child's suckling
5. The milk mother's descendants whether they are born to her children or her descendants have suckled the children (i.e. they are the descendants' milk children)
6. The milk mother's brothers and sisters, whether real or milk (i.e. they are like uncles and aunts)
7. The paternal and maternal uncles and aunts of the milk mother, whether real or milk
8. The real or milk children of the husband of the milk mother, born to another wife (i.e. the milk mother's step-children), and their descendants because the milk 'belongs' to the husband
9. The real and milk parents of the milk father and their ascendants
10. The milk father's sisters and brothers, whether real or milk
11. The paternal and maternal aunts and uncles of the milk father and their ascendants, whether real or milk (2464)

The father of the child that is suckled cannot marry the milk mother's daughters; he cannot marry the daughters of the milk mother's husband (i.e. from another marriage). It is strongly recommended that he should not marry the milk father's milk daughters. It is permitted for him to marry the milk mother's milk daughters but he is recommended not to and he should not behave towards them as though they were *mahram* relatives (2465).

The milk father does not become forbidden in marriage to the milk child's sisters but it is recommended that he should not marry them. The relations of the milk father do not become forbidden to the milk child's brothers or sisters either (2466).

The milk mother is not forbidden in marriage to her milk child's brothers. Neither do her relatives become forbidden to the child's brothers and sisters (2467).

If a man marries a woman, and the marriage has been consummated, he cannot marry that woman's milk daughters (2468).

If a man marries a girl, he cannot marry her milk mother (2469).

A man cannot marry a girl who has been suckled by his mother or grandmother. Also, if a man's step-mother, from his father's milk, feeds a girl, he cannot marry that girl. If he marries an infant who is being suckled, and later his mother, grandmother or step-mother, from his father's milk, suckles that infant, the marriage becomes null and void (2470).

A man cannot marry a girl who has been suckled by his sister or his brother's wife, if the brother 'owns' the milk. The same rule applies if a man's sister's daughters or granddaughters, or his brother's daughters or granddaughters (and their descendants), feed a girl (2471).

If a woman suckles her daughter's child, her daughter becomes forbidden (*haram*) to her husband, her son-in-law (and their marriage consequently becomes null and void). The same rule applies if a woman suckles her daughter's step-daughter: the daughter becomes forbidden to her husband. But if a woman suckles her son's child, her son's wife, who is the child's mother, does not become forbidden to her husband (2472).

If a girl's father's wife (i.e. step-mother) gives her father's milk to her husband's child (i.e. the girl's husband), that girl becomes forbidden to her (own) husband. This rule applies whether the child is her own or that of another wife of her husband (2473).

Rules Relating to the Establishment of the Milk Relationship

The child must be suckled by one woman for a period of time considered sufficient for the milk to have contributed to its growth.

This is generally held to be fifteen times in succession or for twenty-four hours, during which time the child should have received only the milk of the one woman (2474).

The suckling should be vouched for by a number of reliable people or by two men and four women who are known to be honest and of good reputation. They should state that the woman gave the child milk for the stipulated time and that the child had only that milk (2496).

The milk of a dead woman does not create the milk relationship. The milk must be suckled at the breast. The child should be under two (2474).[6]

Recommendations Concerning the Choice of Milk Mother

The mother is not legally obliged to suckle her own child although it is thought better that she should be the one to do so. It is 'meritorious' if the mother does this without expecting payment, but the husband should recompense her for these services. If the mother does ask for payment and expects more than a wet-nurse (*dayeh*),[7] the husband can give the child to a wet-nurse instead (2487).

It is recommended that the *dayeh* should be a practising Twelve Imami Shi'a Muslim. She should be intelligent, of good moral character (*ba e'fat*) and attractive. A stupid woman or one who is not a Twelve Imami Muslim should be avoided; also one who is ugly, bad-tempered or illegitimate. A *dayeh* with an illegitimate child is also to be avoided (2488).

Miscellaneous Rulings and Injunctions

Women should refrain from suckling many children as they may forget which ones they have suckled and *mahram* relatives will marry (2489).

People who become milk relatives should have respect for each other but they do not inherit from each other or enjoy other rights (i.e. those of blood relatives) (2490).

It is recommended that a child should be suckled for two years (2491).

If by suckling a child no harm is done to the woman's husband's rights, the woman can give the milk without the permission of her husband. However, it is not permitted to give milk to a child if the woman would then become *haram* to her husband. For example, a woman cannot feed her husband's infant wife, because if she does, she becomes her husband's mother-in-law and therefore forbidden (*haram*) to him (and their marriage becomes null and void) (2492).

If a man wishes to make his brother's wife *mahram* to him, he should marry an infant for a short period and in that period, observing the conditions stated in 2474, he should give the infant wife to his brother's wife to be fed (2493).

If a man, before marrying a woman, says that through milk that woman is forbidden (*haram*) to him because, for example, his mother has breast-fed her, and his claim seems reasonable, he cannot marry that woman. If he claims this after the marriage and the woman agrees with him, the marriage becomes null and void. This is the case whether the marriage was consummated or not. But if the woman knows about this relationship when the marriage is consummated, she becomes forbidden (*haram*) to the man and does not deserve to receive her marriage settlement (*mahr*). If the relationship only becomes known to her after consummation of the marriage, the husband should give her the marriage settlement (2494).

If a woman before the marriage ceremony (*aqd*) says that through milk she is forbidden to a man, and she is believed, she cannot marry that man. If she says this afterwards, it follows the same rule as in 2494 and the marriage becomes null and void (2495).

Milk Kinship in Iran in Practice

Formula milk was introduced into Iran in the late 1940s and its advent undoubtedly led to the demise of the institution of milk kinship in the middle and upper classes who could afford to buy it. How far the custom subsisted, and subsists, in the rural and urban working classes of the society is undocumented. My own research only deals with the custom as it exists within the living memory and experience of an older generation whose origins lie more in the former landowning class, a relatively élite group. Despite this, as I commented in *Women and Space* (Ardener, 1981: 113), the difference between the rich and the poor in Iran until the mid-1960s was, on the whole, more a difference in degree than a difference in kind: the rich had more of what the poor had less and their life styles, while differing enormously in scale, were based on common values, beliefs and customs. My somewhat limited ethnographic research into the institution from the point of view of Iranian society in general may therefore still indicate how many Iranians did, in fact, think and behave with regard to it.

A wet-nurse/milk mother always appears to have been taken for an infant when it was thought to be absolutely essential: that is, in the case of the death or illness of the mother or the onset of another pregnancy while child was still being breast-fed. There were no examples of the use of the relationship to circumvent strict veiling or to prevent marriages. In fact my informants found the suggestion that it could be made use of for such purposes highly bizarre. This was presumably because there exist, in Shi'ite Islam, much easier ways of effecting the former by means of fictitious marriages (Khatib-Chahidi, 1981: 125–8).[8] For example, servants in Iranian households where there were devout Muslims were made into *mahram* relatives by means of temporary marriage contracts: the servant was 'married' to the son or daughter of the head of household, often an infant who would know nothing about what was being done in his/her name. The servant then became like a son- or daughter-in-law to the household head and to the other members of the family. This permitted practising Muslims to carry out their devotions with a clear conscience in the presence of servants of the opposite sex. It also permitted a female servant to attend to her work without being strictly veiled in front of the male members of the household, which would have hindered her efficiency (Khatib-Chahidi, 1981: 114–6; 125–8).

As far as using milk kinship to prevent marriages went, the Iranians' concern when practising the custom was to avoid a choice of wet-nurse/milk mother which *could* affect future marriage arrangements. No one seemed to have any idea of the extent to which milk kinship affected the prohibition on marriage between persons so related beyond that between milk siblings. Even a man aged sixty who had had a milk mother himself and who, before he became a doctor, had been training to be a *mullah*, had no idea. Thus the detailed Islamic rulings would appear to have borne little relevance to the institution as practised in this century.

As stated above, the illness or death of the mother and onset of another pregnancy were the reasons given for calling upon another woman to breast-feed an infant. Iranian women from the middle and upper classes, unlike their European counterparts in previous centuries (Ross, 1974; Tucker, 1974; Illick, 1974; Marvick, 1974; Flandrin, 1976; Donzelot, 1980; Fildes, 1988), breast-fed their own infants. Examples of the third reason – another pregnancy – were frequent. In such cases the mother's milk was considered as 'bad', because it changed in appearance. It was felt that the change in the mother's metabolism, which caused this change in the milk, was bad for the child being suckled; there was no suggestion that it might be bad for the mother or the foetus.[9]

If Iranian women appear seldom to have given their infants to another woman to suckle, it may be due in part to the fact that it was considered no easy task to find a suitable person. Unlike their European and Ancient Arab counterparts, they do not seem to have been willing to send their infants to the wet-nurse/milk mother's family to be cared for: ideally those from the upper classes engaged a wet-nurse who would come and live in the household; in cases where this was not possible, because of the wet-nurse's own family commitments, she would come to the house at feeding times. These factors posed an immediate constraint on the availability of wet-nurses: they either had to be without family ties or live near enough to come at the required times.

Secondly, as stated in the Islamic rulings, the wet-nurse had to be a person with the right moral and physical attributes. Iranians, like many other people, think that the qualities and defects of the woman who suckles a child are passed on to the child through her milk.[10] A person known to have the right attributes was likely to be a relative or close friend of the family, but since such people might also have children who were potential future marriage partners, they were not considered suitable. Several cases were cited where it would have been easy for a mother's sister, for example, to feed the infant but she was not used precisely because it might affect future marriage arrangements. In only one case cited was a relative used and this was only because they had been unable to find a suitable person outside the family. There are indications, however, that this was a class-related attitude. In less well-off families and in the merchant class in Iran the wet-nurse/milk mother seems more likely to have been a close relative. In the former this probably reflects the inability to bear the expense of a paid wet-nurse; in the latter, perhaps, that jeopardising future marriage arrangements within the extended family was not deemed so important as in the landowning class. Also landowners in Iran, because they 'owned' whole villages sometimes, were in a much better position to know of the right kind of person. Because of their position, too, they were more likely to get someone to agree to allow their wife to be the wet-nurse. Only more detailed fieldwork in a wider section of the Iranian population, however, can determine whether or not these observations are valid.

As might be expected, the wet-nurse who lived in the household came from a lower class than that of the milk child's family. That she was able to stay in the household indicated that something had gone wrong in her own life so that she was not living with her husband or with her own family. Although such women occupied a somewhat ambiguous place within the family of their milk child, in that they were employed in a largely domestic role, they considered themselves to have a much higher status within the family than servants and were treated differently from them. This does not mean, however, that they were respected in the same way as the mother: they remained glorified servants, one of the many family retainers found in large upper-class Iranian households until the mid-twentieth century and beyond. The tie between the wet-nurse and her milk child, nevertheless, cut across natural kin ties: she was the champion of her particular child *vis-à-vis* other members of the family; the child would support his/her nurse when arguments arose within the family involving her.

The wet-nurse who did not live in was likely to enjoy a higher status than her living-in counterpart: she 'belonged' to her own family and the fact that she was able to render such a valuable service to her higher-class neighbour put the latter in a position of being the recipients, rather than the givers – a position of strength in a society where patron-client relationships abound. Such a wet-nurse was not and did not expect to be paid money for her services. This indicated the more equal relationship she enjoyed with her milk child's family. Instead she would be given presents such as material for *chadors* (veils), gold coins which were normally given as gifts rather than in payment of wages, and clothes for her family. Although it appears to have been the norm that the milk child's family was higher class and the wet-nurse's family lower class, several instances were cited of a higher-class breast-feeding mother voluntarily feeding a lower-class woman's child because the former had too much milk and the latter was sick. This was considered a meritorious act.

A few case studies will, perhaps, illustrate the foregoing. The cases cited were actual situations which arose between forty-five and sixty years ago.

Case One — A girl from a landowning family, who had been married at the age of ten or eleven and had had two children by the time she was in her early teens, was breast-feeding her first child. She had so much milk that her breasts were extremely painful. She heard that one of her villagers' wives had picked up an infection in childbirth and was unable to feed her infant. She offered to feed the child and the latter was brought to her for this purpose. The landowner's wife subsequently became pregnant with her second child while she was still breast-feeding (her first child was four months old) which meant that the family had to get a wet-nurse for her first child. The woman selected was from one of the better-off peasant landholding families in a neighbouring village; she was also a *seyed*, descendant of the Prophet, as were the landowner's family. She came to the house four times a day to feed the child. For the last feed at ten in the evening servants were sent to escort her there and back home. Sugar and water were given to the child during the night when she was not available. No cash payment was made to the wet-nurse but her family were exempt from paying their usual dues to their landlord; presents such as material for veils and gold coins at the Iranian New Year (the first day of spring) were given.

Case Two — Another landowner's wife was obliged to get a wet-nurse for her second-born child, who was six months old when she became pregnant with her third. The girl being suckled refused all other food or milk even though she was old enough to do without breast-milk. It was only with difficulty that a wet-nurse was found. She was the second wife of an older man whom she had left after giving birth to a child who, in fact, died after her departure. She remained with the family for twenty years and helped look after the next child as a dry-nurse. She eventually re-married but without the approval of the landowner's family. When the marriage proved unsuccessful, however, she returned to them. Another marriage was arranged, this time with the approval of the family. She now lives in Qom with her present husband.

Case Three — A man now in his sixties had a wet-nurse who used to come to the house because his mother was ill. His mother died when he was five. The nurse then looked after him like a mother until he grew up, despite the fact that she had her own family to care for. This nurse was not paid any regular wage for her services as it would have been unacceptable; instead presents were given in the form of anything she needed for her own family.

Conclusion

Milk Kinship: Its Relevance in Islam

That Islamic jurists have all felt the need to expound at such length on what to us may seem hair-splitting details is, perhaps, more understandable when one considers certain aspects of social life in Muslim countries. In Iran, and in other parts of the Islamic world, ignorance of the laws relating to the prohibited degrees of kinship on the part of men, women and children means inappropriate social behaviour between the sexes. This can, in its turn, affect the devotional duties of practising Muslims for some of whom the mere looking at a na-mahram person while saying their prayers would mean their devotions were nullified and had to be repeated (Khatib-Chahidi, 1981: 114–5). Thus, while one suspects that some of the rulings relating to milk kinship have been prompted by people thinking up hypothetical situations as problems for their religious leaders/jurists to solve, they may also reflect the behavioural implications of the forbidden degrees of kinship for marriage: they represent not so much an indication of whom a person may or may not marry, but of those of the opposite sex with whom one may or may not act in a relaxed manner.

The Iranian Muslim household even in the present time, and more so in the past, is normally larger than that in the West and often comprises members of the extended family, as well as servants. Childbearing may begin for the women in their early teens and continue until the menopause; uncles and aunts (*mahram* relatives) may be the same age or younger than their nephews and nieces; grandmothers may be bearing children at the same time as their granddaughters. In other words, the generational phasing which helps us regulate our social behaviour and govern our choice of marriage partner may be lacking in Muslim society. Although children may not understand the legal implications, or the exact relationship they bear to one another when very young, the *mahram/na-mahram* distinction into which their social world is divided is one easily taught, without any need to go into complicated kinship descriptions.

As regards milk kinship specifically, it will be clear from what has been said that suckling another's child has implications – and uses – which go far beyond merely giving sustenance to an infant in need of it. It can reduce the range of potential spouses quite dramatically, especially when a relative such as the mother's sister or a neighbour was used as a wet-nurse/milk mother. Although my ethnographic data indicates that in recent times in Iran people only became involved in milk kinship relationships in cases of necessity, this should not obscure the fact that in times past the institution may well have been more generally used. The Islamic rulings themselves indicate two important sociological concerns: firstly, the need to incorporate the family of the woman who suckles another's child into the child's family in a special, and irreversible, way; secondly, to ensure that the link thus forged becomes a bar to marriage. In other words, we may well be dealing with an institution which had as part of its *raison d'être* in the past the need to enter into an alliance with a family with whom a link by marriage was to be positively avoided. The ethnographic data I have cited from other societies gives some support to this suggestion.

Data on the royal Rajputs, the Christian Georgians and the tribes of Ancient Arabia, all give some indication that the relationship was used as a means to get friends and allies. Marriages can serve the same purpose but in all the cases cited there may well have been reasons for using milk rather than marriage. For example, the Indian caste system usually only permits marriage within the caste, but milk relationships extended beyond the caste. The Christian Georgians did not approve of marriage with Muslims, but allowed milk relationships with them. In Ancient Arabia, where marriage within the tribe was usual, milk relationship was sought to gain allies in neighbouring tribes.

Milk Kinship: Its Relevance as a Subject of Study

For the Historical Record — If, as would seem likely, the institution of milk kinship has died out, as in Iran, with the advent of dried milk, one is left asking what relevance the study of milk kinship has nowadays. The response, I think, must be that precisely because it has been so little documented it is worth studying for the historical record alone while there are still those alive who remember the custom, many of whom have milk relatives. What, if anything, does this bond mean to them? How does it affect their social relationships?

For Insights into other Relationships — Documenting milk kinship helps fill in the social map of relationships in Islamic society. Detailed knowledge of one type of relationship also sometimes leads unexpectedly to a deeper knowledge of another. I was reminded of this in Turkey recently when talking about the present research. A thirty-year-old Turkish man told me he had a milk sister, his mother's sister's daughter. As in other Muslim societies, cousins are often preferred marriage partners in Turkey. I asked him if he realised that he could not marry this cousin. He replied that he did but that in any case many people felt that it was a bad thing to marry a first cousin on the mother's side of the family – although not on the father's – as they were too closely related. He supposed that in the past they had realised the possible consequences for the children when first cousins married even though they had not known what we now know about genetics. For him it seemed possible that we are indeed more closely related to the mother and her family than the father and his, perhaps because of her milk. This then led on to the choice of milk mother: in his experience the preferred milk mother seemed to have been the mother's sister. Both he and I then realised that this choice could be deliberate: just because it was thought undesirable to marry a mother's sister's child, although permitted in Islam, the mother's sister was used as milk mother to make it impossible for such a marriage to take place. Only further research into the institution and information collected from many informants will indicate whether or not this was the case in Turkey.

To Distinguish Between Milk Kinship and Kinship by Rearing: The 'Fosterage' Confusion — As I mentioned in the introduction, and as was apparent in several examples I have cited in the following section, milk kinship is often referred to as fosterage. Translations of Arabic sources for Islamic Law on the institution regularly use the term 'foster', rather than 'milk'. The English term 'foster', however, is ambiguous: the word 'foster' comes from Old English and now exists only in its original meaning of 'food' in combination with suffixed terms such as child, parent, mother, father, etc.; in this sense it denotes having the specified relationship not by blood, but by virtue of nursing (at the breast) or bringing up (SOED 1973: 796). This ambiguity in meaning poses immediate problems when comparing institutions of fosterage cross-culturally: to make academically valid comparisons we must be sure that we are comparing like with like. My own research into milk kinship indicates that this is not so.

Fosterage as practised nowadays in England does not involve breast-feeding at all but refers to the second meaning of 'foster', the rearing or bringing up of a child who is not your own. Even when wet-nurses were used, they were normally dispensed with when the child was weaned and the breast-feeding did not involve the nurse and child in any form of kinship. In Chamber's Encyclopaedia (1950), in the entry under 'fosterage', we find that it is an Irish custom under which children of freeborn and noble parents were given in early youth to other families to be reared. The tie of fosterage, in such cases, was considered closer than that of blood. When we turn to the Irish sources (ALI, 1869, vol. II; Joyce, 1903; O'Curry, 1873) detailed information on the custom emerges: it does not appear necessarily to have involved breast-feeding since the child went to the foster home at age one or older and remained there until approximately age fourteen for girls and seventeen for boys. It involved the parties concerned in reciprocal rights and obligations: the child's family paid a fee in cattle to the foster family in return for the latter looking after and educating the child in skills fitting to his/her rank and future social standing; provision was made for compensation by the foster parents to the child's family if the child was injured; withdrawal of the child before the period of fosterage was terminated and what had to be done in cases of bad fosterage was also legally regulated. When the foster child grew up, he was responsible for supporting the foster parents if they were old or poor; the same applied in the case of 'literary' fosterage when a boy was sent for his academic education to a foster father – who was often a priest – at a later age (ALI, 1869, vol. II, xliii–xlvi: 147–193; 349).

The Irish case of fosterage obviously differs from that of milk kinship in Islam: it is the rearing and education of the child which creates the kinship in the former; only the suckling of the child in the latter.[11] As a kinship tie it created problems for English rule in Ireland: Tudor governments, always concerned about how to control the unruly Irish, felt that the practice of English settlers marrying with the Irish and adopting Irish customs such as fosterage was contributing to their difficulties (ERE, 1913, VI: 108). Whether or not fosterage in Ireland in times past, along with similar customs practised in Anglo-Saxon England (Thorpe, 1840: Glossary), also represented a legally recognised impediment to marriage does not appear to be mentioned in the sources I have consulted. Both the Irish and Anglo-Saxon cases, however, would seem forerunners of the British boarding-school system which, in itself, is of historical interest.

In Ancient Scandinavia the suckling and rearing of children other than your own was commonplace and regulated by law. The foster father, however, played a more important role than the foster mother and part of his property went to the foster son. Weaker families gained protection by fostering the children of the stronger. The one who fostered was usually in an inferior position. Sometimes an offer to foster a child was made as an overture of friendship (ERE, 1913, VI: 104). Here we have an instance of legally recognised kinship being created by the rearing of the child, in that the child could inherit property from the foster father, unlike in milk kinship in Islam; while at the same time the suckling of the child, in itself, does not appear to be of importance.

Esther Goody (1982) has documented the custom of fosterage in West Africa, where it is practised using kin and non-kin as foster parents. It is seen as a way of improving the character of the foster child and giving him a good training for adult life. When children are placed with non-kin, it is usually for the purpose of providing them with access to skills and patronage which the parents cannot provide. Although some of the societies she cites are Muslim, milk kinship is not mentioned and it does not appear that the fostering which takes place creates a kinship tie which brings with it an impediment to marriage. In fact, in one example cited, a Hausa boy is sent to his father's Ibadan landlord whose daughter he eventually marries (Goody, 1982: 22). Similarly, Wolf and Huang (1980: 113–6) describe the institution of *simpua* in Taiwan where a girl of two or three will be sent to foster parents who take over full parental responsibilities for her from then onwards. This child will normally be destined as a future bride for one of the sons.

In Islam, however, it is often exactly those families into which the child's family would not want to marry which are selected for milk kinship purposes. The same applies in the Georgian case cited: the Christian Georgians did not want to marry into a Muslim family; neither did the Muslims want to marry Christians although legally they could do so. The creation of the milk kinship relationship effectively prevented this ever happening, while at the same time it forged an insoluble link with a trading partner in potentially hostile territory.

Milk Kinship: Its Practical Relevance in the Modern World

A knowledge of Islamic milk kinship, despite the apparent demise of the custom, still has some practical relevance in the modern world where milk banks are commonly used for infants born prematurely. A Muslim couple in Oxford, for example, refused adamantly to allow their premature baby to be fed with the 'mixed' mothers' milk from the milk bank. Those working in the hospital at the time could find no explanation for their refusal. Subsequently when one of the midwives involved heard about milk kinship, she realised the probable explanation: the parents did not want their child to become related through milk to women they did not know. In Sunni Islam, unlike in Shi'a, the baby does not necessarily need to suckle directly from the breast for the milk relationship to come into existence. For several years now there has been concern expressed over the way manufacturers in the West have been promoting the use of formula milk in the developing world with sometimes disastrous consequences for the infants concerned. If breast-feeding is to be encouraged, as opposed to bottle-feeding, then a knowledge of milk kinship in societies where it exists may well be useful.

Looking at Iran in particular, one can wonder if there is a resurgence of the institution in modern times. For the first time in its history Iran is under a totally Islamic regime. Habits and products which are seen to originate in the West are discouraged by those in power. Will this lead to more women breast-feeding and, therefore, having recourse to wet-nurses rather than formula milk when they cannot breast-feed? Will the fact that Islamic behaviour between the sexes is obligatory, at least in public, and has always been so amongst the more traditional and religious sections of society in public and private, give rise to the institution being used to circumvent strict veiling and the segregation of the sexes in the household? In other words, will milk kinship gain a relevance in Iranian society which it did not have in the living memory of those who helped me with my research?[12]

Notes

1. It is clear, however, that there is material published in Russian, e.g. Dragadze (1987) and the sources she cites.
2. Several factors indicate that the tribes had not fully adopted Islamic beliefs and customs. According to Biddulph, infidelity in marriage was not seriously regarded; the women were not secluded; inheritance was equal for men and women.
3. Maine states that the practice of fosterage is 'now known to have been widely diffused among Aryan communities' (1893: 241), but does not give his sources. Did he mean to include most of Europe and much of South West and South Asia in his generalisation, i.e. all areas where Indo-European languages are spoken? Nor does Maine distinguish between fosterage involving suckling another's child and fosterage involving rearing/educating another's child, c.f. my own discussion on this in the Conclusion.
4. For a clear account of the differences between Shi'a and Sunni Islam see Hollister, 1953, Chaps 1–4.
5. I have shortened rulings 2474 and 2496 and omitted rulings 2475–2486 because of lack of space. They deal mainly with finer elaborations of principles already included.
6. Amongst some Sunnis it is certain that the practice of suckling adults in order to establish milk kinship existed in times past (SEI, 1953: 463–4).
7. *'dayeh'* in Persian is the general term for a child's nurse/nanny and means either a wet-nurse or a dry-nurse.
8. It is interesting to note that one informant who thought it bizarre was the same old lady mentioned in my article whose granddaughter was 'married' to her sister-in-law's husband so that the latter could accompany the old lady to Mecca as a *mahram* relative.
9. This accords with the recommendations of the Persian physician Avicenna (980–1036), cited by Valerie Fildes (1988) in her well-

researched book on wet nursing. Kendall (1978: 107), writing about Iranian village women, also mentions this but says that if they became pregnant in the summer, they continued breast-feeding as they considered changing the infant's milk supply was more dangerous than the possible harmful effects of their own milk.

Chloë Fisher, an expert on breast-feeding from the John Radcliffe Hospital in Oxford, told me that when a woman becomes pregnant while she is still breast-feeding, the milk decreases in quantity and changes in quality and composition. Although some people believe that to continue suckling would cause premature labour, there is no medical evidence to support this view. The mother's nipples do become tender, however, which makes suckling painful; also the infant itself often rejects its mother's milk and has to be weaned. None of my informants mentioned this happening.

10. Iranians also think the same about animal milk: although donkey milk is considered to be the next best thing to human milk, it is not given to babies because donkeys are stupid and obstinate; goat milk is given because goats are thought to be intelligent.

11. Although Tudor commentators thought it 'monstrous that the same mother's milk should produce in Ireland the same close affections as did paternity in their own country' (Maine, 1893: 242), I have found no mention in the sources I have consulted that it was the milk that caused the kinship or that it created an impediment to marriage.

12. My own ethnographic research on milk kinship has had to be confined to gaining information from Iranians in exile, living abroad in England and the United States. Because of the Islamic revolution which took place in Iran in 1979, doing fieldwork there is problematic. It would be of great interest to have data from Iran now.

Bibliographical References

Altorki, S., 'Milk Kinship in Arab Society: an unexplored problem in the ethnography of marriage', *Ethnology*, Vol. XIX, No. 2, 1980

ALI (*Ancient Laws of Ireland*), Dublin, Alexander Thom & Hodges, Foster & Co., and London, Longmans, Green, Reader and Dyer, 1869

Ardener, S., *Women and Space*, London, Croom Helm, 1981.

Biddulph, J., *Tribes of the Hindoo Koosh*, Calcutta, Office of the Superintendent of Printing, 1880

Chamber's Encyclopaedia, (New ed.) London, George Newnes Ltd., 1950

Charachidze, G., *Le système religieux de la Georgie paienne: analyse structurale d'une civilisation*, Paris, François Maspero, 1968

Donzelot, J., *The Policing of Families*, London, Hutchison & Co, 1979

Dragadze, T., *'The Domestic Unit in a Rural Area of Soviet Georgia'*. D.Phil. thesis, Oxford, 1987

Encyclopaedia Britannica, Chicago, London, Toronto, Encyclopaedia Britannica Ltd., 1955

ERE (*Encyclopaedia of Religion and Ethics*), Ed. J. Hastings, Edinburgh, T & T Clark, 1913

Fildes, V., *Wet Nursing, A History from Antiquity to the Present*, Oxford, Basil Blackwell, 1988

Flandrin, J.L., *Families in Former Times: Kinship, household and sexuality*, Cambridge, Cambridge University Press, 1979 (French ed. 1976)

Frazer, J.G., *The Golden Bough*, London, Macmillan, 1913

Goody, E., *Parenthood and Social Reproduction*, Cambridge, Cambridge University Press, 1982

Hamilton, C.H., (tr.) *The Heduya, or Guide, a Commentary on the Mussulman Laws*, London, T. Bensley, 1791

——, *The Hedaya*, 2nd. edition with preface and index by S.G. Grady, London, W.H. Allen & Co., 1870

Hollis, A.C., *The Masai*, Oxford, Clarendon Press, 1905

Hollister, J.N., *The Shi'a of India*, London, Luzac, 1953

Illick, J., 'Child-rearing in seventeeth-century England and America', in de Mause (ed.) *The History of Childhood*, New York, Souvenir Press (E & A) Ltd., 1974

Joyce, P.W., *Social History of Ancient Ireland*, London, Longmans, Green & Co., 1903

Kendall, K., 'Nursing in an Iranian Village', in M. Leininger (ed.) *Transcultural Nursing*, New York, John Wiley & Sons, 1978

Khatib-Chahidi, J., 'Sexual Prohibitions, Shared Space and Fictive Marriages in Shi'ite Iran', in S. Ardener (ed.), *Women and Space*, London, Croom Helm, 1981

Khomeini, R., *Resale touzih al-masael*, Qom, Hozeii elmiye-Qom, undated

Lyall, Sir A.C., *Asiatic Studies*, London, John Murray, 1882

Maine, Sir H., *Early Institutions*, (6th ed.) London, John Murray, 1893

——, *Early Law and Custom*, (New ed.) London, John Murray, 1891

Malleson, G.B., *Akbar*, Oxford, Clarendon Press, 1890

Marvick, E.W., 'Nature versus nurture: Patterns and trends in seventh century French child-rearing', in de Mause (ed.), *The History of Childhood*, New York, Souvenir Press (E & A), 1974

O'Curry, E., *Manners and Customs of the Ancient Irish*, London, Williams and Norgate, 1873

Rekhiashvili, S., '*Skhvisshviloba mt'is Ratchashi* (Adoption in Mountain

Ratcha)', in Tsiskari, Tbilisi, 1974

Ross, J.B., 'The middle-class child in urban Italy, in fourteenth to early sixteenth century', in de Mause (ed.), *The History of Childhood*, New York, Souvenir Press (W & A) Ltd., 1974

SEI (*Shorter Encyclopaedia of Islam*), H.A.R. Gibb and J.H. Kramers (eds), Leiden, E.J. Brill, 1953

SOED (*The Shorter Oxford English Dictionary on Historical Principles*), Oxford, Clarendon Press, 1973

Thorpe, B., *Ancient Laws and Institutes of England*, London, The Commissioners on the Public Records of the Kingdom, 1840

Tucker, M.J., 'The child as the beginning and the end: Fifteenth and sixteenth century English childhood', in de Mause (ed.), *The History of Childhood*, New York, Souvenir Press (W & A) Ltd., 1974

Wilson, Sir R.K., *Digest of Anglo-Muhammadan Law*, (5th ed.) revised by A. Yusif Ali, London, Thacker & Co., 1921

Wolf, A.P. and Chieh-Shanhuang, *Marriage and Adoption in China, 1845–1945*, Stanford, Stanford University Press, 1980

6

Working Mothers in Rural Nepal

Catherine Panter-Brick

Dawa Rani, age three, sat in her mother's lap. The *parma*[Nepali] labour group had stopped for a mid-morning meal in the fields: maize flour cooked with water (*chamba*[N]) and maize beer (*jar*[N]), prepared for the workers transplanting finger-millet at 1800 metres' altitude. Syeljom *Tamangni*, the mother, gave her child a little breast-milk, some *chamba* and *jar*, and a puff of her cigarette.

Field notes, Salme 1983
(Individuals cited are given
other names, typical of the area)

This paper presents observations made during a year's fieldwork in rural Nepal, on the behaviour of mothers working in subsistence activities and nursing young children. It asks how successful women are in addressing these dual responsibilities, and what degree of interference in their work can be attributed to the actual time devoted to child care. It also discusses whether discrimination is made against a mother in the labour force and whether the child itself is affected by the mother's activities.

Nursing practices are now firmly recognised to be a crucial aspect of mother-child relationships for their manifold social, demographic, economic, nutritional and psychological implications (Brown, 1970; Nerlove, 1974; Whiting et al., 1975; Leiderman, 1977; Jelliffe et al., 1979; Hambraeus et al., 1979; Lee, 1980; Dobbing, 1981; Lunn et al., 1985; Lancaster et al., 1987).

Attention has recently focused upon the working mother and her dependent children, in both urban and rural environments (Mead, 1970; Popkin et al., 1976; Jimenez et al., 1979; Huffman et al., 1980; Van Esterik et al., 1981; Lawrence et al., 1985;

133

Winikoff et al., 1988; Draper et al., 1988; Levine, 1988; Leslie, 1988 and 1989). My own interest has been to document the impact of a maternity on a woman's working behaviour in subsistence communities, and to examine the child care strategies adopted by pregnant and lactating women who remained active in the work force. I chose my field site in a remote area in the foothills of the Himalayas, where the following conditions were met: village communities were largely self-sufficient and isolated, the difficult mountain environment placed constraints upon food production, women played an important role in the local economy, and child care practices responded to indigenous considerations alone. I worked in the village of Salme (north-west Nepal, district of Nuwakot), only a day's walk from Trisuli bazaar (on the road to Kathmandu) but away from trekking routes to the nearest Himalayan peaks (Langtang and Ganesh Himal). The village had been selected by the French National Centre of Scientific Research research team who carried out a multidisciplinary study of the Salme community from 1979 to 1986 (Dobremez, 1986).

Situation

I will briefly give some background information about the village and its people. Salme lies half-way up a steep hill rising from 1350 to 3800 metres in altitude, and comprises 3070 hectares (of which 69 per cent are forests, 25 per cent terraced fields, 5 per cent pastures, and 1 per cent paths and village area). Two groups inhabit the village. The Tamang (233 families), of Tibeto-Burman origin, operate a mixed agro-pastoral economy: they grow five main crops (rice at the lowest elevations, maize and millet on land surrounding the village, wheat or barley at high altitude), planting and harvesting the crops in succession throughout the year; they also own in total more than three thousand buffaloes, oxen, cows, goats and sheep, which they pen in the fields for the purpose of land fertilisation. The Kami (sixteen families), an Indo-Aryan group which migrated from the plains to the area some five generations ago, are blacksmiths supplying the Tamang with agricultural and household implements in exchange for grain; they also own a little land for growing maize and millet, one buffalo and a few pigs per household.

The two groups, of different historical origin and socioeconomic occupation[1], also contrast with respect to the position of women. The Tamang lifestyle is characterised by a flexible work schedule, very little economic differentiation between households and the lack of a rigid sexual division of labour within the family, in what can be described as a fundamentally egalitarian society committed to relationships of reciprocal exchange (Fricke, 1986; Holmberg, 1989). Men and women share and exchange most household and economic activities, although one finds of course preferential assignments and a few exclusive preserves (see March, 1983). Even though men take responsibility for the herd, sheltering at night in the fields to look after the animals, women help with herding or cutting fodder and may stay overnight in the cattle shelter with their husbands or fathers. On the domestic front, women alone brew beer, but men often fetch water and firewood, cook meals, carry grain to the mill or children to the place of work. In contrast, the Kami organisation of labour shows a marked differentiation of male and female roles, since men alone work in the smithy.

The Tamang woman (*Tamangni*[N]) assumes a greater workload than does the *Kamini*[N]. Her labour is absolutely essential for the household's subsistence: because the Tamang have a diversified economic base with abundant land, animal and forest resources, there are multiple labour requirements on the mountain side, and since they prefer to live as nuclear families, shortage of labour is an important constraint. In particular, the *Tamangni* travels over considerable distances to exploit small holdings in dispersed locations[2] and to reach the best places for firewood or timber. The egalitarianism which marks relationships between the sexes is also apparent between women of different ages and social position in the household, mother and daughter-in-law contributing the same input of work in daily subsistence activities. The blacksmiths, for their part, own fewer resources, and although Kami women work in agriculture and husbandry, such activity only serves to supplement the income earned by the men. Because there is less demand for female labour, and because the expression of *Kamini* social status is to remain at home with the children, one finds that older women stay at home, sending their dependants to the fields. In short, the Tamang woman is valued for her work, whereas the Kami woman is first and foremost a wife and a mother (Acharya et al., 1981; Panter-Brick, 1986).

Nursing and Working Behaviour

In the case of both Tamang and Kami, a woman's economic responsibilities are largely unaffected by pregnancy right up to the birth of the child. When Cyama *Tamangni* expected her first child at the age of seventeen, her family assigned to her light tasks, such as herding, but could not afford to have her work exclusively in animal husbandry: her labour was needed in *parma* (the reciprocal arrangement to work with a group of friends, neighbours or kinsmen for a specified number of days), to till the fields in preparation for the planting of maize. Cyama gave birth in the fields on one of these *parma* days, assisted by her mother, who was also working with the group. Nine months pregnant and the mother of three small children, Mithe *Kamini* went to the forest the day before the actual delivery and carried back a load of firewood weighing thirty-six kilos; her mother-in-law, who spent the day herding one buffalo and supervising the children, had deemed the young woman able to go in spite of advanced pregnancy. So little did working behaviour customarily change with pregnancy that it was very difficult to tell whether or not women were with child, expectant mothers never fussing over their condition, and clothing effectively disguising the changes in the waistline.[3]

Once the baby is born, the mother makes a greater adjustment in her working behaviour. There is, first of all, a period of ritual seclusion during which the new mother (*sutkeri*[N]) is polluting and must remain inside the home. The Tamang isolate her for five days if the baby is a girl, seven days if it is a boy; the Kami correspondingly allow seven days for a girl, and eleven days for a boy. In both cases, the mother or mother-in-law of the *sutkeri* woman may visit her, having assisted with the birth. The husband, father and/or brothers will offer distilled alcohol, rice, chicken meat and a few Rupees after this period of isolation.[4] After this short interval of time, the mother washes herself and resumes her habitual work. She carries her baby in a cot (*jolangue*[N]) made of bamboo, or in a sling made of cloth, propped on the back and supported with a head-strap. She can thus travel to the place of work, hoe, weed or harvest the fields, herd the animals, cut foliage or fodder and carry back a load of grain or firewood with the baby secured on top.

But how does this affect the mother's working behaviour and how much attention does she give the child? Do the *Tamangni* and

Kamini differ in this respect? I kept a minute by minute record of activities on a sample of fifty-eight village women followed continuously throughout the day; each individual was observed for several days during four different seasons of the year (Panter-Brick, 1989).[5] Such intensive and detailed quantitative information is rarely gathered in anthropological fieldwork and constitutes a sound basis for characterising women's working and child care strategies. It helps to examine how a mother's workload, or type of work, influences nursing patterns, or is itself modified by lactation.[6]

The agricultural activity of Tamang mothers presents an interesting set of contrasting situations. There is a marked seasonal variation of work input, with a four-fold increase of agricultural activity in the monsoon, due to a time-pressure for transplanting paddy rice and millet shoots at the beginning of the rains. There are also differences in the organisation of tasks, since a household may work individually or with a labour group, preferring the latter at times of peak activity. Perhaps unexpectedly, nursing patterns (described in terms of the duration of and intervals between daytime feeds) vary little according to the season or social context of agricultural work (Panter-Brick, 1991).[7] The demands of a small baby seem to be satisfied whether the mother works leisurely in the wintertime or intensively in the monsoon, and whether she keeps to her own rhythm or follows one set by a *parma* group. The mother is truly breast-feeding 'on demand'. Over the forty-four days of breast-feeding observed in the fields during the year, nursing bouts for nought to three-year-olds averaged 8.1 minutes at intervals of eighty-seven minutes.[8]

How does the work performance of Tamang women with or without children compare? The minuted observations show that, while differences between women are noted in the winter (when there is little work to be done), pregnant/lactating and non-childbearing women achieve similar time inputs during the monsoon when there is intense work pressure (Panter-Brick, 1989).

Nonetheless, nursing mothers work slightly shorter hours in the fields: in the monsoon, pregnant and non-childbearing women both averaged 5.1 hours of work daily, while lactating mothers worked 4.7 hours (excluding periods of rest: the difference is not statistically significant). It may be that pregnancy, while making the work more difficult, does not curtail a mother's activity, but that lactation reduces her work input in the fields. However, women schedule their nursing sessions and structure their interactions with toddlers to minimise the interference from children. A comparison of the time women spend in rest, in child care, in meals and in toiletry during agricultural labour, shows that nursing mothers look after their child mostly while other women are simply resting and eating, and spend a further 9–10 minutes per working hour breast-feeding. The mother of a small baby, for instance, carries the cot when she begins work in the fields, then places it out of the way once the child has fallen asleep. She will interrupt her work to feed if it cries, but will mostly nurse at mealtimes, even waking the child to offer it the breast. The mother of a three year old (such as Dawa Rani, as described above) similarly interacts with her child in the period of time customarily set aside for meals.

Despite possible interference from children, mothers are reckoned to contribute as much labour as other members of the work force. No discrimination is made against them in barring them from a *parma* group, for instance. In the winter, when there is less work to be done, labour groups are small and two or three mothers may well work a reciprocal arrangement between themselves to work one another's fields in turn. In the monsoon, when every available worker is needed in the fields, larger groups of up to two dozen members are formed, with men and women, young and old, pregnant and lactating mothers working side by side. Each individual contributes a day's work and expects one in return, regardless of the actual time input, effort, expertise, and work efficiency of individual participants. There is little discrimination made on the basis of age, sex, or physical strength and none exist with respect to current childbearing status. Why does this situation prevail among Tamang households in this community? Economic self-sufficiency depends upon the full employment of available manpower and is enhanced by a flexible distribution of subsistence tasks: each family member is equally capable of addressing different responsibilities, exchanging tasks as the need arises, and co-operating with other families.

In contrast to the Tamang, the agricultural work of Kami women shows no significant seasonal variation; the small number of fields, and the absence of paddy rice, keep *Kamini's* work-loads relatively low, particularly in the monsoon. Kami women are also less mobile: they journey less frequently outside Salme, and travel within a more circumscribed area on the mountain side. Their subsistence activity is not modified by current pregnant or lactating status; however, it is influenced by differences in age and household status. Older women work significantly less than younger women: they remain at home and send their adolescent daughters and daughters-in-law to work. In Salme, a *Kamini's* work-load is an expression of her status in the household, which improves with age and with the birth of many children, and is made possible by the lower demand for female labour in their community.

While both Tamang and younger Kami mothers continue to work, the former travel more extensively away from home. How does this affect their respective child care strategies? I will illustrate each in turn. The Tamang mother always took her baby along when working in the fields, unless she happened to work very close to home, or stay away for very little time (e.g. when working in some of her own fields). She usually took older children with her when engaged in *parma*. The day's labour is long, child care responsibilities tend to be shared with other women in the group and enough food for all those present is provided. However, older children, too heavy to be carried but still too young to walk, were sometimes left in the village to play with their peers (this often completed the process of weaning). In the monsoon season, when every able-bodied worker is busy from dawn to dusk in the fields, children who are left behind were often neglected. They ate cold leftovers of hastily prepared *chamba*, and stayed outside the home in front of the closed doors. Houseflies, humidity and heat combine to contaminate these foods. The prevalence of diarrhoea is highest during the monsoon, and the children suffer substantial weight losses (see also Nabarro, 1984). Mortality, resulting from infections of the digestive tract, also significantly increases in the rainy season (Koppert, 1988).

The Tamang mother followed a similar logic when engaged in other activities, carrying younger children with her unless she was away for only a short while or had to bring back a heavy load. During animal husbandry, feeds averaged 7.6 minutes every forty-five minutes, at much shorter intervals than during agricultural work. Herding animals is a less demanding activity, and the mother has the opportunity to look after her child, to groom, wash, dress and nurse. In contrast, fetching firewood or timber from the forest takes considerable time and effort, and is problematic for mothers with small children (the village is at 1870 m, and accessible grounds in the forest are at 2100–2900 m). Many combined such work with husbandry, taking the herd to the edge of the forest and leaving it to graze unattended while they cut a little firewood, carrying the child on top of their load. However, households must make a substantial provision of wood before the start of the monsoon rains. To complete this work more rapidly, they arrange *parma* groups of men and women to cut and carry the stacks of wood, each person bringing back two loads (of 33–48 kg) a day. Mothers also participated in the *parma*. Although they usually managed to leave children behind in the care of relatives, one mother took along her eighteen-month-old child, stating that no one else could look after him in the village, and carried back a load of 50 kg including the child. The mobility and dispersion of both Tamang parents on the mountain side makes it difficult to arrange for an alternative caretaker, especially in the winter and spring when there are still few labour groups involved in a reciprocal and long-lasting exchange. Often, the baby is left alone in the care of his older sibling (Weisner et al., 1977; Nag, 1978; Panter-Brick, 1989).

The child care patterns of Kami backsmiths are somewhat different, firstly because mothers have less outdoor work to complete and, secondly, because fathers and older women usually remain in the village. Because they were usually away only a short time, working in fields close by the village, Kami mothers left their children, even small babies, with the father in the smithy or with other Kami neighbours. Most often, they hung the cot off the roof of the smithy; if the baby cried, the father would call on a pre-adolescent child to take it to the mother so she could breast-feed. Such paternal supervision is more rarely seen in Tamang families, where both men and women are greatly mobile on the mountain side. So while Kami mothers took their children when working in *parma* groups and also when herding, they invariably left them behind when they went to cut grass or went to the forest. Shorter intervals between feeds were also observed during husbandry (forty-five minutes) relative to agriculture (seventy-eight minutes); but while the type of activity influenced the nursing patterns of *Tamangni* and *Kamini* in similar ways, the former carried their children to work much more frequently.

In all, the Tamang mother breast-fed 9.0 times for a total of sixty-five minutes during the period of daily observation; two-thirds (63 per cent) of suckling time occurred during the completion of her subsistence activities.[9] In comparison, the Kami mother breast-fed 9.4 times for a total sixty minutes over daylight hours; only a third (38 per cent) of feeds took place during the mother's outdoor activity. Thus nursing patterns closely mirror the different involvement of women outside the home.

But are such differences of any consequence?[10] It seems that Tamang babies receive more nursing attention than Kami infants, but that they lose their advantage in the second year of life. Tamang mothers, who work outside the home, manage to carry infants and breast-feed on demand, but must increasingly leave older and heavier children behind. Kami mothers, who are more often at home at their children's side, may nurse on demand but may also easily combine supplementary foods with lactation (Panter-Brick, 1991). There is also a difference in the overall length of nursing practices. The *Tamangni* nursed children up to thirty-five months of age, while the *Kamini* stopped nursing when sample children were twenty-five months old. Both women continue to breast-feed into the next pregnancy, since birth intervals average 37.7 months for the Tamang and 29.4 months for the Kami women. It would seem that the *Kamini* stop nursing sooner as a result of becoming pregnant eight months earlier. But why do they become pregnant earlier?

The relationships between a mother's work patterns, nursing practices, fertility, nutritional status and the health of her child have been the focus of recent concern (Durnin, 1979; Prentice et al., 1981; Scott et al., 1985; Chowdhury, 1987; Jones, 1989; Ellison et al., 1989; Ellison, 1990). A discussion of these relationships in the Salme context is in preparation, drawing from actual and day-long observations of individual work and nursing behaviour, rather than recall data or periodic observations on a group of women, and examining nursing duration and interval (per day), rather than referring to the length of lactation (in months). Some intriguing differences between the Tamang and Kami can be listed here.

First, *Tamangni* have lower mean fertility rates (144/1,000) than *Kamini* (237/1,000), bearing an average 4.7 children in their reproductive period. *Tamangni* start childbearing at a late age (21.7 years, as compared with 17.8 years for *Kamini*) and show longer intervals between births. Prolonged and frequent nursing throughout the first two years of life would tend to lengthen the period of post-partum amenorrhoea for both the Tamang and the Kami women (McNeilly et al., 1985). The *Tamangni* also nurse three year olds, but do so at long or irregular intervals since mother and child are often separated. Factors other than lactation intervene to explain differential fertility (Ross, 1984). Tamang marital patterns, whereby the bride often returns to her natal home or sleeps in the village while her spouse stays in the cattle shelter on the mountain side, in stark contrast to those of the Kami, would help reduce fertility to its remarkably low level (Panter-Brick, 1986). In a Tamang population near that of Salme, lactational infecundability was estimated to halve total marital fertility rates from the levels expected in the absence of breast-feeding, while late and unstable cohabitation between spouses further reduced fertility from an expected seven births to just 5.43 per woman (Fricke, 1986: 105–8). Finally, nutritional status and energetic output may also play a part in bringing about fertility differentials (Ellison et al., 1989), although the Tamang have a similar caloric intake to that of the Kami, they experience lower haemoglobin levels and a greater loss of body weight in the monsoon (Koppert, 1988), and sustain a higher expenditure of energy at work.

Second, child health may be affected in different ways. Mortality is high for Salme (271/1,000 for children under five), diarrhoeas and respiratory illnesses causing most infant deaths, digestive disorders with some swelling or emaciation being implicated later on (Koppert, 1988). Two-thirds of child deaths occur during infancy (0–1 year) for the Tamang, only half do so for the Kami. This contrast merits close examination, as it may imply differential nutrition, exposure to disease, or parental care. So far, only the Tamang have been studied in some detail. The fatality rates for Tamang infants would probably be much higher if they were left behind while the mother was at work (Gubhaju, 1985; Levine, 1987 and 1988; Panter-Brick, 1989). They are also considerably higher when birth intervals are short (increasing by 60 per cent for intervals of less than thirty-six months) (Koppert, 1988; Gubhaju, 1986). In turn, birth spacing protects the mother from nutritional exhaustion. Because of uninterrupted maternal activity, with a peak in workload during the rainy season when environmental conditions are much worse, mothers and infants can be considered a nutritionally vulnerable group. But the absence of seasonal food shortages, the long intervals between births and the flexible task – allocation in the family certainly help reduce the risks to their health.

A comparison between the Tamang and Kami should not obscure the variability of mother-child interactions among individuals in the Salme community. The weaning process is a case in point. In Salme, baby boys receive their first supplementary foods at 2.7 months and girls at 3.3 months (Koppert, 1988); as documented elsewhere, working mothers tend to give supplementary foods to their children at an early age (Nerlove, 1974; Levine, 1988; Leslie, 1988). Parents ritually give them some rice cooked with milk, and there after maize *chamba* with condiments, often cooked separately from the main meal since adults have a little fat (*ghee*[N]) added to theirs. They maintain that a child should be weaned (and given its first clothes) after an odd number of months, if a girl, and an even number of months, if a boy (the Nepali custom specifies months five and six; Paneru, 1981). However, there is considerable variation in observed practices (Millard et al., 1985). For instance, Kanmaya *Tamangni* started giving solid foods one month after the birth of her sixth child, because her milk was insufficient and she had reached old age (forty years). She continued to breast-feed for a total of twenty-nine months, and gave birth to yet another child four months thereafter. Ceyba *Tamangni* gave solid foods to both her sons two days after birth, as her 'milk would not come'. When the youngest was born, the grandmother (age forty-eight) took charge of the older sibling (then thirty-three months old); she still placates him by offering her dry breasts now that he is three. Luri *Kamini*, the mother of nine children, breast-fed her seventh child for seventeen months, and her eighth (Suntali) for twenty-two months, introducing solids in both cases after five months. But although she weaned her other children five months before the next expected birth, she continued to nurse Suntali until one month after the next child was born. Luri explained that she had enough milk to satisfy both the new-born baby and Suntali, who so liked milk. Such examples illustrate the range of nursing and feeding practices found among the Salme mothers, an examination of which may well explain women's differential fertility and mortality patterns in Salme.

Conclusions

The observations collected in the village of Salme, a 'traditional' community in rural Nepal, illustrate how mothers manage to integrate dual, and at times conflicting, child care and working responsibilities. Women's strategies were depicted with the help of both quantitative data and ethnographic examples, contrasting the situation of the Tamang and Kami mothers in the community. The observations lead to the following remarks.

In the first place, the quantified observations presented in this paper validate the concepts of 'demand' or 'opportunity' feeding used so widely in the anthropological literature. In Salme, mothers breast-feed for about seven minutes at one-and-a-half hour intervals throughout the day and also feed at night.

Secondly, work patterns are important determinants of child care (Draper, 1976; Weisner et al., 1977; Whiting et al., 1975; Nag, 1978; Draper et al., 1988; Levine, 1988). The type of activity governs the mother's availability for nursing her child, since longer intervals between feeds are recorded for women engaged in agriculture than for those engaged in husbandry. Yet the increased workload of the Tamang mother may not necessarily prejudice the infant: nursing times do not seem to vary between individual and *parma* work or between winter and monsoon. For the Tamang, the compatibility of subsistence work and child care hinges upon the mother taking the infant to the place of work and nursing it during her customary rest periods. Work patterns also govern the availability of substitute caretakers: they entail the mobility and dispersal of household members in the winter, but rally families in large labour groups during the monsoon. In contrast to the Tamang, the Kami have less outdoor subsistence work, are less mobile, and also have a more plentiful choice of alternative caretakers. They adopt another child care strategy, which involves fathers and neighbours in child supervision.

Third, the conflict between economic and child care responsibilities is to a great extent socially constrained or else facilitated. In Salme, although child care may interfere with a woman's work particularly during her agricultural activity in the monsoon, a nursing mother is counted as a full member of the work force. Provision is made for the children at mealtimes and little attention is paid to potential or actual individual differences in labour input. The Tamang community does not discriminate against the working mother, mostly because there is a demand for the labour of all available workers to accomplish multiple or else urgent subsistence tasks. Among the Kami, there is no such demand for female labour, but status differences between the mother and daughter-in-law seem to take precedence over consideration of maternal status.

Last of all, the fact that women continue to work during child-bearing may well have consequences upon the health of the mother and child. Tamang children are particularly at risk of dying during their first year of life, as elsewhere in communities without any medical facilities. They are also at risk if they are born soon after their older siblings. The Tamang mother, whose labour is essential to the household economy, does best by taking her baby along to the place of work, nursing frequently and keeping the infant more or less constantly in her presence. She leaves it behind only when necessary (for example, when carrying a load), with a sibling. Older Tamang children are increasingly left behind, for much longer periods than are Kami toddlers; the child's nutritional status worsens with the provision of poor quality cereal foods, especially in the monsoon when mothers have little spare time to prepare meals and leftover foods are easily contaminated.

In the future, I hope to pursue the contrast between the Tamang and Kami communities, and document the life histories of individual Salme women in order to examine the range and consequences of their different child care strategies.

Acknowledgments

A Leverhulme Study Abroad Studentship and an Emslie Horniman Scholarship from the Royal Anthropological Institute generously funded the field research. The study was undertaken in collaboration with the French National Centre of Scientific Research.

Notes

1. Note that the Tamang are non-monastic Buddhists, who rank as a pure caste (although *matwali*[N]: alcohol-drinkers) in the dominant Hindu hierarchy, whereas the Kami are Hindus and a polluting (*pani na chalne*[N]) caste.
2. Plots are small because they are equally divided between all sons at inheritance. They are dispersed because families must own land at low, middle, and high altitudes (in order to grow all five crops on

suitable soil and at appropriate intervals of time); in this way, the Tamang also spread their risks of harvest failure (brought about by hail, or monkeys).

3. March has compiled Tamang women's life histories, and writes (1990): 'Pregnancy is not announced in any way. It is watched for, and often noted from very subtle cues such as a slight shift in eating or sleeping patterns, or a tighter-fitting bodice. But it is not acknowledged publicly'.

4. The child is then given a name, with reference to a calendar giving the permitted and propitious names for babies born on such a day. Later on, more familiar names may be given, such as Aita Rani for a girl born on a Sunday (*Aitabar*[N]). Urja Rani to denote fair skin (*urjo*[Tamang]: white), Namse raja as in king of the village (*Namse*[T]: village; *raja*[N]: king), *Purne*[N] (new moon), *Prem*[N] *Bahadur* (love), etc. . .

5. The assistants who followed the villagers from morning to evening to note their activities were chosen from within Salme village; they stood some distance away, so that there was minimal interference in the habitual work patterns.

6. Nursing was timed for Tamang children (aged 0.1 to 35 months) and Kami children (aged 1.5 to 25 months) on a total 166 days throughout the year. Ages are known accurately in Salme since time is reckoned according to the Tibetan cycle of twelve (*lo*[T]) years and Nepali lunar months, and since people must remember these dates to choose propitious dates for life-cycle ceremonies (e.g. the first cutting of hair) and to select suitable marriage partners. Age was controlled for comparisons between Tamang and Kami samples.

7. By contrast, Huffman et al. (1980) report decreased maternal attention during peak agricultural activity in Bangladesh.

8. Nursing times refer to the other period of time (in minutes) for which the child was kept on the breast and had opportunity to feed. Nursing duration and intervals are, of course, age-dependent; means are given here simply to characterise breast-feeding patterns. A more precise description of daily feeds is given in Panter-Brick (1991).

9. Observation lasted from 7 a.m. to 6 p.m. in the winter, and 6 a.m. to 7 p.m. in the monsoon. Night feeds could not be measured. Nursing times refer to Tamang and Kami children of comparable age (here averaging one year old) over all 166 observation days.

10. It would be interesting to confirm fieldwork impressions that a Tamang child, so often carried by his mother or siblings, shows delayed motor coordination and unusual passivity, compared to Kami children left in the smithy.

Bibliographical References

Acharya, M. and Bennett, L., '*The Rural Women of Nepal – An Aggregate Analysis and Summary of 8 Village Studies*', vol. II: Field Studies, part 9, Centre for Economic Development and Administration, Tribhuvan University, Kathmandu, Nepal, 1981

Brown, J.K., 'A Note on the Division of Labor by Sex', *American Anthropologist*, 72, 1970: 1073–8

Chen, L.C., Chowdhury, A.K.M., and Huffman, S.L., 'Seasonal dimensions of energy protein malnutrition in rural Bangladesh: the role of agriculture, dietary practices, and infection', *Ecology of Food and Nutrition*, 8 1979: 175–87

Chowdhury, Alauddin A.K.M., 'Changes in maternal nutritional status in a chronically malnourished population in rural Bangladesh', *Ecology of food and Nutrition*, 19, 1987: 201–11

Dobbing, J. (ed.) '*Maternal Nutrition in Pregnancy – Eating for Two?*', London, Academic Press, 1981

Dobremez, J.F. (ed.), '*Les collines du Népal central écosystèmes, structures sociales et systèmes agraires – tome I: paysages et sociétés dans les collines du Népal; tome II: milieux et activités dans un village népalais*', Paris, INRA, 1986

Draper, P., 'Social and economic constraints on child life among the !Kung', in R. Lee and I. DeVore (eds) *Kalahari Hunter-Gatherers*, Cambridge, MA, Harvard University Press, 1976 pp. 199–217

Draper, P. and Cashdan, E., 'Technological Change and Child Behavior among the !Kung'. *Ethnology*, 27(4), 1988: 339–65

Durnin, J.V.G.A., 'Food consumption and energy balance during pregnancy and lactation in New Guinea', in H. Aebi and R. Whitehead (eds) *Maternal Nutrition during Pregnancy and Lactation*, Nestlé Foundation Publication Series, Huber, Bern Stuttgart Vienna, 1979

Ellison, P.T., Peacock, N.R., and Lager, C., 'Ecology and ovarian function among Lese women of the Ituri forest, Zaire', *American Journal of Physical Anthropology*, 78 (4), 1989: 519–26

Ellison, P.T., 'Human ovarian function and reproductive ecology: new hypotheses', *American Anthropologist*, 92 (4), 1990, 933–52

Fricke, T.E., *Himalayan Households: Tamang demography and Domestic Processes*, Ann Arbor, Michigan, UMI Research Press, Studies in Cultural Anthropology no. 11, 1986

Gubhaju, B.B., 'Regional and socio-economic differentials in infant and child mortality in rural Nepal', *Contributions to Nepalese Studies*, 13(1), 1985: 33–44

——, 'Effect of birth Spacing on Infant and Child Mortality in Rural Nepal', *Journal of Biosocial Sciences*, 18 1986: 435–47

Hambraeus, L., and Sjolin, S. (eds), 'The mother/child dyad – nutritional aspects', Symposia of the Swedish Nutrition Foundation XIV, Stockholm: Almqvist & Wiksell International, 1979

Holmberg, D., *Order in Paradox: Myth, Ritual and Exchange among Nepal's Tamang*, New York, Cornell University Press, 1989

Huffman, S.L., Chowdhury, A.K.M.A., Chakraboty, J., and Simpson, N.K., 'Breast-feeding patterns in rural Bangladesh', *American Journal of Clinical Nutrition* 33, 1980: 144–54

Jelliffe, D.B. Jelliffe, E.F.P., Sai, F.T., Senanayaka, P., 'Lactation, Fertility and the Working Woman', *International Planned Parenthood Federation and International Union of Nutritional Sciences*, 1979

Jimenez, M.H., and Newton, N., 'Activity and work during pregnancy and the postpartum period: A cross-cultural study of 202 societies', *American Journal of Obstetric and Gynecology*, 135(2) 1979: 171–6

Jones, R.E., 'Breast-feeding and post-partum amenorrhoea in Indonesia', *Journal of Biosocial Sciences*, 21, 1989: 83–100

Koppert, G.J.A., *Alimentation et culture chez les Tamang, les Ghale et les Kami du Népal*, Thèse de 3ème cycle, Faculté de Droit et de Science Politique, Aix-Marseille, 1988

Lancaster, J.B., Altmann, J., Rossi, A.S., and Sherrod, L.R. (eds), *Parenting across the Life Span: Biosocial Dimensions*, New York, Aldine de Gruyter, 1987

Lawrence, F., Lamb, W.H., Lamb, C., and Lawrence, M., 'A quantification of childcare and infant care-giver interaction in a West African village', *Early Human Development*, 12, 1985: 71–80

Lee, R., 'Lactation, Ovulation, Infanticide, and Women's Work: A Study of Hunter-Gatherer Population Regulation', in M.N. Cohen, R.S. Malpass and H.G. Klein (eds), *Biosocial Mechanisms of Population Regulation*, Newhaven, Yale University Press, 1980

Leiderman, P.H., 'Economic change and infant care in an East African agricultural community', in Leiderman, P.H., Tulkin, S.R., and Rosenfeld, A. (eds), *Culture and Infancy: Variations in the Human Experience*, New York, 1977; 405–38

Leslie, J., 'Women's Work and Child Nutrition in the Third World', *World Development*, 16(11), 1988: 1341–62

——, 'Women's time: a factor in the use of child survival technologies?' *Health Policy and Planning*, 4(1), 1989: 1–16

Levine, N.E., 'Differential Child Care in Three Tibetan Communities: Beyond Son Preference', *Population and Development Review*, 13, 1987; 281–304

——, 'Women's Work and Infant Feeding: A Case from Rural Nepal', *Ethnology*, 28(3), 1988: 231–51

Lunn, P.G., 'Maternal nutrition and lactational infertility: the baby in the driving seat', in J. Dobbing (ed.), *Maternal nutrition and lactational infertility*, Nestle Nutrition Workshop Series, vol. 9, Johannesburg,

Raven Press, 1985: 1–16

March, K., 'Weaving, writing and gender', *Man*, 18(4), 1983: 729–44

—— 'Children, childbearing, and mothering', Paper prepared for the 18th Annual South Asia Conference, Madison, 3–5 November 1989, *Himalayan Research Bulletin*, Special issue on Tamang parenting x(1) 1990

McNeilly, A.S., Glasier, A., and Howie, P.W., 'Endocrine control of lactational infertility: I', in J. Dobbing (ed.), *Maternal nutrition and lactational infertility*, Nestlé Nutrition Workshops Series vol. 9, Johannesburg, Raven Press, 1985: 1–16

Mead, M., 'Working mothers and their children', *Manpower* 2, 6, 1970: 3–6

Millard, A.V., and Graham, M.A., 'Principles that guide weaning in rural Mexico', *Ecology of Food and Nutrition*, 16: 171–88, 1985

Nabarro, D., 'Social, economic, health and environmental determinants of nutritional status', *Food and Nutrition Bulletin*, 6, 1984: 97–105

Nag, M., White, B. and Peet, R.C., 'An anthropological approach to the study of the economic value of children in Java and Nepal', *Current Anthropology*, 19(2), 1978: 292–306

Nerlove, S.B., 'Women's Workload and Infant Feeding Practices: A Relationship With Demographic Implications', *Ethnology*, 13, 1974: 207–14

Paneru, S., 'Breast-feeding in Nepal: Religious and Culture Beliefs', *Contributions to Nepalese Studies*, 8(2), 1981: 43–54

Panter-Brick, C., 'Women's work and childbearing experience: two ethnic groups of Salme, Nepal', *Contributions to Nepalese Studies*, 13(2), 1986 137–48

——, 'Subsistence work and Motherhood – The Tamang in Rural Nepal', *Human Ecology*, 17(2), 1989: 205–228

——, 'Tamang child care and well-being', *Himalayan Research Bulletin*, Special issue on Tamang parenting x(1), 1990: 1–7

——, 'Lactation, birth spacing and maternal work-loads among two castes in rural Nepal', *Journal of Biosocial Science*, 23, 1991: 137–54

Popkin, B.M., and Solon, F.S., 'Income, Time, the working mother and child nutriture', *Journal of Tropical Pediatrics*, 22, 1976: 156–66

Prentice, A.M., Whitehead, R.G., Roberts, S.B., and Paul, A.A., 'Long-term energy balance in child-bearing Gambian women', *American Journal of Clinical Nutrition*, 34, 1981: 2790–9

Ross, J.L., 'Culture and Fertility in the Nepal Himalayas: a test of a hypothesis', *Human Ecology*, 12(2), 1984: 163–81

Scott, E.C., and Johnston, F.E., 'Science, Nutrition, Fat, and Policy: Tests of the Critical-Fat Hypothesis', *Current Anthropology* 26(4), 1985; 463–73

Van Esterik, P., and Greiner, T., 'Breastfeeding and Women's Work: Constraints and Opportunities', *Studies in Family Planning*, 12(4),

1981: 184–97

Weisner, T.S., and Gallimore, R., 'My Brother's Keeper: Child and Sibling Caretaking', *Current Anthropology*, 18, 1977: 169–90

Whiting, B. and Whiting, J. *Children of Six Cultures*, Cambridge, MA, Harvard University Press, 1975

Winikoff, B., Castle, M.A., Laukaran, V.H. (eds), *Feeding Infants in Four Societies – Causes and Consequences of Mothers' Choices*. Contributions to Family Studies, 14, Greenwood Press, 1988

7

Breast-Feeding and Maternal Depletion: Natural Law or Cultural Arrangements?

Vanessa Maher

The intention of this chapter is to take an anthropological look at some of the concepts which inform the discussion of breast-feeding. We are concerned, in particular, with those concepts which are deployed by international agencies in their analyses of what women in developing countries are doing or should be doing. Such concepts appear to originate in Western industrial culture, and are rooted in the particular relationship between science and industrial society which has obtained in the West over the last three centuries. The science which aspires to subordinate 'nature' to industrial ends includes 'reproduction' and therefore women and sexuality as part of its field of action (Merchant, 1980).

In much of the literature (mostly medical, demographic and nutritional) dealing with the gestation, birth and rearing of children, reproduction is treated as subject to 'natural laws' rather than to human choices and cultural pressures (see Raphael (ed.), 1979). Cultural factors, such as the variable configurations of gender relations which determine women's work, conjugal or kinship roles, or the importance of reproduction as a political strategy are rarely discussed. Breast-feeding is treated in a social vacuum, as a 'biologically imperative' function of the 'biological dyad' formed by mother and child (Inch, 1987: 57).

The Medical Model

According to this view, if nature is to be informed by science, science must determine the ideal or optimum role which breast-

151

feeding is to play in child rearing. One has the impression from the medical literature that this role has to be culturally invariable. In reality, the role suggested by 'modern medicine' is based on the cultural assumptions and definitions of gender current in Western industrial societies.

The main assumptions we will encounter are:

a. Women's productive and social roles are secondary to their child bearing and rearing ones, if not incompatible with them.

b. Optimally, each mother should bear a few (fewer than three) children when young (under thirty-five) and care for them herself.

c. An overwhelmingly male medical profession is particularly qualified to advise or even decide on the way children are to be born and reared (by women).

These assumptions do not fit with norms and practice in most developing countries, either in rural areas or in urban ones. They do not even fit women's practice in Western industrial societies. And indeed, breast-feeding, that 'natural' function of mother and child, is at a very low ebb in industrial societies. In Britain in 1980 for example, only 26 per cent of women breast-fed for as long as four months, the period recommended by the Department of Health and Social Security Working party in 1974 (Inch, 1987: 53). In Turin, Italy, the pattern is much the same (see Balsamo, De Mari, Maher and Serini, this volume). A recent turn of the tide is associated with the growing conviction in medical circles that breast-feeding, even in 'affluent' societies, may be of long term benefit to children's health. Models of 'successful breast-feeding' are often sought in developing countries, particularly in rural areas whose breast-feeding customs are compared favourably with the trend to bottle-feeding in 'transitional' and urban areas.[1]

'A substantial amount of what we now know about protection from human milk and the hazards of bottle-feeding has come from physicians to children in the Third World who have recalled our attention to problems which have not been common in industrialised countries since the turn of the century' (Cunningham, 1981: 151). In this work the author suggests, as does Jelliffe, that 'six months of exclusive breast-feeding is probably the ideal defining criterion' (Jelliffe and Jelliffe, 1978: 58; Inch, 1987: 56). This acontextual approach to breast-feeding is accompanied by ethnocentric stereotypes about developing countries, defined as 'traditional societies', which are supposed to be close to Nature. For example, many medical and demographic treatises give us to understand that there is a simple choice to be made between 'artificial' (formula) and 'natural' (breast-) feeding, and that, in situations where there is no artificial milk available, women rely entirely on breast-feeding. In reality, breast-feeding is often not exclusive. In many societies, supplements of various kinds are given to babies, even during the first days or weeks of life (Raphael, 1984. WHO Collaborative Study, 1984).

It is paradoxical that the model of lengthy breast-feeding (for a year or more) which has inspired medical recommendations to Western women occurs in developing countries together with high infant and child mortality. Yct, as we have remarked above, breast-feeding is presented as a panacea for the ills of childhood, and little attention is paid to other variables which may affect the health of children and even the 'success' of breast-feeding itself. We refer to such factors as political and economic insecurity, ill health and overwork of mothers, gender inequality and the dangerous and unhygienic environment that goes with sheer poverty. It is one of the theses of this chapter that infant mortality has probably less to do with women's 'failure' to breast-feed than with poverty and inequitable gender relations. Can it be that the exhortation to women in poor countries to breast-feed for long periods means that women, once again, are being required to meet from their own resources the costs of remedying a situation whose real causes lie in social and political inequalities at both the international and the local level? Vice versa, the reasons why women feed their infants in different ways can be better understood if we consider the social and economic environments in which they do so.

One of the conditions which frequently occurs together with lengthy breast-feeding in developing societies is that of 'maternal depletion', that is, a severe breakdown in maternal health. Of course, I am not positing any simple causal relationship between breast-feeding and maternal depletion here. Maternal health both influences and is affected by the way women feed their children. In associating breast-feeding with maternal depletion. I do not see the latter as the result merely of the 'cumulative effects [on women] of sequential reproductive cycles, including prolonged lactation' which lead to 'progressive weight loss and a prematurely aged appearance' (Jelliffe and Jelliffe, 1978: 62). I intend to re-examine maternal depletion as the result of the total configuration of socio-economic and gender relations in any given society. This approach places women at the centre of our analysis.

It is important to stress that none of the essays in this volume, and this one is no exception, is intended to make a case for or against breast-feeding or bottle-feeding. In bracketing breast-feeding with maternal depletion, my quarrel is not with breast-feeding itself, far from it, but with a simplistic approach to its practice which neglects the multiple roles of women in regimes of gender inequality.

The 'Maternal Bonding' Thesis

Most of the medical and demographic literature concerning breast-feeding and nutrition is generally concerned with the welfare of children, not of women. It is overwhelmingly taken for granted that the welfare of the child depends on the mother. Authors writing on the Gambia, Nigeria and Mali appear to espouse the view of Spence and others (1954) who write in their study of 1000 Newcastle-upon-Tyne families: 'In the study of these families and in attempting to correlate their environments with the health of the children, there emerged one dominant factor – the capacity of the mother. If she failed, her children suffered.' (Spence, 1954, in Hill, 1985: 192)

The mother appears as the only or main caretaker in the child's infancy. The father is not mentioned. Men as fathers are never held responsible for their children's welfare by men as doctors or nutritionists. In the medical literature the tenet of male privilege is rarely called into question. The mother's 'ignorance', need of education, or other inadequacies are assessed as factors contributing to child morbidity. However, in many societies children pass much of their time in the care of women who are not their mother (grandmothers, co-wives of mother, mother's sisters, or children of various ages) and, in theory, other adults including men, are quite capable of caring of small children, given different gender definitions. The following description of the Hopi child's experience may stand for that of many children in contemporary rural and 'transitional' environments in developing countries.

From birth the young of the household were attended, pampered and disciplined, though very mildly for the first several years, by a wide variety of relatives in addition to the mother. These attentions came both from the household members and from visitors to it. In no way was a baby ever as dependent upon his physical mother as are children in our culture. He was even given the breast of a mother's mother or sister if he cried for food in his mother's absence (Eggan, 1970: 117).

When breast-feeding is discussed, it is assumed that women breast-feed 'naturally', but that their various inadequacies or involvement in outside work may lead them to abandon exclusive breast-feeding, or to carry on for a shorter time, thus endangering the child's physical or mental health. To reduce breast-feeding, in this view, is to care less. However, it has been pointed out that the decline in breast-feeding in the cities of developing countries is related, among other things, to the increasing number of institutional births, rather than to changes in maternal attitudes. In industrial countries, the hospital environment is only the first of a series of negative influences which the health services exert on breast-feeding (Laukaran, Winikoff and Myers, 1986: 121).

In the West, the view that a decline in breast-feeding means a decline in maternal 'caring' is linked to the fashionable notion of 'maternal bonding'. According to the adherents of this notion, physical contact between a new-born or young baby and its mother, creates relationship between them such that the mother 'cares' for her offspring, a sort of adult imprinting. Breast-feeding is supposed to enhance the effects of skin to skin contact at birth and so favour 'maternal bonding'. A moderate version of this view is expressed by Jelliffe, for example, when he gives ' "bonding" for protection of the new-born' among the advantages of breast-feeding (Jelliffe and Jelliffe, 1986: 134). More extreme positions, such as that of Vesterdal who attributes child abuse to the absence of 'normal bonding', appear to mean an attachment cemented between mother and child by physical contact immediately after birth, 'a relationship implying unconditional love, self-sacrifice and nurturant attitudes which, for the mother's part, will last a lifetime' (Sluckin, Herbert and Sluckin, 1983: 18).

The socio-biological affinities of this foggy and imprecise notion are easily traced. 'Socio-biologists attribute mothers' major responsibility for child care to the greater maternal biological investment in conception, gestation and lactation' writes Ruth Bleier, citing the socio-biologists Van den Berghe and Barash who claim: 'Among most vertebrates, female involvement with offspring is obligatory whereas male involvement is more facultative' (Bleier, 1984: 35). The idea of 'maternal bonding' is a Western folk notion which sustains other cultural notions such as those of exclusive maternal responsibility for the care of offspring, the biological determination of gender roles and therefore of male political dominance although, and perhaps because, all these notions have come to be challenged.

The 'critical period' version of the notion of maternal bonding, mostly based on the writings of Klaus and Kennell, is severely criticised by Sluckin, Herbert and Sluckin in their book on this subject: 'Contrary to a variety of strongly held beliefs, there is no clear-cut evidence that events around or soon after the time of birth can readily or seriously distort either the development of the infant's personality or interfere with the growth of maternal love and attachment' (Klaus and Kennell, 1976; Sluckin, Herbert, and Sluckin, 1983: 91). The authors include the choice between breast-feeding and bottle-feeding in this observation, remarking that, as far as the emotional welfare of the child is concerned: 'the manner in which parents undertake various care-giving activities is important', rather than the form of feeding (p. 90). Pointing out that strong mother-to-infant bonds are a feature of our culture, (not nature) the authors observe that it is extremely unlikely that they are formed very rapidly or through skin-to-skin contact 'rather than gradually as a result of well-known forms of learning, including exposure, imitation and conditioning' (p. 80).

Vice versa, the socio-biological and frequently the medical discussion of the relationship between mother and child give us to understand that it depends on automatic mechanisms over which mother and child have little or no control. It is therefore different from all other human relationships. To these authors, the care given by the mother, especially in the early period, is almost involuntary, a passive affair. In contrast, male caretaking activities, if they are part of the paternal role are 'facultative' and if they are part of medical practice, are scientific, rational and voluntary, such that doctors have to swear by (Hippocratic) oath to take care of their patients to the best of their ability.

Birth Intervals and Maternal Depletion

In many current medical discussions of breast-feeding in both agrarian and industrial societies, the focus is on the child's welfare and it is assumed that instinct turns the mother into exclusive caretaker. In this context the mother's welfare is taken into consideration only in so far as it affects the quality of the care she can provide. In their important book *Human Milk in the Modern World*, the Jelliffes dedicate a whole chapter to the question of maternal nutrition (Jelliffe and Jelliffe, 1978: 59–83). Although this chapter provides a complex picture of widespread maternal malnutrition, this is not their point. The study is intended to examine the extent to which the mother's state of health can affect the quality and quantity of her milk. The mother shifts out of focus in order to make way for a consideration of the child's needs.

To give a further example of this obscuring of women's needs. The term 'maternal depletion syndrome' is often used in medical and demographic literature on the less developed countries to refer to the breakdown in a woman's health due to short intervals between births. Under such conditions she is often unable to breast-feed or give adequate care to two babies born close together, so that one of them usually dies. Yet Van den Eerenbeemt notes for Fulani in Mali: 'The interval [between births] . . . is important in as far as the mother's health status influences the new-born child' (Van den Eerenbeemt, in Hill, 1985: 97–8). Many agrarian cultures stress the need to distance births, (the Ghanaian word *kwashiorkor* means 'the disease of the deposed baby when the next one is born'). This norm is related to the belief that a new pregnancy 'spoils' the milk, endangering the nursling and compelling the mother to wean it, and/or that semen spoils the milk. According to this view the mother should abstain from sexual intercourse during the breast-feeding period which may last two or three years (Richards, 1956; Swartz, 1973: 73–89; Gray, 1985: 79–86). Short birth intervals are clearly dangerous for babies but it is not clear why, in themselves, they should imperil women, yet it is to short birth intervals that many authors attribute the breakdown in maternal health.

Wishik and Stern contest this:

In reproductive physiology, superfetation is made impossible by the hormonal controls of pregnancy. It is not logical that normal human physiology should make it a requirement that successive pregnancies shall be a detriment or hazard to the host. . . it is possible that the real danger associated with the short interval stems from poverty, deprivation and incidental disease.

Without particular emphasis, the authors mention the woman's 'current lactation' as one of the factors which affects the 'rates of reconstitution of different substances' in her body after delivery (Wishik and Stern, 1974: 73–5). Jelliffe and Maddox who coined the phrase 'maternal depletion syndrome' also considered that interrelated factors, such as undernutrition and chronic infections of various kinds, in conjunction with the demands of menstruation, pregnancy, lactation and a heavy daily work load, could lead to 'premature aging in women'. This last phrase is a somewhat euphemistic reference to the fact that women, under such conditions, die early (Gray, 1985: 96).

Food, Gender and Breast-Feeding

In North Africa, some Middle Eastern countries and most of the Indian subcontinent, child mortality (children dying before they are four years old) ranges between 150 and 250 per 1000. In the rest of Africa the proportion ranges between 250 and 350 per 1000 (*Demographic Yearbook*, 1984: 408–16). The shocking figures on child morbidity amd mortality have laid down the guidelines for the discussion of nutrition in developing countries, and women have been considered more often as bearers and feeders of children than as food producers, workers, or merely as persons suffering from malnutrition and ill health. In food aid programmes, for this reason, women have often been bracketted with children as 'a target group' for supplementary rations. The reasoning behind this policy is that women who are half starved bear low-birth-weight children, and may not breast-feed or look after them properly. 'Young mothers must stay healthy if they are to feed their babies well and produce strong children in the future' writes one expert on food aid to developing countries (Stevens, 1979: 85, 86–101). However, it is commonly observed that food rations intended for women are usually consumed by the rest of the family (Stevens, 1979: 143–5). For this reason some Indian nutritionists have developed a particularly bitter food supplement for mothers which has 'potential non-sharing characteristics'

(Mital and Gopaldas, 1985)!

As we have remarked in the previous chapter, men receive an undue share of family food, while pregnant and lactating women and children may not receive sufficient. 'The position of a husband *vis-à-vis* his wife or children is fixed and food is often distributed according to existing status definitions . . . The senior male members of the household are frequently given the best diet in terms of both quality and quantity and boys often have priority over girls' (Schofield, 1979: 96, see also 81–111).

The evidence for inequitable food distribution within the household is available in studies on many different societies, but receives strangely little attention. (Waldman, 1975: 139–51; Taha, 1978: 137–42; Maher, 1981, 1984). One could say that it appears to be almost universal in agrarian, 'transitional' and low-income urban groups in developing countries (note. 1), if a possible exception is made for some matrifocal West African societies. But inequitable intra-family food distribution was prevalent in the equivalent sectors of European society, too, at least until the second World War (Llewellyn Davies, 1915; Morandini, 1979; Allasia, 1983). Perhaps this is why it is taken for granted, or at any rate constitutes a 'blind spot', in Western medical and demographic literature on developing countries.

The nutritional status of most women in developing countries commonly appears to worsen during pregnancy, the puerperium, and lactation, not only because they are expected to meet these contingencies without extra resources, but often because of food taboos (Wilson, 1973; Eichinger Ferro-Luzzi, 1974). It has often been observed that extreme maternal malnutrition is a cause of low-birth-weight in babies and indirectly of infant mortality. At the same time, it is chilling to note a tone of complacency in the studies that remark on the 'reproductive efficiency' with which undernourished women on the whole produce full weight babies (a slower metabolism enables them to save energy in the first few months of pregnancy) and breast-feed them adequately. This capacity is undermined, according to these authors, only in famine conditions (Jelliffe and Jelliffe, 1978: 65; Prentice, Whitehead, Roberts, Paul, 1981).

Medical studies frequently stress the fact that the milk of undernourished women appears not inferior in quality (only less dilute) than that of better nourished women, or those who have received food supplements. This argument is one of the pillars of the current campaign to defend breast-feeding in developing countries. Its gist is that the women may not get enough to eat, but if they breast-feed at least the children will. The Jelliffes (1978: 80) remark that such efficiency may be to the 'cumulative nutritional detriment' of the mother and Harfouche comments warily: 'The way in which the nursing mother's body compensates for an inferior diet remains to be explored' (Harfouche, 1965: 48). Many women in South Asia show only a modest weight gain during pregnancy and this disappears entirely on delivery. During breast-feeding such women experience considerable weight loss. Some authors have reported a weight loss of up to seven kilos after a year of breast-feeding (Jelliffes, 1978: 64).

The idea that the nursing woman's body manages somehow to compensate for a net loss of vital resources is an optimistic one. Women 'are an unhealthy and badly nourished group compared to men. The fact that there are more men than women in many countries in South Asia is accounted for by higher female infant and adult mortality' (Committee on the Status of Women in India, 1974: 17). This observation is applicable to many North African and Middle Eastern countries, and perhaps some in East Africa, as well as New Guinea. The unfavourable sex ratio is caused not only by greater female mortality in infancy but also by many women dying during the childbearing years. It is the latter which appears to be nearly universal in developing countries. The former appears to be less accentuated in sub-Saharan Africa, in spite of the widespread preference for male children and relative disregard for girls (Tiertze, 1977; Dyson, 1977; Taylor, 1983).

Some anthropologists present data which suggest that in many societies, even 'agrarian' ones, where women normally breast-feed and not under famine conditions, pluriparous women in a poor state of health may find that they have not enough or no milk to give to a new baby. That the baby will die is usually a foregone conclusion, and many anthropologists bear witness to the distress and despair of mothers in this predicament (J. Goody, personal communication on the Lodagaa of Ghana; Gray, 1985: 83–5). Hansen wrote on Kurdish women: 'She was not the only woman I met with who could not suckle her baby 'because of' the continual pregnancies from which women were unable to recuperate, often combined with inadequate or unsuitable food, deficient in protein. The wife who cooks and serves the family meals must make do with what is left over' (Hansen, 1960: 88). That is, 'lactational efficiency' cannot be infinitely renewed under conditions of continuous undernourishment and overwork of mothers. In the meantime the mother's health may become irremediably compromised, so that she may be unable to care for her other children who become more exposed to disease and other difficulties. The synergistic relationship between nutrition and infection as a factor in child mortality has been frequently remarked upon, but high figures of female mortality in many developing countries suggest that women and especially mothers are also at risk.[2]

Fertility and Breast-Feeding: Nature or Culture?

The fact that in many societies women die younger than men and form a smaller proportion of the population suggests that, in discussing breast-feeding in a given society, women must be seen not only in their child-related roles but in the global context of gender relations. However, the misleading emphasis on reproduction in the medical literature dealing with breast-feeding is not unrelated, paradoxically, to the post-war preoccupation with the 'demographic explosion' in developing countries. Women are studied as a function of the quantity and quality of their children. An enormous number of studies are concerned with the relation between nutrition and fertility. It is as if, by controlling the former, the writers, governments and international development agencies hoped to control the latter. For example, an OECD (Organisation Européenne pour le Commerce et le Développement) study on *Relationships between Fertility, Child Mortality and Nutrition in Africa*, 'deals with various aspects of malnutrition and focuses in particular on problems of weaning, lactation and birth-spacing. The purpose of analysing these various factors is to devise a feeding policy for infants and young children which will lead ultimately to the formulation of a consistent demographic policy' (Mondot-Bernard, 1977: 12). Similarly, a World Health Organisation study is entitled, *Workshop on Breast-feeding and Fertility Regulation* (1982).

In this context, breast-feeding has emerged as the *trait d'union* between nutrition and fertility, the miracle of 'nature' which can resolve at once the problems of feeding children adequately, and of reducing their number, since, under certain conditions, breast-feeding may have a contraceptive effect. Jelliffe's estimate that breast-feeding may reduce conception by a third has been much quoted. However, there are many indications that amenorrhoea and anovulation during breast-feeding may vary idiosyncratically, and not only with nutritional status or levels of the hormone prolactin (Mondot-Bernard, 1977: 67–96; Hennart, Hofvander Vis and Robyn, 1985: 179–87).

B.M. Gray remarks that Enga (in New Guinea) are acutely aware of the fallibility of breast-feeding as a system of contraception and women observe a post-partum taboo on sexual intercourse which may last three years. This is a frequent finding among peoples who stress the importance of adequate birth intervals, particularly in Africa south of the Sahara. Given the frequent coincidence of the breast-feeding period and that of post-partum sexual abstinence, it appears unwarranted to suppose that where there are long intervals between births, it is actually breast-feeding that provides protection against conception (Swartz, 1973: 80; Gray, 1985: 84–5).

The Misuse of the Concept of 'Natural Fertility'

Nature is a term which recurs in twentieth-century as in eighteenth-century medical treatises when the writers discuss women and/or reproduction (Bloch and Bloch, 1980: 25–41). The concept of 'natural fertility' is often used erroneously to define situations of high fertility. The writers who use it in this way assume that neither women nor men engage in any decision making where having children is concerned, nor, according to this view, do cultural factors intervene in the process. Natural fertility, claim these writers, is experienced by populations 'not using any form of deliberate birth control' (Van den Eerenbeemt, in Hill, 1985: 83; Hill, 1985: 57–9). The nomadic and settled populations in Mali described by Alan Hill and colleagues, are considered 'non-contracepting' by these authors, who attribute the birth interval and the number of children to biological factors plus breast-feeding.

It is hazardous, however, to assume that fertility reduced by the contraceptive effects on undernourished mothers of a two-year period of breast-feeding is 'natural'. First of all, as we have intimated above, the fact that the mothers are undernourished is, to a certain extent, a cultural not a natural fact. Further, the length of the breast-feeding period is highly variable cross-culturally and varies even within Mali itself. Its contraceptive effect depends on several factors, some of which, such as the frequency of feeds, may be the result of the mother's decisions or be cultural in origin. There is, at any rate, no good reason to assume that fertility reduced by breast-feeding by undernourished mothers is any more natural than say, that reduced by *coitus interruptus* in seventeenth-to ninenteenth-century Europe.

Behind the misuse of the concept of 'natural fertility' lies the assumption that the only 'cultural' or 'rational' forms of contraception are the mechanical and hormonal devices diffused during the last century in the West. But these forms are probably responsible for only a part of the drop in fertility over the last century in the West itself, where nuptiality rates declined for decades in some areas between 1870 and 1930, where the proportion of unmarried women grew even more, where abortion and *coitus interruptus* have probably remained important means of birth control, and where stress and urban living have apparently been responsible for a certain degree of sterility. Livi Bacci points out that in 1971 most Greek, Yugoslav and Italian immigrants to Australia were using withdrawal as a contraceptive method, and that in spite of this Italians had no more children than English immigrants (Livi Bacci, 1980: 345, 338–9). In Czechoslovakia and Hungary, withdrawal is the most common method, and the frequency of abortion in many countries in Eastern, Southern, and even Northern Europe (Denmark) suggests that, here too, many women do not use hormonal or mechanical contraception (Heitlinger, 1987).

It would certainly be difficult to gather information on the delicate subject of birth control in the course of a large-scale research project, such as that of Hill and colleagues. But it cannot be assumed *senzaltro* that, in the West African societies in question, neither women nor men limit births. Their methods may not be recognisable as 'contraceptive' by Westerners, but it is likely that they are used as intentionally as any in use in the West. Among the former methods are probably abstinence (assured in part by the spatial separation of spouses and by polygamy), delay in marriage for males, and even clitoridectomy and infibulation (practised in 56 per cent of African societies named in the Ethnographic Atlas), as well as abortion and other 'folk' methods (including breast-feeding) practised by women (Oldfield Hayes, 1975: 617–33; El Dareer, 1982; Koso-Thomas, 1987: 12). The populations wrongly described as practising 'natural fertility' rarely have more than six to eight children per family, yet a woman who stays married from age fifteen to age fifty has the potential to have around seventeen children (if she does not breast-feed nor use any method of contraception, nor resort to induced abortion). In Metro Manila all women: 'preferred . . . abstinence, withdrawal, limited contact, folk methods and reliance on breast-feeding' (Simpson-Hebert, Cresencio and Makil, 1986: 166–8) to mechanical or hormonal methods of contraception.

On the other hand, it seems reasonable to suppose that where women occupy a subordinate position in a society which expresses values emphasising the importance of having many children, high fertility, far from being 'natural' is, rather, imposed on women. Swartz points out that in some (patrilineal) groups in East Africa, to have many children is a sign that a man is on good terms with his kin, and is not the victim of witchcraft or of vengeful ancestors. Women may feel pressured willy-nilly into having many children for the husband's kin-group, or for other social reasons. Women's ambivalence towards the maternal role, towards the bearing of many children and the cultural preference for males has been documented for many Middle Eastern and South Asian societies (Maher, 1984: 116–7; Minturn and Lambert, 1964: 232–5; Granquist, 1950: 79). This ambivalence is not to be attributed merely to the fact that women have more children than they want. Many women appear quite aware that obligatory high fertility is only one aspect of overall gender inequality. Thus, having many children may be the main source of power and esteem for some women as well as being advantageous for men. But in some societies women are perceived to grow weaker and die earlier than men. And they actually do, as we have noted above (Granquist, 1950: 62 and 72; Gray, 1985: 95–9).

Cultural Norms and Women's Practice

If we take into account gender definitions as a whole, it becomes clear that, in some societies, women are less valued from birth, that in most they have no access to positions of political or control over collective decision making, and that in many this situation is reflected in the fact that they do not enjoy social or economic independence. They work extremely hard, in agriculture or in salaried work, and they are skimped of food and other resources, including medical care, although they bear the main physical burden of reproduction. In the light of the above observations, we should view women's behaviour in the field of reproduction and child-rearing, not as determined by 'nature' but as conditioned by cultural priorities (not always to the advantage of women and children) and by personal choices. Breast-feeding, in spite of the impression we might gain from the phrase 'it obtains where there is no artificial alternative' (Hill, 1985), appears to be an area which is particularly subject to cultural manipulation and personal judgement. That is, its practice cannot be regarded as 'natural' or other forms of feeding be considered 'artificial', in contrast.

In the previous chapter we pointed out that it is frequently men who determine the rules for breast-feeding, but that day-to-day decisions are made by women themselves who may turn breast-feeding to their own advantage, establishing important matrilineal relationships, creating symbolic values, and so forth. The summary of an article by Millard and Graham on weaning in rural Mexico points out that villagers make:

> conscious weaning decisions based on maternal and child health. . . Women in two Mexican villages use principles conveyed by oral tradition to guide their decisions on weaning. They do not blindly follow unarticulated beliefs as implied by other studies. The principles that guide weaning inform a mother of the effect of continued lactation, under specific conditions, on the child at certain stages of biological and psychological development. . . . Villagers' decisions are situational rather than determined by the child's chronological age. The outcome, according to lactation histories of 285 women is a heterogeneous pattern of ages at stopping breast-feeding (Millard and Graham, 1985: 171–88).

As well as the breast-feeding and weaning decisions which take into account maternal and child health, there are many more decisions, taken as often by men as by women, which refer to symbolic values and the structuring of social relationships. Jane Chahidi points out that the notion of milk kinship, with the implication that women may nurse babies other than their own, has been used until recently in many contemporary Eastern European, Middle Eastern and North African societies to prevent certain marriages and to promote alliances between families of the same or different rank (Chahidi, this volume). Lucy Rushton has analysed the way Greek women regard breast-feeding and weaning as determining the confines of the self (of both mother and child) and its relationship to society, such that a baby precociously weaned may harm others by its tendency to envy them, whereas a mother overtaxed by excessive breast-feeding may herself cast the evil eye on others (Rushton, 1988).

These beliefs broach the possibility that a mother may overtax herself by excessive breast-feeding, that is, that there is a sense in which the amount which the baby needs may be too much of a drain on the mother's resources. Such a possibility is rarely mentioned in the medical literature. But this notion is frequently referred to by women in those 'agrarian societies where social support and women's work provide a context for successful breast-feeding' (Millard and Graham, 1985). We also find it in the areas of recent urbanisation where most women breast-feed their children for at least six to nine months, especially the women from low income households (75–85 per cent in the Philippines according to Simpson-Hebert, 1986).

Creyghton has analysed the notion of 'bad milk' among Northern Tunisian peasants. 'Bad milk' results from a mother's attempting to feed her child when she is hot and tired from carrying wood, and it causes illness in children (Creyghton, 1981). In Beirut, Harfouche reported that women in low income households thought a woman's anger or fatigue would make her milk hot and liable to harm her infant. A pregnant woman's milk was regarded as 'poisonous' and should not be fed to her children. The milk of a sleeping mother is 'the milk of laziness', 'dead milk', and so impure and harmful. That is, when a mother is under stress and needs to rest, she should not try to breast-feed. Harfouche himself noted: 'The harmful effects of "poisonous milk" on the suckling infant may be a manifestation of malnutrition vaguely expressed by pregnant lactators' (1964: 59). Again, the Philippine women in the RMAF study believed that a mother's milk was unsuitable for her infant if she were tired, angry or unhappy, hungry, 'cold' (after doing laundry by hand in cold water) or 'hot' (if she had been out in the hot sun), ill or pregnant (Simpson-Hebert, 1986: 56–7).

The examples are legion. They probably include most cultures where women are overworked, underfed and bear many children. On the other hand, these beliefs appear to be an implicit recognition that, in order for the child to be properly nourished, the mother needs to breast-feed in a relaxed and reassuring situation so that the 'let-down' of the hindmilk is not inhibited. The medical studies which report these beliefs often cite them as one of the obstacles to breast-feeding to be ironed out by 'scientific' instruction! (Harfouche, 1965; Simpson-Hebert, 1986)

Breast is Best but not Enough

It is under these circumstances of undernourishment and overwork that women in the overwhelming majority of cultures supplement their breast-milk (with gruels in Africa, rice-water in South East Asia and herbal teas in Mesoamerica) often from the first weeks of a baby's life, or even the first days. The WHO Collaborative Study (1981) showed that in most of the countries studied, up to half the infants were receiving supplements by the age of three months. In rural areas the incidence of such supplements was generally lower, but even in those communities (rural India excepted) the practice was widespread. One study made in Nigeria remarks on the widespread practice of supplementation although mothers of all sections of Nigerian society breast-feed at least for several months. The conclusion is unusual:

> Biologically, the welfare of the mother is more important to society than that of the child. In traditional societies, breast-feeding is essential for the survival of the infant, but early introduction of other foods and fluids must reduce the nutritional demands on the mother. Although such foods and fluids may increase the immediate risk of disease and malnutrition, this could well be counterbalanced by the improved ability of the mother to give good care. Information on this point is lacking, but it may be relevant that of 50 children admitted to Ibadan hospital with severe malnutrition, almost all came from the poorest levels of society and 49 of the 50 had been breast-fed for at least nine months. Obviously the capabilities of the mothers had been severely taxed.

In this light, Hill's view that women breast-feed where there is no 'artificial alternative' needs qualifying. These women, like many others, combine breast-feeding with artificial supplements in various ways. The authors of the Nigerian study say: 'This study shows that in Nigeria as in other developing and Western countries, early supplementation of infant milk intake is common. Although some urban women are now breast-feeding for a shorter period, it appears that the main change has been that these mothers are now tending to use commmercial rather than traditional products for supplementation.' Whether the former are any more 'artificial' than the latter is open to question, unless ethnocentrically, we are to regard non-western countries as the realm of nature. 'From this study' says the oft cited article on Nigeria 'we can draw no conclusions about the costs and benefits of this change' (Orwell, Clayton, Dugdale, 1984: 129–41).

I have cited this article at length, because in some ways it goes against current trends, particularly in its consideration of the burden which exclusive breast-feeding places on the mother, and in its attempt to specify the time limit beyond which exclusive breast-feeding or inadequate supplementation can be damaging for both mother and child. Most unusual of all is its assertion that: 'Biologically, the welfare of the mother is more important to society than that of the child'. Since culturally influenced behaviour and personal decision making are once again mistaken for biology, one might suspect a medical or demographic authorship. Indeed the authors are from a Human Nutrition Research group, Department of Child Health, University of Queensland, but also from 'an independent consultant market research organisation' and the research was 'sponsored by Nestlé S.A., who gave the authors complete access to the data.'

Despite this unpromising sponsorship, their remarks on the danger of prolonged exclusive breast-feeding are largely borne out by other studies. Thus, a study on southern Brazil entitled, 'Is prolonged breast-feeding associated with malnutrition?', citing others in Indonesia and Kenya, observed that in a sample of children aged twelve to thirty-five months, the prevalence of malnutrition was smallest in those who had been breast-fed for three to six months and worse in those breast-fed for longer. The nutritional status of those still being breast-fed at the time of the survey had a lower weight for length than those who had been totaly weaned and those being breast and bottle-fed presented intermediate levels (Victoria, Vaughan, Martines, Barcelos, 1984: 307–14).

A study in the Sudan also concluded that there may be advantages in bottle-feeding after six months, because available supplementary foods are indigestible or unnutritious (Taha, 1978). This is one of the conclusions of the Philippine study cited above, which also found that, despite a higher incidence of diarrhoea, mixed-fed and bottle-fed infants seem to do as well as breast-fed ones. The factor which distinguishes well babies from chronically ill ones is the higher income of the parents. Since their study favours breast-feeding, for economic, contraceptive and other reasons, the authors deplore the overemphasis given by researchers to the protection which breast-feeding may afford against illness. They have found that mothers expect their milk to protect infants from all illness and lose confidence and give up breast-feeding when their children fall ill. On the other hand both exclusive breast-feeders and 'mixed' (breast and bottle) feeders appeared to derive a contraceptive effect from breast-feeding, because, in practice, the latter breast-fed several times a day (Simpson-Hebert, 1986: 121–8).

A study of breast-feeding in Dar-es-Salaam, Tanzania, also found that the average birth weight increased and under-five mortality decreased substantially with rising income. The nutritional status of high income children tended to be better, and infection rates lower, regardless of the mode of feeding. The duration of breast-feeding decreased with rising income. The proportion of children breast-fed for more than twelve months decreased from 89 per cent in the lowest to 30 per cent in the highest income group (Mgaza and Bantje, 1980: 10–1).

Thus, in the absence of adequate income and the conditions it implies, such as a hygienic and safe environment, good food, piped water, proper housing and a high level of parental education, the babies breast-fed longest did not appear to enjoy proportionally better health, rather the contrary (see also Raphael (ed.), 1979). Here too, the general conditions in which children are fed appear to count more than the mode of feeding. We may remark, further, that in many societies, the amount of breast-milk that women provide for a child does not vary for two years or more (400 ml for over two years among the Chimbu of New Guinea), a phenomenon which leads us to suspect undernutrition of older babies and overtaxing of mothers, conditions which their respective mortality rates confirm (Jelliffe and Jelliffe, 1978: 64–6).

Other Forms of Infant Feeding

The availability of substances considered by a given society to provide an acceptable supplement or alternative to breast-milk does not necessarily lead to the abandonment of breast-feeding. Breast-feeding is sometimes preferred in cultures where animal milk is available, sometimes not. Examples of the former could be the African nomadic cultures described by Hill and colleagues, most of South East Asia and sixteenth-century Britain. The United States during the last hundred years and Iceland, between the sixteenth and the nineteenth centuries, appear to have been examples of the latter (Hastrup, this volume).

As we have remarked, in some societies, breast-milk has been considered dangerous for the infant under certain circumstances. During the frequent periods in European history when wet-nursing was common, (from the Greeks and Romans onwards) the breast-milk of some women was considered to transmit undesirable characteristics to the infant. Animal milk was liable to transmit worse ones, quiet apart from the fact that it was not pasteurised. Indeed, rather than being considered an 'alternative' as it is to some extent among African nomadic tribes, animal milk in sixteenth-century England, though probably not more microbe-ridden, was considered a last resort when all others failed.

The practice of wet-nursing gave to breast-feeding certain class connotations (which are less emphasised though not always absent in societies practising milk kinship). This is perhaps not unrelated to the plethora of beliefs current among women (and until recently large sections of the medical profession) in Western industrial nations, according to which breast-feeding may damage women's health. It is as if breast-feeding were considered a form of work which upper class women should be spared. We have suggested in the previous chapter that breast-feeding is actually curtailed in some stratified societies because it interferes with the conjugal relationship as a status-conserving structure. It is a paradoxical finding that well-to-do English women in the sixteenth century who bore more children because they did not breast-feed, and lost proportionally more children than did the less prolific breast-feeding (and wet-nursing) poorer women, actually died younger (see Maher, previous chapter). '"as the Renaissance advanced the image of the nursing Virgin waned in popularity". Believing that sexual intercourse could corrupt the milk, but that the conjugal debt had priority above the welfare of the infant, the church had condoned wet-nursing. Rich women who wanted to feed their infants had a battle, especially with husbands and friends' (McLaren, 1985: 27–8). Many women, interviewed in a recent study in Turin, echoing this statement, explained that they too had been advised by doctors, husbands or friends not to breast-feed or to stop doing so, in their case, because of the risk to their eyesight, the shape of their breasts, or because of illness, tiredness or minor mishaps.

Maternal Depletion, Work and Breast-Feeding

In Turin work was rarely mentioned as a reason for not breast-feeding, although women's work is often given as a general explanation for its decline. That is, not working and not breast-feeding may both indicate the claims to status of a woman or her husband in certain social milieux. In fact, the question of the relation of women's work to breast-feeding is a vexed topic and is often treated in the medical literature in a cavalier and approximate fashion. Only when a woman's activity is carried on outside the home, for a salary, is it regarded as having damaging implications for childbearing and breast-feeding, probably because the woman is thought to have broken through gender confines and become 'more like a man'. Again, we may suspect the intrusion of Western folk notions concerning gender roles. These ideas may underline the importance of a woman's conjugal role vis-à-vis her roles as worker, kinswoman and so forth: 'a woman's natural place is in the home, having babies and caring for husband'.

No distinction is made in the medical literature between paid and unpaid work, work for the family or work for strangers, work carried out far from home and work nearby, agricultural work or industrial work, seasonal or continuous work. Since the gender role is defined in purely reproductive terms, what women do for the household is rarely called work, but rather 'looking after the children' 'keeping house', a natural extension of their conjugal and reproductive role. The result of this analytical confusion is to render women's work invisible, a paradoxical result indeed when we consider that in large areas of the world and notoriously in areas such as sub-Saharan Africa, where some celebrated studies of infant nutrition have been carried out, women are responsible not only for farming and trading, but also for fetching water and firewood over long distances and for labour-intensive food-processing.

Of course, these are areas where women, with few exceptions, breast-feed for more than a year, so that their work is not called into question by demographers, nutritionists or medical experts. Such work barely enters into the nutrition-fertility-mortality equation. Yet most of the cultures characterised by a heavy female work burden, high fertility and lengthy breast-feeding are also those with a high rate of infant mortality (as well as a high rate of maternal mortality and relatively low female life expectancy

(Tiertze, 1977; Dyson, 1977; Gray, 1985). This fact appears to escape the advocates of breast-feeding and maternal care as a panacea for the ills of children in developing countries.

The authors of the studies on Fulbe in rural Mali provide us with an example. They describe approvingly the fact that after a long period of breast-feeding, mothers wean their children gradually onto a diet of animal milk which, the writers believe, has a certain antibacterial action. In spite of these precautions infant mortality is around 360 per 1000 live births. The lowest mortality, among the Seno-Mango Fulbe, still means that 32 per cent of children die before age five. It is difficult to understand why the authors consider this model of infant feeding to be particularly desirable, unless it is because it resembles that prevalent in the industrial West, whatever the results for Fulbe babies in Mali (Van den Eerenbeemt, 1985; Hildebrand, 1985).

Conditions of work, including the attitudes of employers and fellow-workers, may affect breast-feeding. In large cities, such as Metro Manila, the very logistics of getting to work in overcrowded buses, dealing with pollution and unpredictable hours, may discourage women from taking their babies with them, and so prevent breast-feeding (Simpson-Hebert, 1986: 63–4). Further, in many countries and in many of the workplaces where women are employed, they are not allowed to breast-feed in public and no special time or place is set aside for them to do so. Interviewees in Turin said that although, under Italian law, women with infants have the right to arrive late at work or leave early, and to take up to two hours a day for breast-feeding, hardly anyone does so for fear of provoking the resentment of employer and colleagues. A breast-feeding mother would be considered to require 'time off work' to breast-feed, and would risk losing her job. Yet the Tanzanian study, cited earlier, claims that: 'mothers' employment has little effect on the duration of breast-feeding. Low income employed women more often stop earlier than low income unemployed women. But in the high income group the opposite was found' (Mgaza and Bantje, 1980: 11).

The inhibition of breast-feeding appears to be one aspect of industrial work relations in developing countries and is not inherent in the fact that women are 'working outside the home'. This hypothesis is borne out by Panter-Brick's study of breast-feeding in Nepal where women are involved in heavy agricultural work. Women work with others and do not hesitate to breast-feed in 'public'. Under these conditions, women do not stop breast-feeding but neither do they work less than anyone else (Panter-Brick, 1990, this volume). Women who are self-employed and work at home are (according to the Philippine study) also more likely to breast-feed than women working under industrial conditions. The problem lies not in the work itself, or even in 'work outside the home' but in capitalist industrial relations.

Vice versa, women who work are not the only ones who may give up breast-feeding. Taha remarked of his Gezira sample that they tended to turn to bottle-feeding though they 'did not work' (1979: 199). In some developing countries it is the women with more education, higher income and longer residence in the city who breast-feed for the shortest time whether they work or not. In contrast, in some Western industrial countries these are the women who breast-feed longest (Oakley, 1979: 323). In some developing countries many women do not enjoy good health either in childhood or as adults because of an unhygienic environment, malnutrition, lack of medical care, overwork, high fertility or a combination of some of these factors. Breast-feeding, which certainly taxes women's physical resources, may be perceived as work to be avoided if equivalent services can be provided in some other way. In Western societies, the important factor appears to be a perceived competition between breast-feeding and other relationships, especially the conjugal one. This perception is related to the isolation of the nuclear family and to the complexity of urban life and the stress which accompanies it, a stress doubled for those women who carry out both wage-work and domestic work. Perhaps among the Western women who breast-feed are those who can evade either one or the other, being sustained by kin, spouse, friends and a life-time of good health.

More important both in the developing countries and in Western societies is, however, the configuration of gender relations in which breast-feeding takes place. This has been changing in different ways in different societies. Many studies have noted the frequently deleterious effects of economic development on women's land rights and work burden. In particular, the increasing involvement of rural societies in the cash economy has often meant a shrinkage in the subsistence sector managed by women and a corresponding concentration of economic power in the hands of men (discussed in the introductory chapter). These developments have thrown into relief the dependent status of women and the fact that their access to land and cash is often mediated by men, for whom, under the new conditions of commercial production, they appear to represent, even or particularly as family members, an infinitely exploitable work-force (Ahmed, 1985).

Conclusions

To point out as do the Jelliffes (1978) that breast-feeding constitutes a great saving to a national economy, is to ignore the worsening conditions of women and children in developing countries. It is to suggest that women should provide more resources while their own share continues to diminish. Nevertheless, the vast majority of women in developing countries do not need to 'discover' the importance of breast-feeding and continue to breast-feed for long periods even under unfavourable conditions.

Mike Muller in the War on Want Pamphlet *The Baby-Killer* on the promotion and sale of powdered milks to the Third World pointed out that, to the average low-income family in Egypt (which stands for many developing countries), the cost of baby milk when the child had reached three or six months, could constitute half the father's salary. This led to the practice of over-dilution and so forth. But, as I have suggested above, the fact that the cost of feeding a baby comes to weigh on the father's salary, rather than on the mother's health, may be a clue to the trend away from lengthy breast-feeding in many developing countries. Cash, in many developing countries, is controlled by men and often spent on items of consumption which do not benefit women and children. Overburdened mothers find, in many cases, that they have lost access to the means of producton and control over the product of their own work, to the advantage (in particular) of husbands. Under such circumstances, women may find in bottle-feeding one means of transferring to men some of the cost of reproduction, which they have been bearing alone on an ever slimmer budget of food, cash and vitality.

To a certain extent, to resort to bottle-feeding may be seen as an attempt to save children, since it may be increasingly difficult for women in poor health to breast-feed adequately under conditions of unprecedented family and wage exploitation, as well as in the stressful environment of shanty towns. The advertising for milk formula played on the anxiety of women facing these problems. The health of bottle-fed babies, particularly of those who have been breast-fed for the first few months of life, does not appear to be always worse than that of breast-fed ones (although the determining factor appears to be income and general environment). Certainly, for women themselves, there may be an element of self-preservation in bottle-feeding at least some of the time, in view of the multiple roles (including that of mother to other children) which women carry out in developing countries.

The increasing importance of the conjugal relationship in certain social strata, and the modification of systems of social control in situations of emigration and high mobility may put paid to the possibility of abstinence and lengthy breast-feeding. (This appears to be true of many immigrants to Britain, both from Africa and from the Indian sub-continent). At any rate, the problem cannot be posed in the terms suggested by much of the medical literature, of whether breast-feeding or bottle-feeding is good or bad, and which should be assumed by health care experts as a rule of behaviour to recommend to mothers, irrespective of the social and individual personalities of mother and child.

Although few anthropologists have addressed themselves to this problem, the circumstantial data brought to light both by anthropologists and psychologists allow us to conclude that the 'conditions', both subjective and objective, in which infants are fed are an essential element in whether a certain form of feeding can be considered 'good' or 'bad'. Among these conditions are the complexities of economic and gender inequalities. The attitudes represented in much of the medical literature, doubtless contain an element of unselfconscious male projection and envy with regard to female sexuality (which we have not examined in this chapter, but which is considered, for example, in Balsamo et al. above). The 'medical model' as regards breast-feeding appears to belong to an outdated positivist tradition, which is anthropologically interesting but highly dangerous if it is to inform policies towards women. It may be too costly for women to regard it merely as an object of analysis and not as an attitude to oppose and overcome.

Notes

1. In this essay, the terms 'nomadic-pastoral', 'agrarian' and 'industrial' refer to productive forms, the terms 'rural' and 'urban' to modes of settlement, and the term 'transitional' to 'agrarian' or 'rural' societies where wage-labour, cash-cropping and urban styles of consumption have made considerable inroads. I also use the term 'transitional' to refer to urban populations of recent immigration, settled in shanty towns etc. I never use the term 'traditional societies', which is recurrent in the medical literature on breast-feeding.

2. I have recently met Astier Almedom and read her important articles on weaning in Ethiopia which could provide an interesting commentary on some of the theses of this book (Almedom, 1990). She and Alex de Waal have observed that Eritrean women in Sudanese refugee camps, lacking transitional foods for older infants, tend to 'unwean' their children, at what personal cost and with what outcome for the children we can only know in the long term (Almedom, and de Waal, 1990, 22: 489–500).

Bibliographical References

Ahmed, I. (ed.), *Technology and Rural Women: conceptual and empirical issues*, I.L.O., London, Allen and Unwin, 1985

Allasia, R., *Terra e Famiglia in Racconigi, Piemonte, 1900–1940*, Tesi di laurea, University of Turin, 1983

Almedom, A., 'Infant feeding among low-income households in Ethiopia: I. The weaning process; II. Determinants of Weaning The Ecology of Food and Nutrition, 1990

—— and De Waal, A., 'Constraints on weaning: evidence from Ethiopia and the Sudan; *Journal of Biosocial Sciences*, 1990, 22

Bleier, R., *Science and Gender: a critique of biology and its theories on women*, Oxford, Pergamon Press, 1984

Bloch, J.H. and Bloch, M., 'Women and the dialectics of nature in Eighteenth century French thought', in MacCormack, C. and Strathern, M. (eds), *Nature, Culture and Gender*, Cambridge, Cambridge University Press, 1980: 25–41

Cameron, M. and Hofvander, Y., *Manual on Feeding Infants and Young Children*, Protein-calorie Advisory Group of the United Nations System, Second Edition, New York, 1976 *Committee on the Status of Women in India*, 1974, cited in Nelson, N., *Why has Development*

Neglected Rural Women: a review of the South Asian literature, Oxford, Pergamon Press, 1979: 37

Creyghton, M-L., *Bad Milk: perceptions and healing of a children's illness in a North African society*, Ph.D. thesis, University of Amsterdam, 1981

Cunningham, A.S., 'Breast-feeding and morbidity in industrialised countries', in Jelliffe, D.B. and Jelliffe, E.F. (eds), *Advances in International Maternal and Child Health*, Vol. I, Oxford, Oxford University Press, 1981: *128–68*

Demographic Yearbook, Geneva, 1984

Dyson, T., 'Levels, trends differentials and causes of child mortality: a survey,' *World Health Statistics Report*, Vol. 30, no. 4, 1977: 83–92

Eggan, D., 'Instruction and affect in Hopi cultural continuity', in Middleton, J., *From Child to Adult: studies in the anthropology of education*, New York, Free Museum Press, 1970: 109–33

Eichinger Ferro-Luzzi, G., 'Food avoidances during the puerperium and lactation in Tamilnad', *Ecology of Food and Nutrition*, 1974, Vol. 3: 7–15

El Dareer, A., *Woman, why do you weep?*, London, Zed Press, 1982

Eerenbeemt, M-L. Van den, 'A demographic profile of the Fulani of central Mali with special emphasis on infant and child mortality', in Hill, A. (ed.) *Population, Health and Nutrition*, 1985: 79–104

Granquist, H., *Child Problems among the Arabs*, Helsingfors, Söderstrom and Co, 1950

Gray, B.M., 'Enga birth, maturation and survival: physiological characteristics of the life-cycle in the New Guinea Highlands, in MacCormack, C.P. (ed.), *The Ethnography of Child-birth*, London, Academic Press, 1985: 79–86

Hansen, H., *Daughters of Allah: among Moslem women in Kurdistan*, Copenhagen, Nationalmuseet, 1960

Harfouche, J.K., *Infant Health in Lebanon: customs and taboos*, Beirut, Khayats, 1965

Heitlinger, A., *Reproduction, Medicine and the Socialist State*, Macmillan, London, 1987

Hennart, P., Hofvander, Y., Vis H. and Robyn, C., 'Comparative study of nursing mothers in Africa (Zaire) and in Europe (Sweden): breast-feeding behaviour, nutritional status, lactational hyperprolactinaemia and the status of the menstrual cycle', *Clinical Endocrinology*, 1985, 22: 179–87

Hilderbrand, K., Hill, A.G., Randall, S. and van den Eerenbeemt, M.L., 'Child mortality and care of children in rural Mali', in Hill, A.G. (ed.), *Population, Health and Nutrition in the Sahel: issues in the welfare of selected West African communities*, London, Routledge and Kegan Paul, 1985: 184–207

Hilderbrand, K., 'Assessing the components of seasonal stress amongst the Fulani of the Seno-Mango, Central Mali', in Hill, A.G. (ed.), *Population Health and Nutrition*, 1985: 254–88

Hill, A.G. (ed.), *Population, Health and Nutrition in the Sahel*, London, Routledge and Kegan Paul, 1985

Inch, S., 'Difficulties with breast-feeding: mid-wives in disarray', Report on Meeting of Forum on Maternity and the Newborn, 2 Dec 1985, in *Journal of the Royal Society of Medicine*, Vol. 80, Jan 1987: 53–8

Jelliffe, D.B. and Jelliffe, E.F., *Human Milk in the Modern World: psychological, nutritional and economic significance*, Oxford, Oxford University Press, 1978

——, 'The uniqueness of human milk up-dated: ranges of evidence and emphases in interpretation', in Jelliffe, D.B. and Jelliffe, E.F., *(eds.)*, *Advances in International Maternal and Child Health*, vol. 6, Clarendon Press, Oxford, 1986: 129–47

Jelliffe, D.B. and Maddox, J., 'Notes on ecological malnutrition in the New Guinea Highlands', *Clinical Paediatrics*, 3, 1979: 432–38

Klaus, M.H. and Kennell, J.H., *Maternal-infant Bonding*, St. Louis, Mosby, 1976

Koso-Thomas, O., *The circumcision of women: a strategy for eradication*, London, Zed Press, 1987

Laukaran, V.H., Winikoff, B., Myers, D., 'The impact of health-services on breast-feeding: common themes from developed and developing worlds', in Jelliffe, D.B. and Jelliffe, E.F.P. (eds) *Advances in International Maternal and Child Health*, vol. 6, Oxford, Clarendon Press, 1986: 121–28

Livi Bacci, M., *Donna, fecondità e figli*, Bologna, Il Mulino, 1980

Llewellyn-Davies, M., *Maternity: letters from working women*, London, Virago, 1978 (First ed. 1915)

MacCormack, C. (ed.), *The Ethnography of Child-birth*, London, Academic Press, 1985

—— and Strathern, M. (eds), *Nature, Culture and Gender*, Cambridge, Cambridge University Press, 1980

Maher, V., 'Work, authority and consumption within the household: a Moroccan case' in Young, K., et al., *Of Marriage and the Market: the subordination of women in cross-cultural perspective*, London, CSE (1981) republished Routledge and Kegan Paul, 1983

——, 'Possession and dispossession: maternity and mortality in Morocco', in Medick, H. and Sabean, D. (eds), *Interest and Emotion: studies in kinship and the family*, Cambridge, Cambridge University Press, 1984: 103–28

McLaren, D., 'Marital fertility and lactation, 1570–1720', in Prior, M. (ed.), *Women in English Society, 1500–1800*, London, Methuen, 1985: 22–53

Merchant, C., *The Death of Nature: Women, Ecology and the Scientific Revolution*, Berkeley, California University Press, 1980

Mgaza, O. and Bantje, H. (eds), *Infant feeding in Dar-es-Salaam: Tanzania country report for the International Union of Nutritional Sciences Study, 'Rethinking infant nutrition policies under changing socioeconomic conditions'*, Dar-es-Salaam, Tanzania Food and Nutrition Centre, 1980

Millard, A.V. and Graham, M.A., 'Principles that guide weaning in rural Mexico', *Ecology of Food and Nutrition*, 1985, Vol. 16: 171–88

Minturn, L. and Lambert, W.W., *Mothers in Six Cultures*, New York, John Wiley, 1964

Mital, N. and Gopaldas, T.G., 'Habit survey of a culturally acceptable mother food in Gujarat, India', *Ecology of Food and Nutrition*, Vol. 16, 1985: 243–52

Mondot-Bernard, J.M., *Relationships between Fertility, Child Mortality and Nutrition in Africa*, Paris, OECD Development Centre, 1977

Morandini, M., *Terra e Famiglia in Fagagna, Friuli, 1900–1940*, Tesi di laurea (unpublished), Università di Trieste, 1979

Nelson, N., *Why Has Development Neglected Rural Women: a review of the South Asian literature*, Oxford, Pergamon Press, 1979

Oakley, A., *Becoming a Mother*, Oxford, Martin Robertson, 1979

Office of Population Censuses and Surveys, *Infant Feeding, 1975: Attitudes and Practice in England and Wales*, HMSO, London, 1978

Oldfield Hayes, R., 'Female genital mutilation, fertility control, women's roles and the patrilineage, in modern Sudan: a functional analysis', *American Ethnologist*, 1975, Vol. 2, no. 4: 617–33

Orwell, S., Clayton D. and Dugdale, A.E., 'Infant feeding in Nigeria', *Ecology of Food and Nutrition*, 1984, Vol. 15: 129–41

Prentice, A.M., Whitehead, R.G., Roberts, S.B. and Paul, A.A., 'Long-term energy balance in child-bearing Gambian women, *American Journal of Clinical Nutrition*, 1981, no. 34: 2790–9

Raphael, D., (ed.) *Breast-feeding and Food Policy in a Hungry World*, London, Academic Press, 1979

——, 'Weaning is always: the anthropology of breast-feeding behaviour', *Ecology of Food and Nutrition*, vol. 15, 1984

Richards, A.I., *Chisungu: a girls' initiation ritual*, London, Faber and Faber, 1956

Rotberg, R.I. and Rabb, T.K. (eds), *Hunger and History: the impact of changing food production and consumption patterns on society*, Cambridge, Cambridge University Press, 1983

Rushton, L., *Breast-feeding and the Evil Eye in Greece*, unpublished typescript, 1988

Schofield, S., *Development and the Problems of Village Nutrition*, London, IDS, 1979

Simpson-Hebert, M., Cresencio, E.N., Makil, L.P., *Infant Feeding in Metro Manila: infant feeding decisions, infant health and family planning among low income families*, Ramon Magsaysay Award Foundation Research Report, Vol. I, Manila, Philippines, 1986

Sluckin, W., Herbert, M. and Sluckin, A., *Maternal Bonding*, Oxford, Basil Blackwell, 1983

Spence, J., Walton, W.S., Miller, F.J.W. and Court, S.D.M., *1000 Families in Newcastle on Tyne: an approach to the study of health and illness in children*, Oxford, Oxford University Press, 1954

Stevens, C., *Food Aid and the Developing World*, London, Croom Helm, ODI, 1979

Swartz, M.J., 'Some cultural influences on family size in three East African societies', *Anthropological Quarterly*, 1973, vol. 42: 73–88

Taha, S.A., 'Household food consumption in five villages in the Sudan (Gezira)', *Ecology of Food and Nutrition*, 1978, Vol. 7: 137–42

Taylor, C.E., 'Synergy among mass infections, famines and poverty', in Rotberg and Rabb, 1983: 285–301

Tiertze, C., 'Maternal mortality (excluding abortion mortality)', *World Health Statistics Report*, Vol. 3, no. 4, 1977: 312–9

Victoria, C.G., Vaughan, J.P., Martines J.C. and Barcelos, L.B., 'Is prolonged breast-feeding associated with malnutrition?', *The American Journal of Clinical Nutrition*, 39, Feb. 1984: 307–14

Waldman, E., 'The ecology of the nutrition of the Bapedi, Sekhuniland (South Africa)', *Ecology of Food and Nutrition*, Vol. 4, 1975: 139–51

Wilson, C., 'Food taboos of child-birth: the Malay example', *Ecology of Food and Nutrition*, 1973, Vol. 2: 267–74

World Health Organisation, *Contemporary Patterns on Breast-feeding: report on the WHO collaborative study of breast-feeding*, Geneva, 1981 and 1984

Index

Accati, Luisa, 10, 76, 77
Acharya, M., 135
Achterberg, J., 53
advice on breast-feeding from other
    women, 30–1
agriculture, 6, 7, 99, 100–1, 103
Ahmed, I., 174
aid programmes, 158
Akbar, Emperor, 110
Allasia, R., 159
Altorki, S., 19, 110, 114
Anderson, J., 97
animal milk, 28, 98–9, 101, 170
Ardener, E., 92, 93, 102, 103
Ardener, S., 19, 91, 102
Ariès, P., 96
artificial methods of baby feeding
    in Iceland, 9, 24–5, 96, 97–9, 102,
    103–4
    see also bottle-feeding
Assenoh, A.B., 16
At-Tabari, 10, 22, 26
Aztec women and breast-feeding, 24

'baby-milk scandal', 3
Badinter, E., 96
Bandelloni, A., 59, 61
Bantje, H., 169, 172
baptism, 71
Belloni, C., 65
Biddulph, J., 111
birth(s)
    process of, 92
    spacing of, and maternal depletion,
        157–8
Bleier, Ruth, 155–6
Bloch, J.H. and M., 162
blood in milk, 83
Bordo, S., 81
Bott, E., 15
bottle-feeding, 2–4, 7–8, 61, 174–5
    supplementary, 67–9, 167–9
Bottone, E., 61
Bourdieu, P., 91
Bowlby, John, 26
Brazil, 168
breast pumps, 69

Breiðfjörð, Sigurður, 95
Britain see United Kingdom
Brown, J.K., 133
Burghart, R., 22, 28
butter, 98–9
Bynum, W.C., 10

Callaway, H., 91–2
Cameron, M., 5
cash, access to, and gender roles, 7–8,
    173 4
Cattaneo, G., 60
Charachidze, G., 111
Charnay, J.P., 43
children
    mortality of, 4, 95–6, 139, 142, 158
    and property inheritance, 11
    see also kinship
    choice of breast-feeding: in Italy, 63–5
cholostrum, 9
Chowdhury, A.A.K.M., 141
Christian imagery see religious
    imagery
Clastres, P., 104
clitoridectomy, 18, 163
contraception, 161–4
counting, absence of, 51–2
cows' milk, 98–9, 101
Creyghton, M.-L., 166
crying children, 79
cultural elaboration of breast-feeding,
    9–10
Cunningham, A.S., 152

Davin, A., 86
demand feeding, 1, 74, 77
depletion see maternal depletion
divorce, 7
Dobremez, J.F., 134
doctors, attitudes to breast-feeding of,
    2, 3, 13–14, 32–3
    in Italy, 59–61, 64, 72, 79–82
Donzelot, J., 120
Dragadze, T., 111–12
Draper, P., 134, 144
dress: in Khmir culture, 40–1
Durnin, J.V.G.A., 141

181

Books about women by members of the Centre for Cross-Cultural Research on Women, Queen Elizabeth House, Oxford include:

Narrowing the Gender Gap
G. Somjee

Gender, Culture and Empire
H. Callaway

Images of Women in Peace and War
Edited by S. Macdonald, P. Holden and S. Ardener

Anthropology and Nursing
Edited by P. Holden and J. Littlewood

Roles and Rituals for Hindu Women
Edited by J. Leslie

Rules and Remedies in Classical Indian Law
J. Leslie

Visibility and Power
Edited by L. Dube, E. Leacock and S. Ardener

Wise Daughters from Foreign Lands
E. Croll

Arab Women in the Field
Edited by S. Altorki and C. Fawzi El-Solh

Growing Up in a Divided Society
Edited by S. Burman and P. Reynolds

The Perfect Wife
J. Leslie

Women's Religious Experience
Edited by P. Holden

Food Insecurity and the Social Division of Labour in Tanzania
D. Bryceson

Caught Up in Conflict
Edited by R. Ridd and H. Callaway

Perceiving Women
Edited by S. Ardener

Margery Perham and British Rule in Africa
Edited by A. Smith and M. Bull

The Incorporated Wife
Edited by H. Callan and S. Ardener

Fit Work for Women
Edited by S. Burman

For a complete list of books in the **Berg Cross-Cultural Perspectives on Women** series please see page ii.